GRANNY DUVAL

'She must have come from somewhere'

Sue Pickrell

GRANNY DUVAL

'She must have come from somewhere'

Copyright © Sue Pickrell

First published 2024

ISBN: 978-0-6458689-8-2

All rights reserved. Without limiting the rights under copyright reserved above, no part of this publication may be reproduced, stored in or introduced into a database and retrieval system or transmitted in any form or by any means (electronic, mechanical, photocopying, recording or otherwise) without the prior written permission of the owner of the copyright.

Original illustrations/ Photographs by [Name of Artist/ Illustrator/ Photographer]

Published with the assistance of Angel Key Publications

https://angelkey.com.au

Acknowledgements

Deb Collumbel, Pauline Webby, Pam Brown, Jillian Openheimer, John Aitcheson, John Ferry, Hope Strudwick, Patricia Bartholomew-Locke, Judy Quinn, George Partridge and Stephen, Monica Wright-Burgess, Carol and Robert Lesley, Rodney Clarke, Margaret (Marge) Fermor, Peter Hooper, Penne Pemberton, Geoff Cummins, Greg Livermore of Anaiwan Local Aboriginal Land Council, Steve Widders, Patsy Cohen, Dr Mark Moore at the University of New England, Bruce Moore, Tom McClelland, Harry Allie BEM AM, Victor Fermor, Larissa Behrendt, Professor Margaret Somerville, Megan Truesdale, Andrea Warden, Marilyn Wood, Walcha Council, Uralla Shire Council, Colleen Johnson, Bruce Brand, Melinda Parker, Julian Pickrell, David Liddle and Vision Australia. Every single person contributed. Thank you!

Granny Duval — Sue Pickrell

Author's Note

Throughout this work I have consulted with several Aboriginal Australians, all of whom are of the same clan group—see the photo captioned 'In loving memory'. I have tried to report accurately the content and spirit of the stories they imparted to me over thirty years while I lived in Nundle.

Along with these personal stories I have included my historical research and imaginative, fictional stories to bring the history alive.

I believe that the lives of the families written of here deserve to be celebrated, otherwise the stories may be lost—which will inevitably occur, as several of us are well into our eighties! Compiling this work since 1986 has taken me on a vast learning curve, which has been both a challenge and a blessing. It has been a privilege to work with such Australians—they have fine families.

It should be noted here that any land 'taken up' by white settlers has *never* been ceded to the Australian government.

Throughout the book, I have tried to avoid giving offence, but if offence is experienced by a reader, I apologise.

I advise Aboriginal and Torres Strait Islander readers that this book contains names and images of people who have died.

Sue Pickrell, Googong, New South Wales, March 2024.

Dedication

To Trish Bartholomew-Locke, Rodney Clarke and Marge (Margaret) Fermor, thank you for helping me to understand!

Contents

Acknowledgements	iii
Author's Note	v
Dedication	vii
From Mary's Great-Granddaughter	xiii
Foreword	xv
Introduction: The Search	xvii

Part One
What Was Life like for the Aboriginal People Back Then? — 1

Chapter 1
A Child Is Born — 7

Chapter 2
Introducing Bidja — 25

Chapter 3
Disaster at the Billabong — 29

Chapter 4
They Had Lived Nearby for Eons in Deep Time — 31

Chapter 5
The Hanging Rock Cemetery Gathering — 35

Chapter 6
The Seat of Government Was 400 Miles Away — 39

Chapter 7
Explorers, Soldiers and Surveyors in the Corridor — 43

Chapter 8
The Cedar Cutters and Bidja at the Coast — 47

Chapter 9
The Howl of the Dingo: A True Account — 53

Chapter 10
Black Men Met White Men on Their Country — 59

Chapter 11
Moving In and Taking Over 65

Chapter 12
Hostilities in the Bush 73

Chapter 13
Aboriginal Vengeance v. Law and Order 85

Chapter 14
The Maitland Gold Reward 89

Chapter 15
The 'Asiatics' 93

Chapter 16
Nathan Burrows: Establishing Runs and Stations 97

Chapter 17
A General Practitioner in the 1850s 103

Chapter 18
Warrigal 109

Chapter 19
The Crafting of the Stone Axe 117

Chapter 20
Bushrangers and Rogues: Bakers Downfall 125

Chapter 21
Two Strong Men Wrote 127

Chapter 22
Missionaries Worked under Tension 131

Chapter 23
A Journalist Reported 135

Chapter 24
The End of the Dancing 137
Timeline of Events in Northwestern New South Wales, 1818–1923 141

Image Album
THE STORY OF GRANNY DUVAL 145

Part Two
　These New England Families and Individuals Made a Difference　153

Chapter 25
　The Black Matriarchs　155

Chapter 26
　Two Felons: Maurice Quinn and James Duval　167

Chapter 27
　The Toffs and Two Orphan Boys　179

Chapter 28
　Foley's Folly　185

Chapter 29
　The Bartholomews　189

Chapter 30
　The Fermors　197

Chapter 31
　The Wright Families　203

Chapter 32
　The Morrises, and the Morris Name Change　205

Chapter 33
　The Lesley Family　209

Chapter 34
　The Clarke Families　211

Chapter 35
　The Partridge Families　215

Chapter 36
　These Went to War; Being Aboriginal in Australia　221

Chapter 37
　The Historian Professor Margaret Somerville　225

Chapter 38
　Commissioner Macdonald　227

Chapter 39
　Uncle Joe 'Doc' Woods　231

Chapter 40
William Wynter of Taree — 235

Chapter 41
A Missionary Who Made a Difference — 237

Chapter 42
The 1920s on Gog's Top — 241

Chapter 43
Mixed Ancestry Marked Two Women's Lives: They Spoke Up — 245

Chapter 44
Marge Fermor nee Bartholomew Was Not Stolen — 251

Chapter 45
The Bush Kids the Welfare Missed — 255

Chapter 46
The Two Beardies: Men with Agricultural Influence — 261

Chapter 47
Bush Justice — 265

Chapter 48
Seeking Sanctuary — 267

Chapter 49
The End of the Story? — 269
Bibliography — 273

Appendix 1
Tom McClelland OAM's Poetry about Nundle and Hanging Rock — 277

Appendix 2
A Language Lost in Time — 283

Appendix 3
Aboriginal Spirituality — 287

Appendix 4
Historical Background: Wool — 289

Appendix 5
Capturing the 'Breelong Blacks' Bushrangers — 293

Appendix 6
Myths and Legends of the Goldfields — 297

From Mary's Great-Granddaughter

I acknowledge the peoples of the nation and pay my respects to their Elders past and present. I also wish to acknowledge Sue for putting together this book about my great-grandmother Mary Quinn. Sue has worked on this book through thick and thin and has had a lot of barriers and perseverance in understanding the Aboriginal culture and anything she could about my people's hardships and what our Elders endured, so I really appreciate all your hard work—it is marvellous what you can achieve if your heart is in what you are doing.

Pat Bartholomew-Locke, Anaiwan Elder

Etching of Nundle, 1891

Foreword

First and foremost, I would like to acknowledge the dedication and energy of Sue Pickrell, who has authored *Granny Duval: She Must Have Come from Somewhere* following a conversation with Trish Locke nee Bartholomew in 1986.

It is through the hours, days and years of hard work that *Granny Duval* has come to fruition.

I am honoured to introduce this book that details Aboriginal families' history in the Nundle area of the New England region which borders the ancestral lands of both the Kamilaroi and the Anaiwan peoples.

Nundle and its surrounding district is an area with a rich and fascinating cultural heritage that has often been overlooked or forgotten.

Granny Duval is a testament to the dedication and hard work of author Sue Pickrell, who, through her commitment to research as recorded in this work, honours many aspects of this district's local history, which can now be shared with a wider audience.

For too long, the stories as well as the experiences of the Indigenous families who lived in this region have been neglected, ignored or even silenced.

Through meticulous research, Sue and many dozens of contributors to this book have brought these stories to light. This has helped to give voice to those who have for various reasons and circumstances been silenced for too long.

The history of the Aboriginal people of Nundle is not only a story of resilience and survival, but also a story of cultural richness and diversity. From the land and its resources to the language and customs, the Indigenous culture of this region is an integral part of the broader Australian cultural landscape.

Sue's research and writings have also captured stories of Nundle's colonial past and delved into how white settlement of the area impacted the local Aboriginal community, specifically those who had cultural and historical ties to the ancestral land of the Anaiwan people.

Granny Duval: She Must Have Come from Somewhere has been a motivator for Sue, who has made a personal commitment to ensure these stories are told and will never be forgotten.

Additionally, *Granny Duval*, I feel, will reawaken stories of both the old and the untold. I believe Sue's storytelling will encourage descendants of the featured families to reclaim and retain pride in their Aboriginal identity.

I hope that this book will not only provide a deeper understanding of the Aboriginal history of Nundle but will also serve as a reminder of the ongoing need to acknowledge, respect and celebrate the cultural heritage of all Indigenous peoples.

It is my sincere hope that *Granny Duval* will contribute to a greater awareness and appreciation of the rich cultural legacy of both the Aboriginal and the non-Aboriginal people of Nundle and the surrounding areas. Further to this, I hope this book will inspire future generations to continue to learn, honour and celebrate these important histories.

Steve Widders, Anaiwan Elder

Introduction: The Search

In 1986, I was interested to know about the Aboriginal people of the district around Nundle and Hanging Rock. I was asking questions. Someone in Nundle said to me, 'My grandchildren are asking me about the Old People, but I don't know anything to tell them.' That comment sent me seeking out the people and their stories, with the help of Aboriginal Elder Patricia Bartholomew-Locke and others, over the next thirty years. Other stories came up as we went along, until 2018. I found that there are nine surnames of Aboriginal people living in the Nundle and Hanging Rock area of lower New England, New South Wales. They identify as Anaiwan people of lower New England—mostly.

The main source of the following stories is the Aboriginal Elder Patricia Bartholomew-Locke. When Aboriginal people are trying to identify a person or a family, when sorting out the relations of the past, they tend to ask 'she must have come from somewhere'?

For further information about other Anaiwan families of lower New England, see Waters & Moon 2016 (pp. 104, 105, 115–117); all the families are descended from Maryann Quinn.

White researchers might ask to see family trees, but Aboriginal Australians do not necessarily connect relatives together by genealogy as white people do. First, their older relatives are most often known as their Auntie, Uncle or Granny—terms that are used respectfully. Adults are known by their relationships rather than by a written document. They care more about the way things are in practice than about words in a strict family tree governed by blood relationships. For Aboriginal people, family trees are more like circles than straight lines, which seems consistent with Aboriginal ways of thinking. Genealogical confusion can also be the result of people marrying several times and of names taken that did not follow any standard pattern.

Second, relationships among Aboriginal people often have not been recorded or formalised in writing, because shared memories are enough. Third, due to low literacy and the passage of time, any written records that do exist are not necessarily accurate. Finally, as a people who traditionally did not use writing and may have limited literacy today, Aboriginal people may distrust anything written down on paper, saying that in the memory 'it was much safer'.

Hope Strudwick's amazing collection of family records, including some very old photos, has been greatly appreciated as I tried to collate all this information in my own mind and record it—hopefully accurately—so that these Aboriginal people's stories, the memories of them, are not lost. They were the 'Old People' whose identities I was seeking back in 1986.

Part One

What Was Life like for the Aboriginal People Back Then?

Thirty years before the birth of a certain Aboriginal child of the Anaiwan (shortened form of Nganyaywana) people, their extended country in northern New South Wales was invaded. They were living on the land mass known as the Great South Land. It was described by Europeans as 'without inhabitants', the 'land belonging to no one' or 'terra incognita.' There were thousands of Aborigines there at the time, occupying the land—in fact, they had been there for at least 40,000 years! But in 1788, white British men came in ships from across the seas. The fleet consisted of nine vessels, bringing a human cargo of 1,400 convicts accompanied by their officers under the captaincy of Arthur Phillip. White men moved into the New England area in the 1820s.

Whatever one's personal attitude towards Australian Aboriginal people, it cannot be denied that a great many of them and their children were deliberately displaced, relocated and killed. The land they walked on became no longer open to them. The writers of the nineteenth century recorded the landing and what followed as 'invasions'. "The name "Invasion Day" does not just reflect an Aboriginal and Torres Strait Islander perspective. It also reflects the meaning of "invasion" within a European system of law — international law as it operated in the eighteenth and nineteenth centuries."[1] The word was acceptable then and is still useful to describe what took place. Many were violent assaults, more than we of the twenty-first century perhaps wish to acknowledge. Changes were enforced on Aborigines with the rifle and the horse, while dreadful acts of retaliation haunted the lives of early squatters and settlers as they developed settlements on their appropriated land.

For millennia, the Aboriginal people had been killing food animals and gathering native edible vegetables, but their previously natural environment was altered by the newcomers—and that persists until now. The Indigenous inhabitants were decimated as a great many fell to the same diseases that were rampant in Europe in the 1700s and 1800s. Some had also been warring among themselves in a limited way for thousands of years. There were widespread reports of starvation, too.

The cultural practice of infanticide also occurred—female babies were not always valued. This meant there were few adult females. The Aboriginal women who were violated by marauding white men often became sterile, another direct cause of a reduced number of women in the population. There is historical evidence of this, and it is what happened in the other colonised lands during that period. The green environment in which the Aboriginal people and their children had lived changed rapidly when the white men arrived, and they had no way to adapt. However, there were eventually some positives (as reckoned by European thought) that flowed from the coming of the English sailors to Terra Australis. When, in the nineteenth century, stable government was finally established, some Aborigines received some schooling and health care, and the freedom from fear of bad spirits, as well as some freedom from fear of their enemies. The institutionalising of children who were thought to be vulnerable may have had some practical benefits for many Aboriginal people. For example, Marge, age ninety, declared: 'If the government had not looked after me, I would have been dead in the gutter.' She grew up in three different institutions. Babies and girls survived when missionaries looked after them. However, the care of the children was not always protective in these homes. Many children were shockingly abused in 'care'. Young adults and children in care were also seriously harmed by being forbidden to speak their own languages, which amounted to a loss of identity. In effect, the Aborigines became non-existent and officially almost invisible in their own country.

This work reconsiders past events. The era covered is 1820–2020. It is about what happened, from prior to 1815 up to the twenty-first century, to one family line that eventually swelled to include a great many people. At one stage, there was a policy towards Aborigines that aimed to assimilate or integrate them into the white colonial community of the day—even though there was a ruling that Aboriginal people could not marry white people. The assimilation policy is still deeply resented today.

What is past cannot be changed. However, it can be discussed. It can be understood and appreciated. Injustices can be acknowledged and, to some extent, addressed. This is the very least that is needed for all Australians to live in peace and to be healed of the burden of our colonial past.

Questions that need answers

How are the lower New England Aboriginal families of the twenty-first century descended from one baby born in northern New South Wales around 1820? How did the Aboriginal people of this area confront and survive the many changes that occurred in their lives? Who are they today? How well did their culture survive, and what is their future in the twenty-first century? How can black and white Australians work together towards a stronger and richer future for the whole Australian nation?

***

Years before the James Duval family moved from the Walcha district in New South Wales to Hanging Rock—fifty or so years before—a baby was born on Rimbanda Station in northern New South Wales. Two Aboriginal tribal adults, Milbona and Corumba, with their children, formed one group within the larger Anaiwan clans who made up the Ingleba people, who later occupied lower New England. It was their daughter, Maryann, whose story forever became that of being an ancestor of Granny Duval. Her descendants consist of at least nine families (counted by surnames) of the Nundle and Hanging Rock district of northern New South Wales.

There are several mysteries in the background of Maryann, who is believed to be the ancestor of the Aboriginal families of lower New England, New South Wales, according to family knowledge and records. Several queries have been solved to the author's and assistant researcher's satisfaction; Aboriginal Elder Patricia Bartholomew-Locke and I have worked on this together since 1988. Our work was carried out long before the widespread use of the internet and before the publication of the Bullcorronda Report in 2016. The Aboriginal people in this part of New South Wales are the Anaiwan people of the Armidale, Walcha, Uralla and Guyra districts and southwards, including Ingleba and the Hanging Rock and Nundle districts. They are from nine families: Quinn/Morris, Duval, Bartholomew, Clarke, Woods, Partridge, Fermor, Pacey, Ninness and Brand. All people in these families have some Aboriginal blood and were raised in an Aboriginal family, and they usually identify as Aboriginal. They are the people of lower New England or 'people of the snow country' (Anaiwan Elder Steve Widders, opening the Aboriginal memorial in Nundle in June 2016).

The Caucasian or non-Aboriginal sides of these families came to Australia from Europe—one of the first European settlers was from England and had a French ancestor, and another was a convict from Ireland. The events described in this book happened in the land corridor between the Hunter River Valley, the Macleay Valley and the Great Dividing Range, southeast of Tamworth in northern New South Wales, including the Nundle and Hanging Rock district. The geographical corridor being discussed is bounded by the New South Wales east coast, from Port Stephens to Taree and the Manning River coast, and extends northwest to Walcha and Peel River and south to Nundle, Hanging Rock, the Barnard River and Tuggolo Forest.

The family members are Aboriginal because they grew up in their Aboriginal families, not because they might have a dark pigment in their skin. It is their family upbringing and cultural inheritance that have given them their Aboriginal identity. In the twenty-first century, they usually identify as Aboriginal, many having been acknowledged as such by their peers in the Anaiwan Local Aboriginal Land Council.

This strongly identifying fact matters because of the cultural nature of identity and identifying:

- Aboriginal people do not like being assumed or identified to be someone else other than who they really are; this is a view held strongly by Aboriginal people. It is offensive to be misidentified. For example, a blond German would never accept being identified as an Englishman just because he looked white and spoke English, as many Germans do!
- Due to European intervention, Aboriginal people have lost so many years in time, so much country and place, and the truth of their original identity—particularly their language, which is a strong identifier—that they hold what is left very dear.
- It is discourteous for someone to try to dispel another person's possibly mistaken notions of their identity. In Aboriginal culture, it is very important to know who you are and where you came from—your identity is with your land. This was particularly important in the Nundle district, where the Anaiwan people were usually said to be Kamilaroi, which wasn't true. (The Kamilaroi were more numerous and had a reputation so were considered more significant.) The Anaiwan did not (and still do not) want to be known as Kamilaroi—it was an insult.
- The reality of 'being Aboriginal' involves 'identifying as Aboriginal.' This acceptance must come from being recognised by Aborigines of the local Land Council who can attest to one's familial connections. The group decides who is Aboriginal, not the individual.
- Aboriginality has nothing to do with skin colour; it is in a person's upbringing—their true family. 'It's a family thing,' said Stan Grant[2]. Inherited Aboriginality is not removed by 'stealing a child from mothers and placing him within the white culture'; it simply gives the individual two ways to live. However, the result can be that for the rest of their life, the individual lives with profound confusion about who they are, living in two worlds at the same time.

The author comes to this work with a Biblical worldview, understanding that all people are made in the image of the Living God, having personality, the ability to communicate, think, feel, speak, and act in history, and therefore they are equally precious. I also believe that truth (i.e., facts) matters, that justice must be done so that we Australian people can live together in peace, and that hurts can be healed with the grace of God—that is, there is no absolute need to carry past hurts forever. However, epigenetically, there may be wounds or effects of trauma that remain over generations. Traumas can be forgiven and forgotten; however, there are two sides to forgiving and forgetting. Forgiveness must be given *and* received—a two-way action is essential. This needs to be acknowledged.

There is a mythical youth, Bidja, whose story runs through the book.

Notes

1. https://psnews.com.au/the-law-of-words-is-invasion-day-the-right-name-for-26-january/32242/
2. Stan Grant said this in a TV Interview in 2020

Chapter 1

A Child Is Born

A child was born. She was perhaps named Maryann. She ultimately had seven children with Maurice Quinn, the Irish convict of Rimbanda Station.

The story of Granny: who was she?

Maurice Quinn and Maryann's daughter, Mary Elizabeth, went on to become the ancestral grandmother of the families surnamed Quinn, Bartholomew, Brand, Duval, Fermor, Clarke and Lesley, as well as others of the Nundle and Hanging Rock district, including many families of the Ingleba, Walcha and Uralla districts. She married a James Duval, and as an older woman, she was known as Granny Duval. Regarding her mother, we can call her Maryann Quinn, but there is no document to verify her relationship (perhaps her first) with Maurice Quinn. (Most relationships are documented.)

Maryann: a child was born

A shriek of the black cockatoo was heard in the dawn on Rimbanda Station, a property north of Tamworth, New South Wales, in around 1820. The young woman, Milbona, woke in the early dawn feeling more uncomfortable than any day before. Her grandmother was with her, so she was not alone. She was in a hollow near a north-facing granite boulder. The sun would warm her a little when it came up.

The baby's birth took place in the bush. This child became Maryann Quinn—Granny Duval's mother.

The possum-skin cloak slipped from her shoulders as she moved into a squatting position. Her grandmother sat quietly beside her for encouragement; she would not interfere with the birth process. She helped her with some pain control by pouring cold water on Milbona's abdomen. The grandmother's culture and experience governed the whole process. The young mother was relaxed, though fearful of evil spirits that might hurt her baby. She walked everywhere the tribe went, so she was strong and supple. The child entered the cold world with a gasp.

After delivering the child and the placenta, the mother was 'smoked'[1] with burning herbs and eucalyptus leaves to help her recovery, and she quickly returned to her usual day with her baby by her side. The baby was tenderly wrapped in a soft new possum skin and placed carefully in a coolamon.[2]

The grandmother may have buried the placenta nearby in the belief that this kept the child connected to the land. The echidna that scuttled across the track at the time of the birth went unnoticed, but it would become the totem of the Anaiwan people.[3] The child's father was named Corumba.

The little girl was born in around 1820, and there is a notion in the family that her Aboriginal name was Mahrakah or Mahrakan. Somehow, this became the similar-sounding English name Maryann. In accordance with tribal tradition, the Aboriginal name would likely have been taken from a natural feature, a tree or an animal, or from what was happening nearby at the time.

∗∗∗

There was an observer that day, Bidja, who stood silently, watching but unseen, resting one foot on his knee, his long spear by his side; a yellow dog curled up in the weak sun nearby. He watched in spite of the taboos—an Aboriginal man was not allowed anywhere near a childbirth—but he understood what was happening: that a special connection with his people had just occurred.

∗∗∗

Milbona quickly learned how to care for her child. It was her grandmother that she turned to most of the time, as was the custom. The father, Corumba, would not be involved at all in the child's care—that was not the work of an Aboriginal warrior. Much later, the child was referred to as Maryann on a baptismal certificate; no white men would be passing through or nearby for another fifteen years.[4]

The women of the tribe were happy with the little girl's progress. Soon she was toddling everywhere.

However, there was always the chance of a raid by Kamilaroi men.

One day there was a raid by men from the plains in the west. They came to steal young women—fresh blood, not their relatives—to be wives for their young men. There was a serious skirmish between the warriors. Maryann was afraid, but she settled down after the invaders left, even though they had captured two young women, who had somewhat willingly gone with them.

Annual migration: it was in the newspaper

The Elders decided that it was time to go across the high plateau as they had observed the change in the wind and knew that cold weather would be soon coming on the tops. They would make their seasonal migration to move their camp[5] across the range and down to the beach (Macleay River/Kempsey area).' They had read the signs in the colouring of the casuarina leaves. This decision made everyone happy, as food was plentiful on the riverbank. There were plump oysters on the rocks and fish in the saltwater. The flies, called March flies by the white men, were 'too merry saucy' for them up in the range; they would be free of them at the beach.

But it took them several days to get there; there were nursing mothers and small children who couldn't travel fast. The children were eager to go as they knew they would enjoy playing on the warm white sands while their parents were out on the river fishing. The adults would easily catch juicy fish for their people to feed on. The men would make canoes, and the boys would learn how to catch fish using their long spears. The children couldn't wait!

The youth, Bidja, was there that day, one of the older children in the tribe, so he had responsibility for the younger boys. He would soon teach them all he knew. He would sit with them and show them how to fashion a child-sized spear. They all were excited about going to the saltwater!

At the beach were trees that had branches down near the ground. The young boys loved climbing them and swinging out over the water. They had to be brave to let go of the liana vine and let themselves fall in. They were always a little scared, for they had heard tales of the dangerous creatures which lived in the deep water. The little girl would play on the pile of seashells at the beach that archaeologists would later call a midden.[6]

Maryann was weaned when she was around four years old, and from then on she grew long and lanky. She didn't know that there was another child about to come into her family. Soon it would be time to talk about whom she would marry. The arrangements would be complex, made when the child was very young; the various relationships were talked over by the Elders. There were very strict rules about marrying, and these had to be observed, or swift retribution would follow. It seems that from ancient times, the Elders had instinctively understood something of the possibility of inbreeding—marriages between close relatives producing imperfect or 'damaged' children.

When the casuarinas[7] changed colour, the weather was changing, and the observant Aboriginal Elders knew it was time to leave the beach. It was time to return to the tops of the range, for the hot weather would come soon; it was always cool in the Barnard River valley when the weather was too hot on the beach.

The talk at the camp at night was about the white strangers who were beginning to come onto the Rimbanda country up on the top of the range. The black men were counting on the fact that when they arrived there the next day, there would be meat—young wallabies, unafraid, certainly not expecting any disturbance. They would also be able to feast on the 'sweet green pick' growing where the men had lit small fires at the end of the summer, fires that had burnt slowly in the dry grass because the night dews damped them down. This firestick farming was not dangerous. The next day they pushed their way through the bracken fern out onto the marsupial track and followed it all the way. The women collected native raspberries as they went, and stopped to dig out some juicy yam daisies (these were root vegetables, and were called murnong).[8]

The children ran happily ahead, chasing each other up and over the rocks, through the creeks and over patches of new sweet grass. They were all hungry when they arrived at a camping place further up the mountain. When they camped that night, it was cold, but their possum cloaks kept the children a little protected. The adults curled up with their dogs near the small fires the men had lit at dusk.

The following morning, the tribespeople clambered up the last hills before they stopped and looked across the plateau towards their traditional lands—their country and home. They were shocked to see fierce fires raging (this was not in accordance with the Aboriginal use of fires). As they went closer, they saw fat pale creatures—round, woolly four-footed animals. The white settlers were certainly making their presence felt! Two white men rested in the shade, just watching the fires.

The tribesmen were enraged at the white strangers because their food animals grazing on the grass that was meant to be food for wallabies. They let fly with their spears. The two shepherds fell where they sat; some sheep were slaughtered too.

The noise of the hollering and whooping frightened the mob of sheep, which ran pell-mell in every direction. There was neither fence to keep the animals in nor any rock walls to define the 'white man's land.' Hostilities had accumulated—for some time, the people had seen their standing string traps destroyed and their means of catching their food broken down by these new creatures. On that terrible day, the children experienced the first threat to their livelihood.

Young Maryann was amongst the tribal family group on this dramatic day when the Aboriginal men killed the shepherds and the flock was scattered.

Did Bidja notice the young child Maryann amongst the group? What did he think of her? He may have worried what might happen if the white men got to her when she was older. White men already had a bad reputation for their behaviour with women.

In the township nearby, the newspaper recorded the white men's views.

The Sydney Herald (1831)

The bellicose attitude of the aborigines on the tableland, as elsewhere, began when their localities became overrun by the stock of the squatters. The blacks naturally resented the intrusion of the whites with their flocks and herds, and both parties soon commenced a war of extermination. Fearing the firearms of the intruders, the natives rapidly slaughtered the stock, and, when opportunity presented, the shepherds and herdsmen as well. In retaliation, the conquering whites, while making application to the Government for assistance, which they scarcely expected, ensured the granting of such relief in other ways.

Some additional excerpts from the Sydney Herald, 1831–1842

We hear numerous outrages have been commenced by the aborigines in the newly discovered country northeast of Liverpool Plains.

Two men belonging to John and Francis Allman were murdered at Yarrowyck, and their sheep taken away.

We have been informed that the blacks of New England drove off 1,400 sheep, the property of Mr Windeyer, but they were all recovered with the exception of 50 or 60, which the savages had slaughtered.

Poor Kelso has lost six to seven hundred sheep again by those infernal blacks who have nearly ruined him.

The blacks to the number of five hundred have been about Peter McIntyre's Byron Plains station for the last five weeks. Last week they commenced driving off the cattle, four hundred head of which are missing. They also attacked a shepherd, who saved his life by killing one at the first shot, after being wounded in the head by a spear.

Letters have been received in town stating that 'the blacks had attacked the station of Robert Ramsay Mackenzie (Salisbury), murdered a shepherd, driven off thirteen hundred sheep, and burned down two huts. The district is without police, Mr Commissioner Macdonald and his party having been ordered by the Governor to proceed to

Moreton Bay, Queensland.' (New South Wales was policed from far away, from Queensland.)

The Aborigines feasted well that night on the sheep that had been killed.

Young Maryann had seen her first white men that day. She had no idea that that ultimately she would be pregnant with the child of an Irish convict Maurice Quinn, who was an assigned man.[9]

✱✱✱

In 1838, the laden ship sailed from Plymouth towards the Great South Land. Many weeks later it arrived in New South Wales.

It is thought that Maurice Quinn was off-loaded in Newcastle harbour on the mouth of the Hunter River, New South Wales, with other assigned men, and that the group then took a smaller craft up the coast, put ashore at the fledgling settlement of Port Macquarie and then walked the many miles from the coast under guard. They followed the Nundle Spur up—on foot—onto the tops of the range and marched across the plateau to the station known as Rimbanda, the place where Maurice would live the rest of his life. There were some stations they passed along the way, Congi, near Wolka (now Walcha), being the first station in that district. The stations were located on Aboriginal tribal land: after all, the land was never purchased or even leased from the true owners. Permission was never asked; neither was the land ever ceded to the white men. This practice—land-grabbing by the government and by white individuals—has been the main source of discontent amongst Aboriginal people, not surprisingly, since the time of early settlement until today.

From 1835, white men were making inroads into the country that they wanted to use for their grazing animals and to make homes and gardens for themselves. The Aboriginal people in the area were seen as a nuisance who, if ignored, might simply go away altogether, melting into the bush.[10]

By the time he met her at Rimbanda Station in 1839, Maryann had developed into the beauty that attracted Maurice Quinn. She was about nineteen. The convict was soon aware of the young black girl, and he was determined to have her for himself. There was no demonstration of affection between the two—Aboriginal culture did not allow such behaviour. If they had been in the bush together, she would have insisted that he walk a little ahead of her which was their custom. He would not have 'had his way' with her at all—her brothers would have slaughtered him without ceremony. She had grown up on country and was strong and healthy. She knew how to survive in the bush away from the tribe, which she proceeded to do as she and Maurice became closer.

The Aboriginal women camped near the homestead had some food from the whitefella boss's missus in return for working with the animals, in the garden or in the house, and Maryann may have been one of them.[11] Maryann bore at least seven children to Maurice Quinn. The Aboriginal people were beginning to 'try to live in two worlds, two different cultures'.

As adults, Maryann's children were unique at the time in that they had Aboriginal blood and culture as well as Irish heritage; several of them had fair skin. The women were called matriarchs in the literature of the Walcha district. Between 1820 and 1850, great changes came into the lives of these people. They successfully straddled two generations and two lifestyles! The old tribal ways were disappearing—they began to use English ways and language, to dress like the white people and to eat the easy-come food that was given sparingly to the camp workers. This was tea, sugar and flour—a diet described much later as nutrient-free—and occasionally some meat, as some cattle were slaughtered on the property to feed the various hands working there. It is unlikely that any of them was paid wages at all—their situation was almost slave labour, with just enough food to keep them anchored to the station. The dietary changes are responsible for the obesity that has afflicted many older Aboriginal adults since the time of colonisation. The non-payment of wages has been the source of deep feelings of injustice because state governments tended to accumulate these Aboriginal workers' wages 'to be remitted at some stage in the future', which mostly never happened. At its worst, this practice was called 'nigger farming' and was prohibited. Some effort has been made by the state government in recent years to identify and pay the lost wages.

Sadly, some adults and children fell from diseases brought by the settlers. (These were illnesses that Europeans did not understand at that time.) Other changes occurred as proud men of the tribe lost their authority and dignity. They no longer knew or practised their traditional way of life. They struggled to adapt. However, a few Aboriginal men got work as station hands. They were athletic - a boon to the station management because they knew the local country around there so well.

By 1855, Maryann was rearing at least seven children—Mariah, Mary Elizabeth, Sarah, Bodella (called Jessie), James, Patrick and Hugh. The older women of the group successfully spanned two cultures—a great achievement. It became their responsibility to keep the Anaiwan Aboriginal culture alive in the people's hearts. They came to be respected as Matriarchs.

It seems that Aborigines were treated surprisingly well on Rimbanda country. It is also said that there are still many Aboriginal graves on Rimbanda Station. Maurice Quinn's grave is there too—he was killed by a lightning strike while out in the paddock at the age of sixty-nine. Maryann and Mrs Stitt, the station manager's wife, went to look for him. They found him, just a heap on the ground. He was buried where he fell. Aboriginal people are often fearful around cemeteries, where there might be spirits.

***

Bidja, looking on, felt spooked when he remembered it all. He seemed to feel all the dying and grief that had been concentrated on that one hillside …

***

Several Aboriginal graves have been located on Rimbanda Station. There were so many burials out in the bush there—a great many unrecorded deaths. A memorial has recently been placed there to remember Maurice Quinn.

While their children were growing up in the camp, at the fireside each night, the Aborigines would yarn at their small fires. The full black sky was peppered with tiny spots of light—the stars and constellations that told them of a Creator's hand in their beginnings. Byamee was the Creator spirit in whom many Aborigines in northern New South Wales believed, understanding that the wonderful country into which they had been born, on which they had hunted and where their family's needs were provided with great abundance came from the Creator. The Anaiwan have characteristically been a thankful people.

Granny Duval's family

One of the daughters of Maurice Quinn and Maryann was Mary Elizabeth Quinn, usually called Mary. She was born at nearby Winterbourne Station in 1842; she would eventually become known as Granny Duval. As she was Maryann's daughter, her grandmother was Milbona, a tribal woman.

She was a Quinn by birth, but she grew up to marry an Australian-born young man, James Duval, whose father was a French sailor from the SS *Lady Kennaway*. (Some marriages are acknowledged to have occurred; other relationships are recognised in conversation.) In the Aboriginal world, adult women are usually known by their cultural marriage name. Family connections are held to strongly and with respect.

James Duval at Rimbanda

One evening, tired and footsore, a hungry young man named James Duval arrived at the station. He was a young felon from the township of Sydney, 260 miles away. He was fleeing from the law.

James had escaped from a work party—which had meant heavy long days when he was always hungry! He walked into the Rimbanda Run from Branga Plains Station, a distance of some thirty miles. (Branga Plains was a beef cattle station managed in cooperation with the Catholic Church.)

Among those around the camp in the creek bed was Bidja, along with another family group. From them, James found welcome. Bidja was curious about the newcomer—the young white man—where did he come from?

James's parents—who were somewhat lacking in parenting skills—had ended up residing in two jails, for murder and for drunkenness, their three children running loose on the streets of Sydney town. At Rimbanda, having tramped in, James set his eye on young Mary Elizabeth Quinn, and she was soon pregnant. In spite of his rough upbringing, James cared for Mary, his woman; he had a good, strong character. He looked after her, marrying her at the Roman Catholic Church in Walcha in 1862 or 1863. It was this Mary who became known as Granny Duval.

In that period the white population was extending over the creeks and gullies—gold had been found in the waterways in the district, and there was good grazing country that satisfied the would-be squatters.

Mary and James were excited to welcome their first baby, also called James, but sadly he died. They bore their grief stoically. Mary went on to bear twelve more babies. James and Mary found it hard going until James got a job away from Walcha/Ingleba, to the south, at Hanging Rock above Nundle, in the ranges. James was later employed on Goonoo Goonoo Station, working the sheep and helping out in the shearing shed when needed. (See Appendix 4.)

Sometimes (we might imagine), James would bring the children an unmothered lamb to be fed; the girls, especially, just loved having a pet. Perhaps a goat was milked for the children—and for the lamb. James enjoyed learning about the sheep and how to care for them out in the paddock. He needed this knowledge later on when he became a shepherd.

The Duvals had six live children by 1870—six babies had been registered in Armidale. Six more children came; who were registered in Tamworth and baptised at St Nicholas's Church.

Mary had the skills of a midwife. She was called on during emergencies, even by members of the white community—though her own babies had been born in the bush as she had back in the 1820s, with just a grandmother waiting nearby, keeping watch.

Mary was rearing her children at the diggings and camps. The first four Duval children were named Kate, Elizabeth, John and Ada. The others were Louisa, Margaret, Hannah, Mary, Agnes, Catherine, Claude and Francis (not in birth order; thanks to the Holmes family for these details).

By 1883, on the diggings, Mary had four children in the Hanging Rock School—Kate, Elizabeth, John and Ada. The small community was dependent on gold, but the diggings were languishing. They were in drought at that time, and the diggers desperately needed water to wash the 'stuff'. The population of their community was 500; a great many of them being Chinese.

Later, the Duval family were living in Duncans Creek, above Woolomin village. James was working as a carpenter at Foley's Folly, a small community that vanished due to the forestry plantings of 1952.

In 1885, there was a catastrophe: James became ill. He was taken to Sydney, but he died. (He had travelled to Sydney on the gold escort and by rail—a long slow journey for someone so ill.) He was buried at Rookwood Cemetery in Sydney. This left Mary to raise her large family with very little support. He had only been forty-four. Sadly, they could never go and visit his grave; it was too far away.

After James's death, Mary began living at Ben Halls Creek, a community of smallholdings near the Barnard River, with seven of her children. She would have been hiding the children down in that community to avoid the Welfare, the officers who drove around the country looking for 'half-caste' children to take from their homes, from their mothers. Like the other mothers, Mary was afraid for her children, who could be taken, never to be seen again. This practice resulted in much grief in the families. At the time the authorities considered it better for the Aboriginal children's welfare, but that has always been disputed by Aboriginal people. Some stolen children did return home after reaching the age of sixteen—but their lives had been changed forever.

In 1886, a letter came. Because of poverty, Mrs Duval was unable to pay the required school fee. In a note written by the school inspector of the time—she had written asking that her debt be cancelled—he described her as 'half caste, now widowed', which showed that there was some practical compassion towards a struggling Aboriginal family. This mark of respect was not forgotten because it was so unusual.

Although James's death had left Mary Duval with a large family to raise and no income, there were some family members nearby. During this time, Mary's sister, Jessie, met a Jack Cook and may have married him. Jessie, who was a high-spirited young woman, had been so deeply disturbed by an event—a massacre on the Ingleba reserve—that she left her family behind, setting off to the south. Jack Cook was a refugee from the incursions of the Australian Agricultural Company shepherds in the Birpai and Worimi country inland from Taree and Port Stevens. Jessie and

Jack were part of a gold diggers' settlement, the Barrington River community. She too reared a large family—so there were many cousins, all living nearby! Having some family nearby is very important to Aboriginal people so that their culture is kept strong.

One day when we were talking together, Patricia said, 'Granny Duval, Mary, was known for her storytelling; she had a gentle nature and a quiet voice. She could not read or write. When she was telling children about a place or a route track to somewhere, she would draw a "mud map" in the earth. It was said that wherever she had been, you found her "pictures written in the dirt". Also, she was the best finder of honeybees, from anyone—this made her very popular!'

As an older woman, she wore a 'topknot', a crocheted hat. She probably wore her hair long as was the habit of Aboriginal women. She was proud of her looks—her skin was fair like her father's. She was an able horsewoman and usually rode side-saddle. (These are her great-granddaughter's recollections.)

Being a practical woman, she always knew where clay could be found in the bush; she used it for her clay pipe and for whitewashing the hearth. The fireplace or hob in humble homes might be as wide as the room. A huge log would be hauled into the house from outside to burn away slowly over days and weeks. The hearth was whitewashed annually, usually in spring.

Patricia's mother, Meg, remembered: 'One of her favourite things to do was sit with her friend Jimmy Crimp and quietly smoke away in silent companionship out on the porch. They would speak the Anaiwan language there—but she never used it in the house.'

In 1890, Mary and James' Duval's daughter Hannah was married to an Adam Bartholomew. When their first child was due, Mary rode out to Hannah and Adam's small home and delivered her own first grandchild, a boy they named John.

In the 1920s, Granny Duval was elderly and not at all well. She was living with her son Claude and his family at a Giro property.[12] It was remembered that one day Claude was to take his wife Sarah to hospital in the sulky as she was due to give birth, but that day they couldn't cross because there was a 'fresh' in the river—the water flow was too strong and they couldn't get across safely. (There had been a storm up the valley overnight.) So Granny Duval took charge of the situation as Sarah went into labour.

Meg, who was a child at the time, recalled:

Of course, the children there didn't realise that a baby was soon to be born. Granny sent them all out of the house 'to collect bark to start the fire in the morning—there is a storm coming'.

When they got back, she told them, 'Look at what the angels have brought us.'

The children found a new baby sister wrapped in one of their grandfather's soft flannels and laid in a Dutch oven hanging at the back in the fireplace to keep her warm. Their oohs and ahs were shushed when their grubby bare feet touched the white hob. But they simply had to have a quick look at the new baby sister! (This was Ethel May Brand nee Duval.)

In 1923, Granny Duval was staying with Claude and Sarah near Gloucester, New South Wales. There were other family members there too. She suffered a long debilitating illness. She died at age eighty-one of 'senile decay', with the family all around her. She was buried in Gloucester Cemetery.

During the 100 years between 1820, when Maryann is presumed to have been born, and her daughter Granny Duval's death in 1923, their family had expanded into a large group that included Morrises, Wrights, Bartholomews, Clarkes, Partridges, Ninnesses, Lesleys, Brands and many more from Walcha, Ingleba, Hanging Rock, and Nundle in lower New England. They were all Anaiwan people.

Family tree of Trish Locke

Five generations from an Aboriginal baby in the 1800s to Aboriginal Elder Trish Locke.

Gen. 1.   Milbona and Corumba's child 'Maryann', who married Maurice Quinn and had seven children.

Gen. 2.   Maryann and Maurice's daughter Mary Elizabeth (Granny Duval; born at Winterbourne Station in 1842), who married James Duval in 1863 in Walcha, New South Wales, and had twelve children.

Gen. 3.   The Duvals' daughter Hannah (Annie), who married Adam Bartholomew in Nundle in 1890; her brother Claude Duval, who married Irish woman Isabella McCanna, of the Wallabadah district.

Gen. 4.   Claude and Isabella's daughter Isabel (called Meg), who married John Bartholomew of Nundle.

Gen. 5.   Meg and John's daughter is Elder Patricia Bartholomew-Locke of Armidale, New South Wales.

Some of these relationships are documented.

Notes

1. 'Smoked': An Aboriginal custom. Smoking involves eucalyptus leaves being burned; the smoke containing the aroma of the heated oil is considered to be health-giving or protective.

2. Coolamon: An Aboriginal carved wooden 'dish' used for all kinds of carrying purposes—even for safely carrying sleeping babies.

3. Echidna totem: An Aboriginal person's totem animal became specially revered. It could never be eaten by that particular person, for that would be disrespectful.

   There may have been a cultural taboo that Aboriginal names were not to be spoken out loud (as a protection from spirits). This may have been one reason why Maryann's tribal name was not even remembered; another reason could have been that there was no written document to record it except the registration card, which was presumably not completed until some time after she was born.

4. More on Mary's birth and baptism: according to the note on p. 43 of *Citizenship and Indigenous Australians* (edited by Peterson & Sanders), 'One of the first children to be baptised by Bishop Therry was Mary, daughter of Corumba and Milbona. When Therry baptised Maryann she was living in Windsor and her parents were noted to be "natives".'

    The author believes that, since priests visited communities only every so often to baptise children and marry couples, and Father Therry only arrived in Australia in 1820 and would probably have been stationed at the Windsor Catholic Presbytery when he baptised a group of children among whom Maryann stood out, she may have been six years old, not newborn at all—and thus not born in 1820. However, she was certainly baptised and registered as Catholic in 1820.

5. She grew up in the camp: 'camp' means a place as well as a specific group of people. A camp could have been large—200 people—but more likely much smaller and made up of family members or a couple of clans. One language or dialect would be spoken among the people. A campsite would be decided by the Elders. The camp would move according to the availability of food plants and animals and the suitability of the climate or environment—for example, in autumn, firestick farming was carried out to encourage sweet new grasses to attract young wallabies in spring to make them easier to kill. The camp would have been located on country, with relatives nearby. On country: in Aboriginal English, 'country' usually refers to an area perhaps something like 'homelands' to a white person, and 'the' is not included as 'country' is understood to mean a specific area connected to family and culture. Importantly, a people's country would have been defined by the main language spoken there.

6. Midden: A large pile of discarded shells and rubbish; left on the coast, these have become very interesting to archaeologists. People's rubbish says a lot about their diet, habits and so on. After a very large group had eaten together over years and years, the midden could be extensive—a wonderful resource for later research.

7. Casuarina: Australian native tree; the leaf tips' changing colour indicates a change in the seasons.

8. Yam daisies: Indigenous vegetables, also called daisy yams or murnong. They have a yellow daisy-like flower and a fleshy underground tuber that is a sweet food if cooked. They grew widely on the slopes, on the plains and in the valleys in New England country and west of the Great Dividing Range. Yam daisies are good food that the Aborigines enjoyed. The small tubers had to be cooked before eating to reduce toxicity. Sheep ate the whole plant, which did not regenerate. Almost every plant was eaten out by the first small mobs of sheep that were driven across the land, so murnong became very scarce, and many Aborigines went hungry. There are three kinds of yam daisies, two kinds of figs, lily roots, raspberries, cherries, lilly pillies, nuts, seeds of certain grasses, cabbage tree tops, native bee honey, and witchety grubs, along with shellfish, crustaceans, scrub turkey, eggs of python and emus, and some water birds.

9. Assigned man: Settlers could apply to have a convict labourer assigned to them to work on their property. Initially it was expected that much of the early agricultural and stockwork, and the building of the colony, was to depend on convict labour, so that in 1840, when the transportation of convicts from Britain was stopped, there was a resulting serious shortage of labourers. Chinese coolies were soon employed to do the work, and even men from South America. Aboriginal men, too, for the first time, were employed to do the stockwork, at which they were particularly skilled, being strong and athletic and knowing the country so well.

10. Walkabout: It was the Aboriginal custom to 'go walkabout,' apparently leaving for some ceremony or funeral, maybe many miles away—a custom the whitefellas found very irritating, particularly when the Aborigines were 'employed'. This habit alone showed the marked differences between the white and black people's points of view. Also, walkabout was sometimes led by the Elders of a group when food was becoming short. They read the seasons and moved the whole group on to where bush fruits were just ripening or animals would be

grazing on grass patches burned the year before that would now have green shoots.

11. Domestic service after settlement: it became customary for local young Aboriginal women to be instructed in menial work around and in the homes of the white settlers; otherwise, there would have been people camping nearby and wanting to be fed, so this employment served to even things up to some extent—some work for some food was a kind of justice—and it was the white people's way of using people. However, there was often exploitation and abuse. Early on, the authorities envisaged that there would be a blending of the two races so that eventually the overall colour of the population would be white. Another view held in the 1800s following the scientific work of Charles Darwin and others, who had ideas that became accepted by the white scholars of the time, was that the dark-skinned people would die out. In Torres Strait, the Indigenous people themselves observed to scientists that their numbers were dwindling. (See Russell (ed) *A Trip to the Dominions: The Scientific Event That Changed Australia*.)

12. Giro Station: Rough country used for raising cattle by the Australian Agricultural Company, located in the foothills of the Great Dividing Range adjacent to the properties of Nowendoc, Kunderang and Callaghans Swamp. The source of these stories is Patricia Bartholomew-Locke, who is five generations from Maryann. Claude Duval was her maternal grandfather. Several generations of the family were living together at Giro in the 1920s.

Chapter 2

Introducing Bidja

Indigenous Australians may believe in mythical figures who are part of their life experiences and are different to harmful spirits. They are sometimes called Bunyips, Yowies, Hairymen or even Clevermen. There are probably other names too, though spoken of in language (Aboriginal language), of course.

Throughout this work is a young Aboriginal man who is a keen observer of all that is going on. He is deaf and mute, so he spends a lot of time alone, watching and wondering. He has to figure a lot out by himself—however, he does experience the full range of feelings at the time. If he must have a name, we can call him 'Bidja.' It is up to the reader to interpret the young man and who he was—and whether he was real or not! He is included in the story using the Aboriginal customary thought or their belief in mythical creatures and events—so use of imagination will be necessary by the reader; of course he is fictional. The black men interacted with him, but to the whitefellas, he was invisible. For a white person to be given Aboriginal stories, they must be a believer, that is, they must show a genuine respect for the speaker.

Australia's Aboriginal people may use a rich array of beliefs, stories and imaginings in daily life; when they are sharing thoughts and memories, they may speak of a rich assortment of realities, thoughts and ideas that contain mysteries beyond the thoughts and experiences of an average twenty-first-century white person. Bidja could easily have sprung from such a background. However, a proud white man, a person with rational thought might dismiss such ideas out of hand, as ridiculous. Bidja was visible to Aboriginal believers but invisible to the white people, who did not understand or accept the uniqueness of Aboriginality. Some of the Aboriginal people called him Bidja. They understood that Bidja was somehow one of them. But there was a mystery about him too, something they did not quite understand. He saw what was going on, the changes, and puzzled about their meaning for his people and for himself. He was mute but could make himself understood when necessary, gesturing with his face and hands. He had been a witness, from a distance, to baby Maryann's birth in around 1820, yet was apparently also present in 2009 at the Hanging Rock Cemetery, interacting with Auntie Meg Bartholomew nee McCanna.

He identified with people who were suffering, like the cruelly treated convicts and the miners who were raising families 'on the diggings' and were dirt-poor or starving. These people worked hard for extremely little. He may have interacted with the families noted in this book—the Quinns, Duvals, Bartholomews, Fermors, Ninnesses, Clarkes, Morrises, Wrights, Partridges, Paceys and others—though none have ever seen him, and they have no stories about him.

Bidja enjoyed sitting in on a good yarn, though the people were a little nervous of him because he was different.

***

That morning, the camp was stirring early. The children and the mothers were to gather the sweet red fruits that grew near the billabong. Bidja would be among them. He would carry one of the smaller children on his shoulder. There had been rain overnight, but the track was dry. The children skipped along, some holding hands. The bigger ones held onto the cleverly woven grass baskets—something to put the fruit in. Little did they know that something would happen that day, something so terrifying that the youngest never forgot it and the bigger children would never go near that billabong again! Indigenous Australians can have a belief in mythical figures in their life experience, that is, something other than harmful spirits.

Notes

- Bunyips and yowies are mythical creatures found in stories told to children as warnings, for example, not to wander away from the camp. But one was apparently seen by young Bobbie, who is described in Chapter 50 of *Tales at Old Inglebah*. Jamieson writes that the bunyip was real. See also *The Wallabadah Manuscript* (Telfer and Milliss). These creatures have other names in different languages or dialects.

- Earning or establishing trust: Family stories, especially mythical tales, are never shared with a white person until substantial trust has been established between the storyteller and listener. This trust only occurs when white people learn to 'listen with blackfellas' ears'.

- This event could have occurred in the early 1800s. Ingleba means 'whirlpool of crayfish'. The rainbow serpent lives in deep lagoons and waterholes and represents the water element; the Nganyaywana word for rainbow serpent is kabulgan. It is a creature that will devour people who approach its home unless they are medicine men. There used to be a kabulgan in Walcha in a pool just below the waterfall near where the hospital now stands. (Wording used with the permission of the Jamieson family of Limbri).

- Hairymen: This term is difficult to explain. A Hairyman might have longer hair growing on his face and arms and have magical or mysterious powers which had been passed to him on the death of an older Hairyman.

Chapter 3

Disaster at the Billabong

As they approached, the children saw that the billabong water surface was very still. The light breeze hardly disturbed the casuarinas. The plump bush raspberries were red and shiny in the sunlight. The mothers had gone to dig for the sweet yams growing by the creek while the children collected the fruits in a basket.

They stood together at the edge of the water.

A child spoke up loudly. 'We can put our feet in the water—my mother told me!'

'No, we can't,' said another. 'This is scary place!'

'The raspberries are sweet though.'

'Yes. When you get all that juice on your face, you look like a blackfella!' said the second child. 'Look! The water's trembling! Stand back!'

'I'm not frightened!'

'I think there's a bunyip in there—my grandfather said!'

'It's lovely and cool. I can see the bottom and the little gudgeon swimming.' The first child put his toes in the water.

'But something's there … look, it's coming!' said the other. 'Where's Bidja? He'll know if it's safe.'

'Our mothers aren't looking—let's do it. We can paddle.'

There was a sudden rush of water and a big black mouth! The child with wet toes disappeared.

'Where's Bidja?' said the other, looking around desperately. 'He'll save us!'

But Bidja was off lying against a big rock in the warm sun, daydreaming about a young woman he'd seen in the camp.

The children huddled together, crying. 'My brother! My brother! Where has he gone?'

They hunted around in the long grass and everywhere, but they couldn't find him. 'What will our mothers say?' said one.

'Grandmother will be crying,' said another. 'She loved that naughty boy; she loved his adventurous spirit, even though he got us into trouble.'

Then Bidja came over and told them not to panic—but he couldn't find the missing child either.

The luscious red fruits they'd gathered were spilled, forgotten. The girls cried; the boys whimpered all the way along the track back to the camp. The day had been meant to be fun, but it had turned into a disaster.

Bidja went back to the billabong in the evening to have a better look around. The tall grasses had been nibbled, which told him that there was certainly something big living nearby—and perhaps in that billabong! But he would keep that thought to himself when he told the story.

Chapter 4

They Had Lived Nearby for Eons in Deep Time

In the corridor, not far away from the billabong 'where the great sadness' took place (a child had been taken), the group of Anaiwan people that Granny Duval's ancestors came from were living on Ingleba reserve, Walcha, northern New South Wales.

***

An old Aboriginal woman had some children sitting at her feet. She told them a story:

> *A woman spent the day collecting the tiny seeds of the barley grass in her coolamon. She very carefully ground the seeds until they became a powder. Then the woman stirred the powder with a little of the water which she had carried up from the riverbank. She made the dough into muddy-looking grey balls, waiting until the hot fire died down so these cakes could be cooked in the hot ashes.*
>
> *Aboriginal Grannies taught their children to make use of the barley grass seed. They carefully planned the seeding, watering and gathering of the barley grass seed. The harvest would fail in the hungry times when the rains did not fall. When that happened, the people would often go to sleep hungry. Then the marsupials they wanted for tucker*

would go far away because there was little green pick for them, and getting food for hungry men and children became harder and harder.

Sometimes the men might have to hunt for days just to get one kangaroo or possum. It was possum fat that the people craved—just like you do.

But when the first flocks of white men's sheep were driven through the land, there were so many of them that they gobbled every blade of grass before them. Then began our times of great hunger. The yam daisies completely disappeared. We never saw them growing again.

As the children grew, they understood that they would be able to help their people survive when they were hungry—for they had been taught well by their Grannies.

Years later at Ingleba Primary School, King Yarry Campbell was telling the children about their heritage. He said, 'We believe that from time long ago, there was peace between other tribes and our people, who had come together and moved onto the good country, around here. There were times of great hunger. When barley grass and the kangaroo grass seeded, they would grind them up for bread. Our people were the first bread-makers in the history of the world. They never went hungry, for the children had been taught well; our people became survivors.'

Notes

- ❖ In 2018, the Anaiwan people of New England, New South Wales, were believed to be made up of two main groups—a northern group, and a southern group centred on Ingleba in lower New England. The families in this story are of the southern group.

- ❖ The camp would have consisted of a large family group of 50–100 people, including women and children. They would probably have spoken one language, in this case, the Anaiwan language.

- ❖ Memories held by the generations were kept fresh in songlines as well as by storytelling and by the collective tribal memory of generations. Songlines are paths through the land, not just songs. Songlines reinforced Aboriginal memory and culture.

- See https://www.ted.com/talks/elizabeth_loftus_how_reliable_is_your_memory? June 2013

- '"Generations"? Aboriginal Hair samples were taken with permission in the early 1900s and analysed at the Australian Centre for Ancient DNA, with DNA researching to establish whether Aboriginal tribes actually tramped very widely over the continent as has always been stated by authorities and others. Professor Alan Cooper at the Centre (at University of South Australia, The Heritage Project 1927-1964) found that over very long periods of time they got to know the country so intimately and in great detail. Their research found that at the Top End the people had not moved widely geographically at all. This resulted in them storing extraordinary details about the landscape in their minds as they told their stories including the details which developed fine traits in memory which they passed on to their offspring, which has become an amazing Aboriginal trait of memory retention about the natural environment; the white men seem to be unable to develop the skill to the same extent; this helps establish a more accurate passage of time-something about which many white researchers still disagree fundamentally, arguing over how long Aboriginal tribes have inhabited the Continent. It all affects our National Story. However Cooper's work and conclusions have been often disputed.

- They had had plentiful plants to harvest until mobs of sheep ate out every green shoot, killing out the whole spread of nutritious indigenous vegetables.

- 'From their woven dilly bags, the gins sprinkled seed food over the ground—it lay in little hillocks, already swelling and creeping to repeated applications of water which the gins poured on them to "make wungee and the same walkabout grass to grow". (Alice Duncan-Kemp, 1910; see *Dark Emu, Black Seeds* by Bruce Pascoe, pp. 32, 146)

- King Yarry Campbell was married to Elizabeth Quinn (Morris). It is likely that Elizabeth was a decendant of Mary Ann (Quinn) p.126 Unknown newspaper [photo on www.facebook.com/profile/100063617414591/search/?q=King%20Yarry]

- ❖ It is believed that these Australian Aborigines were probably the very earliest people on earth to make bread. In New South Wales, researchers have discovered 36,000-year-old ovens and grindstones that were used by Aboriginal Australians who turned seeds into flours for baking. That is well ahead of other civilisations that started baking early on, like the Egyptians, who began making bread around 17,000 BC. (*Dark Emu: Black Seeds*, pp. 32–33)
- ❖ See also Chapter 19, which discusses R. H. Mathews's descriptions of nineteenth-century Great Eastern Ranges Aboriginal resistance.

Chapter 5

The Hanging Rock Cemetery Gathering

In September 1993, a group of people met in a grass clearing just west of Hanging Rock, near Nundle.[1] In and around Nundle, word had gone out that Hanging Rock Cemetery would be visited by the council and members of parliament. The overgrown, neglected cemetery at Hanging Rock had been prepared for the visit by the families of people buried there. It was a very special day for all of them. Some locals, under Tom McClelland's leadership, had worked hard for months to get rid of the encroaching pine forest seedlings and blackberry brambles. Some discarded headstones had been found and replaced, as had the ironwork surrounding some of the burial plots. Tom's general research was combined with the author's when hunting for these families' records. We went to the courthouse and local church (it was long before we had the internet), but some of the documents had been destroyed by fire. Just a few years later, the same documents would no longer be available to the public as some showed very private information.

***

Bidja, a dark-skinned youth, waited beneath the casuarinas, watching all the activity. He knew who the people were, but what was written on that rock in the clearing? It seemed to have something attached. People were reading the words out, calling out the names there— 'Mary Clarke, James Duval, Marion Mahoney, Emma Williams, Edward Ward …'. There were eighteen names. Many of these referred to Aboriginal people.

A small older Aboriginal woman noticed him.[2] She was generally known in the family as Auntie Meg, although her baptismal name was Isabella and she had a nickname, Dickie; white members of the community called her Meg. Everyone was respectful to her. She was there that day with her daughter, Patricia (Trish for short). Meg had made sure Trish remembered the family stories—she had faithfully passed them on to her.

A tall white man who looked as if he was important stepped from a smart black car. After a few introductions and handshakes, he moved forward to cut the cord that had been strung across the entrance to the cemetery.

He then spoke to the crowd. Bidja read his lips.

'I'm proud to be here today,' he said, 'remembering the Aboriginal people of Hanging Rock and Nundle. So many have died in the past, buried in this cemetery—carefully placed off to the side away from the goldminers and diggers who had also died and were buried here.'

Some family members were not sure which relation was buried at Hanging Rock or where they were—but at least they now had the names of those who were believed to be buried here. More importantly, they had a place to visit where they could respectfully think about family members who were long gone but not forgotten.

Bidja wondered about the sincerity of the white man. What was he saying? Did the tall man really know about his people who were buried there? What did he know about them? It was all such a long time ago.

Auntie Meg[3] approached him and talked quietly; she could see that he was curious. He tried to read her lips. She told him something of her life when she was raising several children out at Cowsby on the country she called home. She told him:

When my children were young, the whitefellas were taking our children away from us—they didn't want 'yellow children' ('half-castes') here at all. We mothers were all very frightened. My husband John had been away in the army, and, after being discharged, he got a good job keeping the boiler going at the big girls' school in Armidale. One day the school matron told him, 'The Welfare are coming tomorrow to take your children.' So in the middle of the night, we packed the kids, the pet lambs, two ducks and the dogs into our old Essex ... and we drove away from our home into the dark and very cold bush. We knew of a big tin shed out there. We made it to our new home. It was rough, but our children were all safe from the Welfare.

The people gathered around Meg—she was like an Elder to them. They were all talking at once, each one trying to tell their own story of family members they recalled with love and affection. They all had family members in common and came from large families, and many had married within the overall group. There were people there with the surnames Duval, Bartholomew, Fermor, Clarke, Partridge and some others. The name Granny Duval came up in their various conversations, and they tried to remember who she was. Where had her family come from? Meg knew about her. Granny Duval had been her great-grandmother.

It was an exciting day for them all. They hadn't seen each other in years, and soon Granny Duval and her story were lost in all the chatter, swept away with other memories of the past.

Bidja saw that it wasn't all excitement. He was aware of a feeling of deep sadness in the gathering, in spite of the excitement at meeting up with friends and family.

He thought that Granny Duval might be kin to him somehow. Perhaps he would work it out one day. Maybe he would even meet her on his walkabout.

They picnicked together that day, appreciative of the work that had been done. However, the weather was getting cold and snow was forecast. Soon they had to bundle up the leftovers, get into their various cars and trucks and head for home. Goodbyes echoed all over the valley that afternoon. This same group of people would never again meet up like they did on that special day in 1993.

Notes

1. The author, a newcomer to the Hanging Rock district, was there that day—and very curious as to who these Aboriginal people were. I didn't understand the significance of what I was witnessing. The experience was another catalyst for my research as I realised how very little I knew.

2. Bidja: The Aborigines at the gathering could have seen him, and might have talked about him for the rest of their lives. However, the 'tall white man' would not have seen him because he was not a believer; he was not privy to their stories, their beliefs, so to him, the boy was mythical, not real. Meg, who lived in both worlds, conversed with Bidja while tacitly accepting the white people's views. She understood.

3. Meg Bartholomew: The great-granddaughter of Granny Duval; the words are from her daughter Patricia Bartholomew-Locke, who is a central figure in this book.

Chapter 6

The Seat of Government Was 400 Miles Away

The Aboriginal people of the tablelands were effectively silent, their voices not heard. No one in authority was interested.

Meanwhile, the government—sitting in Sydney town, many miles away—was asserting its authority, appointing various commissioners and authorities to keep people under control.

The authorities from across the oceans were also having a considerable say about events in the Great South Land, also called New Holland. The first colony, which turned out to be unsustainable, was established inland from the harbour, Port Jackson. But a more successful garden site was established to the west, now the Parramatta area.

It was reported in New England and in the *Maitland Mercury* that there were only 500–600 Aborigines in lower New England from the end of 1836. But twenty years later, there were 1,100 settlers, so the Aboriginal people were outnumbered, and the white people were dominant because they had horses and muskets.

Initially, settlement was discouraged, but when gold was found, Gold Commissioners were assigned to collect licence fees. They had a small force of police to assist them. The licence fee was a type of 'fine' meant to discourage squatting. When Aborigines encroached on what the settlers saw as their land, there could be violence; they didn't see eye to eye at all. They had completely different ways of thinking. And many paid with their lives. But it was too late to prevent the worst of the violence.

While the unnoticed, unacknowledged Anaiwan people were living out their various lives in the bush 400 miles north of Sydney town, the Myall Creek Massacre took place in their general area, near Bingara. It appalled Governor Gipps. It was 1883, and Governor Gipps was a broken man when he took ship home to Britain. He had tried in vain to stand up for justice being meted out for the killings at Myall Creek—but the wealthy squatters were far more powerful than he was. (*Wallabadah Manuscript*, Telfer and Milliss, pp. 173–174)

Between 1837 and 1846, Governor Gipps had announced that he had received instructions that inquests were to be held into any violent deaths of Aboriginal people resulting from conflict with white men. He noted that some atrocities had been recently committed beyond the frontier and stated that 'as the Aboriginal possessors of the soil from which the wealth of the country has been principally derived and as subjects of the Queen, whose authority extends over every part of New Holland, the natives of the colony have equal right with the people of European origin to the protection and assistance of the law of England'. (See *Bingara Advocate* 1965, article by L. L. Payne; Telfer and Milliss, pp. 173–174.)

The two races were getting closer to each other, geographically—but getting in the other's way at the same time; previously unseen black-skinned men encountered the explorers in northern New South Wales.

The English government had given these explorers the job of keeping the peace, providing soldiers, as well as convicts to be labourers. Major Innes was in charge. They were to explore and map the new land, in the hope that adventurous people would come from Britain and settle there.

Beyond Hanging Rock: in the corridor

Men such as Innes and John Oxley were the first to interact with the Aborigines within the corridor. They paved the way for the development of the Australian Agricultural Company, which was Australia's first public company.

Initially, encounters with Aboriginals were not hostile. Here are some firsthand reports:

In 1818, John Oxley became surveyor general; he wrote in his journal: 'We heard the natives call close to us; on being answered, they immediately presented themselves to the number of ten, taking care to show us, by lifting up their hands and clapping them together, that they were perfectly unarmed.'

In 1823, Major Innes was managing a group of convicts when he wrote of the Hastings and Macleay valley people: 'I consider the natives to be very friendly. Numerous tribes for sixty miles, around constantly, visit us and can be employed to apprehend any deserters.'[1]

Neither Major Innes nor John Oxley became afraid of the Aboriginal people. Also, their use of the word 'natives' was not derogatory—this was how people spoke of Indigenous people in the nineteenth century. They were merely using language to convey facts.

However, when Aboriginal people were taking vegetables from plots growing on the north shore of the river, and one of the gardeners—a convict—was murdered, many white people became anxious.

Note

❖ Innes said he 'reached an agreement with the natives to administer justice in the matter in their own way'. There is evidence that this is exactly what happened. (See Frank O'Grady's *Major A. C. Innes*.) The native police were managed from hundreds of miles away at Moreton Bay, Queensland. They were usually mounted. When they were dispatched to go after an Aboriginal 'criminal', they could be dealing with a tribal member—a relative. Thus, the order caused inner conflict for the 'traps', as they were called. Their particular skill was in following the tracks of people they were to hunt down and capture. Once caught, the accused person might be fastened to the trackers' stirrup leather and have to keep up with the horse. A group of captured Aboriginal men might be chained together with iron collars round their necks.

All this would happen without any kind of trial to determine whether they were actually guilty and before any sentence was handed down. They might also be locked up for extended periods of time. It was usually assumed that because they were black-skinned, they were guilty and fit to be punished. Some were hanged. (See Chapter 43.)

Chapter 7

Explorers, Soldiers and Surveyors in the Corridor

Agricultural commerce would soon be established in the north. The two men most significant in this development were employed by the Australian Agricultural Company. It was 1826.

The first man was Richard Dangar, whose work encouraged more Huguenots to come to Australia. Huguenots were fleeing from the Catholic persecution of Christians in Europe. It was said that Dangar sometimes stood up for Aborigines; however, he chose not to do so after the Myall Creek Massacre.

In 1838, the second man, Robert Dawson, was a pastoralist and a 'common man'. He was also something of a scientist in mindset; he made accurate observations and recorded them in his book *The Present State of Australia*. At that time, there was huge interest in the new science of anthropology. It was said of Robert Dawson that he 'was the first Anthropologist of the Aborigines'—that he lived with the Birpai people of the Taree coast—and his book was described as 'an outstanding record of Indigenous life in Australia at a time when the ancient beliefs and customs were still alive and visible throughout most of New South Wales'.

Following his meeting with one elderly black man, Dawson wrote:

I was much amused at this meeting and above all delighted at the prompt and generous manner in which this wild and untutored man conducted himself towards his wandering brother. If they be savages—thought I—they are very civil ones; with kind treatment we have not only nothing to fear, but a good deal to gain from them.

I felt an ardent desire to cultivate their acquaintance and also much satisfaction from the idea that my situation would afford me ample opportunities and means for doing so.

He wrote, 'The treatment of Aborigines in colonial times was generally atrocious—they were subject to abuse, exploitation, and cold-blooded murder—regarded as subhuman and not recognised at all as the Traditional Owners of their lands.' He stated, 'For a long time no serious attempts were made to study their languages or to understand their culture—their beliefs, customs … On the contrary the focus was on "civilising them" by imposing upon them the European way of life—they were classed as savages.'

This was the case until well into the twentieth century. An important scientific expedition involving researchers from Europe was mounted in Australia in 1914. (See Russell, L.(ed). *A Trip to the Dominions : The Scientific Event that Changed Australia*) These expeditions and a conference that was also held were the origins of the idea, which came to be held by so many in the wider Australian community, of the black men being so weak and so few that they would die out, which was the excuse usually given for removing Aboriginal children from their mothers and from the camps. Also, cross-cultural marriages were forbidden by law. The government of the day definitely did not want hosts of 'half-caste' children spoiling their efforts to whiten the whole Australian population. The White Australia Policy was just around the corner!

At one stage, the authorities wanted the whole population to be white. The authorities made it hard for Aborigines to live in peace on Australian soil at all and genuinely persecuted them. On the other hand, they wanted the two races to combine to bring about a 'white-out' effect, or assimilation. Later, however, they did *not* want the races to combine, so intercultural marriage was forbidden. Later still, they again removed 'children at risk' from their homes, deeming their mothers, the conditions or the surroundings unfit for them. (See Chapter 36 for more information about 1914 and various regulations imposed by the authorities.)

Notes

- ❖ See Dawson, *The Present State of Australia 1830*. Copies of the 1987 version are facsimiles. The book is about Aboriginal languages, weapons, families, death and religion, as well as intertribal relations and interactions with the colonists.
- ❖ See Harrison, *Shared Landscapes*, a report combining the activities of settlement and colonial activities with the geography and Aboriginal interaction, covering northwestern New South Wales.
- ❖ The use of the word 'half-caste' is not acceptable today as it is considered derogatory, insulting, or demeaning. Sometimes Aboriginal people themselves use the term 'yellow men', indicating non-white skin colour.
- ❖ See Rolls, *A Million Wild Acres*, an enjoyable and informative read about the bush and the changes in northwestern New South Wales.
- ❖ On 'developing our own anthropology', see Russell, L. (ed) *A Trip to The Dominions*.
- ❖ Philip Gidley King: The Aborigines were the people who showed the Australian Agricultural Company surveyor, young Philip Gidley King (with his father), the best route for a road from their coastal lands up to the tableland. It was just a line of carved trees, going straight up Hungry Hill through Nowendoc to Walcha. The road is still in use today and was a great achievement.

Chapter 8

The Cedar Cutters and Bidja at the Coast

This chapter is set between 1816 and 1870. After 1816, the Aboriginal people, who only eight years earlier had enjoyed sovereignty over their own country, could find no foothold in that land. As the northeastern New South Wales country was explored—opened up—the white men that Aborigines encountered were cedar cutters, ruthless men with few scruples; they had been soldiering overseas, had been discharged and needed an income.

In 1810, huge cedar trees had still been growing thickly fifty miles into the hinterland. After this, various Aboriginal people worked with the cedar cutters in exchange for tobacco, tea, sugar, flour and possibly rum. The country was steep and rough, but Aboriginal people could reach the trees more easily than the white men. Trees were cut down, and bullocks were used to haul logs to the riverbank, where the strong water flow would wash them downstream when the floods came.

The cedar cutters lived rough, in squalid camps. Perhaps the Aborigines didn't realise that those in the camps were not much different from themselves—the cedar cutters shared their food and may have shared women too. White men who had served in the army in Abyssinia (Eritrea), discharged from the army in the 1860s, finding themselves with no income, trekked north into the forest looking for cedar trees—there was a market for the good timber. These men could be brutal—they had muskets to 'protect themselves from the savages' and would swiftly mete out justice, as they saw it.

✳✳✳

Bidja was on walkabout. He had run from the older man who had taken his girlfriend. He was heartbroken. Near the river, he heard a woman crying in terror, shrieking in anguish. She was being held by a couple of cedar cutters—rough men who had abused her, hurt her, and tied her to a tree. Her cries touched Bidja's heart. He fled from the riverbank horror and the cedar cutters as he heard the woman's shrieks, which drove him up the mountains, down into the valleys and across raging creeks. He could not forget her cries. Following animal tracks, he tramped determinedly towards the new settlement of Port Macquarie. It was a long way.

At the edge of a cliff top he stared, wide-eyed with amazement.

He was on a headland, and the spread of the blue ocean in front of him quite took his breath away. From the clifftop, he saw the Irish convict Maurice Quinn, a skinny white man. Though Bidja was not visible that day, he came face to face with Quinn—who didn't realise it. Their paths would cross again.

✳✳✳

On his papers, Quinn was described as 'an Irishman from Limerick, Southern Ireland'. His conviction document states that he was born in 1810; a labourer, he was tried in March 1837 and arrived in Australia on SS *Calcutta* to be indentured to a Mr and Mrs Stitt of Rimbanda Station, Bendemeer, New South Wales, in 1838. Mr Stitt was the station manager.

On his committal papers, Quinn was described like this:

Maurice Quinn
Complexion: dark ruddy
Scars: right eye, right wrist, and left forearm
Eyes: hazel grey
Hair: dark brown
Height: 5 ft ¾

Crime: burglary and robbery

Transportation

Conditional pardon

It also said his sentence was to be commuted in 1850.

In 1836, back in Ireland, thousands of miles away, across the ocean, a man broke into a cottage. He stole a shirt and some fancy socks. 'These look pretty good,' he thought. 'I could easily sell them down the street and get myself some baccy.' But he was caught, arraigned, and sentenced to transportation across the seas. (Major crimes called for hanging!) That Irishman was Maurice Quinn, who, straight off the cutter, gasped in the fresh air when he'd finally got his bare feet onto dry land and could get his balance again. In chains, he tramped all the way from Port Macquarie penal settlement.[1] The officer was on horseback; but there was no mounted transport for Quinn. His fair Irish complexion suffered horribly in the harsh sun—all he could do to soften the pain of sunburn was rub in some mutton fat. The smell was not good, and much later he realised why some of the 'gins' (Aboriginal women) smelt so bad! ('Gin' was a colloquial term, said to come from the women drinking gin—which someone must have been supplying!)

There were Anaiwan people living in the range in the (then) Bendemeer and Walcha areas. At Rimbanda Station, Maurice saw the Aboriginal camps for the first time in his life. Much later, one young woman in particular caught his eye.

By 1838, the young Aboriginal woman, Mahrakan, then about eighteen, and the Irish convict Quinn were drawing closer together.

Descendants of their daughter Mary Elizabeth and her husband James Duval became associated with Ingleba people following their marriage. Later, in the 1870s, they settled down in the Hanging Rock Diggings and Nundle communities.

✲✲✲

Looking on—seeing the sick old men moving around below him—Bidja thought to himself: Back at the camp, I'll show them. From the clifftop, I'll tell them, I saw strange-looking people milling around on the white sand.

They had huge animals, like kangaroos, but much bigger! And they swam in the saltwater—like giant fishes! The spirits looked like men but were pale-skinned, not dark like us! And some of them were all tied together with pandanus twine—like old, old men. They couldn't walk straight—they were sick!

I'll tell them there were other animals, like big kangaroos, that looked like good tucker, but they moved slowly. If we could catch one, it'd make a good-tasting meal—enough for everyone.

There were huge canoes too, I'll say. I think the spirit-men came in the canoes.

I was afraid of what might happen if they caught me, I'll say—but they didn't even see me!

***

There were always different points of view about what was happening 'in the bush'. Here are some comments overheard on a Sydney Street after the Myall Creek Massacre trial.

Countryman: 'Well, they have hanged the man this morning.'

Citizen: 'Yes, I understand that they have!'

Countryman: 'It's a damn shame. But we have fallen on a safer game in our part of the country.'

Citizen: 'Indeed, pray what is that?'

Countryman: 'Oh, we poison them.'

Citizen: 'Good God, poison them?'

Countryman: 'Yes—we have done so with a good many already and serves them right, too!' (20 December 1838, quoted in Milliss, p. 558)

***

On the cliff top, Bidja knew that he needed to catch up with his wider family back on the (Barnard) River. His grandparents had reared him to respect the women of the camp. He'd had some training in fighting, although he was not keen on the idea of fighting at all and, anyway, not much warring went on anymore; the government and the missions had insisted that the Aboriginal and white people live in peace.

His people had finally been forced into submission.

When Bidja arrived back in the camp, following his fraught trek to the coast, he was the centre of attention as he told them all about his walkabout. They sat around taking in his wild gestures and the faces he pulled. There was much serious conversation about what he was telling them.

However, when he caught up with his grandparents, he was most anxious to ask them about his mother. Grandfather had told him a little about her, but now that he was grown and had been out on his trip on his own, he wanted more details. Grandfather was an old man of great wisdom and was much respected in the tribe. Bidja was very curious. He'd been told something about his mother, but the story was incomplete. One day he would know the whole story—something terrible must have happened to her. Any wrong must be righted; payback would fall to a family member. And his faithful yellow dog was always at his side.

Note

1. Port Macquarie penal settlement. See Lieutenant Stephen Partridge, described in Chapter 34.

Chapter 9

The Howl of the Dingo: A True Account

In the area around the camp, not far from Wolka (later Walcha) district, a local skirmish took place. As usual, the causes of the conflict were land and Woldja (Eagle Hawk), one of the leaders of the tribe.

From time to time, the Anaiwan Aborigines dealt with differences between themselves and a group of Kamilaroi people. Donald Jamieson, the first white child born on Ingleba Station, recounted the story. It was told to him by his father, Francis Jamieson. 'The Himberrong clan of the Anaiwan people were sandwiched between the Dunghutti or Thungatti of the Macleay River Valley and the highlands and the Gumbaynggirr tribe of the Hastings area, including the Eastern Falls country. There was many a clash between these two tribal groups, often over territorial boundaries.' (From *Tales at Old Inglebah* by Donald Jamieson; used by kind permission of the Jamieson family.)

The following is an account of a battle between some Himberrong (Anaiwan/Ingleba) men against neighbouring 'Moonbi' men. The Himberrong were a clan of the Anaiwan people. This was oral history recorded from local knowledge during the early twentieth century (and used with permission). It would have taken place around 1910. Donald Jamieson wrote: 'One night, the mournful howl of a dingo was heard way out on the range.'

The Anaiwan clan did not usually venture far over the Moonbi Range to the west, but they claimed the land; and on the other hand, the Moonbi clan claimed all the land to the top of the range. If they ventured across these lines, there would be trouble!

The story is recorded in Jamieson's family history, *Tales At Old Inglebah*:

A group of Anaiwan warriors camping on the area in question were sighted by a Moonbi hunting party. Being few in number, they knew they were not strong enough to attack with any hope of success, so they hurried back to their own camp which was located near a creek at the foot of the Moonbi Range not too far from where the village of Moonbi is today.

When they returned to the camp, the hunting party informed the rest of the clan that the Himberrong men were once more trespassing on their hunting grounds. The whole tribe lost no time in preparing themselves to go forth and settle the question—forever.

Leaving the women, children, and younger men behind, the Moonbi warriors set out at about sundown, intending to travel through the night and attack the enemy camp just before dawn. As the camp would be full of women and children, the Moonbi warriors expected an easy victory.

Whipperoo, 'Great Kangaroo', and Mungengarly, 'Goanna', were two of the leading men in the Anaiwan clan at that time. These two were never likely to be caught napping, as they knew whenever they were in this that part of the country they were likely to be attacked, so they were prepared for such a contingency.

It was the black man's love for fire which lost the battle for the Moonbi before it had begun. It did not matter if it was hot or cold or summer or winter—even if they were only still for only a few minutes, they would start a little fire.

If the Moonbi men had been content to rest before attacking the camp without lighting any fires, they would have won the day!

On the northern side of the Ingleba camp stood a high mountain—the highest point of land for some miles—with the hills on either side falling away, so they had a good view of the country both up and down the creek.

Two sentinels were always waiting on the top of this mountain, standing guard, day and night. There were another two on watch at the camp itself to inform the others immediately if they saw any danger. They had agreed that if the enemy was sighted, their warning signal would be a smoke signal during the day or a dingo howl, twice repeated, during the night.

If the Moonbi men had been content to rest before attacking the camp, without lighting fires, they would have stood a very good chance of taking the Ingleba men by surprise. However, the two watchers on the mountain saw numerous fires spring up, and they knew at once what it meant!

The watchers in the camp below heard the mournful howl of a dingo ring out in the night air. It was repeated from the mountain twice more. They hastily began rousing the rest of the camp. The women and children were sent back across the creek and into the hills in charge of the old men who couldn't fight.

In the midst of these preparations, the two sentries had come down from the mountain and reported what they had seen.

Learning how long the fires had been lit, allowing for the time the enemy would be expected to remain where they were, and the time it would take to travel the distance to the camp, the Ingleba men decided they had about two hours to wait before they were attacked. They made good use of the time at their disposal.

A short distance down the creek, the mountain came down to a beaten track almost to the water's edge. The leaders of the men knew that the Moonbi would follow this track as it was the best for walking and they could travel it without making much noise. It was here they chose to make their stand. Half the Himberrong warriors, led by Mungengarly, circled around so they could close in behind the Moonbi as they entered the pass between the creek and the mountain. Whipperoo took the other half so they could bar the way out of the pass. The men at the rear were to wait until they heard the tribe's battle cry before making an attack.

It was an hour before daylight when the Moonbi decided it was time to make a start. The warriors made ready their weapons and silently resumed their march, expecting to find the enemy camp sleeping. They entered the narrow pass, which enabled three men to walk side by side.

Silently black shadows dropped from the mountainside and closed up behind the Moonbi. Some minutes passed and the first of the warriors was about to emerge into more open ground when a spear thrown from only a few yards whistled through the air, and he fell without a sound.

At the same time, the war cry of the Anaiwan rang out on the still night air, immediately answered by the warriors behind the enemy as they sent a shower of spears.

The Moonbi men had no chance. Some made a desperate stand, but being trapped between the creek and mountain and attacked from both front and rear by their foes was a hopeless fight from which very few escaped. Others had made good their escape as soon as the attack began, climbing the mountain. Others leapt into the creek and were soon swallowed up in the scrub darkness.

It was some years before the howl of the dingo was heard again in that part of the country to signal that a fight was on!

Bidja was there too that night, watching the sentries as they watched the Moonbi men sitting calmly around their small fires, never dreaming they would soon be roundly defeated.

Notes

❖ Ingleba/Anaiwan v. Kamilaroi—a border dispute. In a nutshell: the Moonbi clan claimed that the Ingleba people were trespassing on Moonbi hunting grounds. The Anaiwan maintained that the area in question was part of their hunting grounds and were prepared to back up their claims with nulla-nullas, boomerangs and spears.

❖ Aborigines were scornful of the white people's way of building a huge fire when a small one was enough. But if the Moonbi men had been content to rest before attacking the camp without lighting *any* fires, they would have won the day!

- ❖ The Anaiwan group was called Himberrong from ancient times—so the names are interchangeable.
- ❖ Ingleba: The Anaiwan clan did not usually venture far over the Moonbi Range to the west, but they claimed the land and would sometimes go as far as halfway from the top of the range to where Weabonga is located. Weabonga is the Nganyaywana word for swamp gum.

Chapter 10

Black Men Met White Men on Their Country

When Aboriginal men met white men on their country, Bidja was there—just watching the events.

The following is a first-person account of an event that occurred in about 1842 near the Macdonald River in the Walcha district.[1] It is told in *Tales at Old Inglebah* by Donald Jamieson and is used with the permission of the Jamieson family at Limbri.[2]

This is an account of a real-time meeting of Himberrong (Anaiwan) men Bungaree (James Dixon) and Chief Yarry (Campbell) with four settlers in 1842, the earliest recorded encounter.

They were working on the building of their house, which they were anxious to get finished before the winter set in. ... [Two men assisting Bill, Jack Coe, not his real name, and George, who never went by any other name.] They were both vague about their past lives and where they came from and nobody cared much. They were both good willing workers. ...

[Mr Connel, the boss of the white men suddenly] said, 'What do you think of that, men?' ...

The men turned in the direction indicated and saw a sight which caused them considerable uneasiness. For coming round the shoulder of the hill was a long line of Aboriginals, warriors in the lead, in single file. Behind them came the young men, then the gins, old and young, and then piccaninnies of all sorts and sizes, but no dogs. In all the accounts I have read about the tribes throughout Australia, I have always noticed dogs mentioned, mostly mangy dingoes, but this tribe had none, mangy or otherwise. It was not until years later when they were partly civilised that they had dogs and they were obtained from the white people. (Warrigal says that the Aborigines took whole litters of dingo pups and raised them to be domesticated according to their lights—see Chapter 18.)

Jack Coe stared, then gasped and said, 'shall I get the guns boss?'

The guns were two single barrel muzzle loaders and a smooth bore Enfield rifle, which they used for shooting any game they came across.

'Don't be silly, Jack,' said the boss. 'What use would those three ancient things be against two hundred spears and as many boomerangs? No, we must try other means if they approach us. They may not be hostile if we treat them properly. Our trouble will be, that we will not be able to understand their language, or they ours.'

Between where they were building and the granite hill there was a line of black ash timber, [tall and] … very dense. Between this timber and the hill was an open space which was sheltered. … and it was here that the natives had their permanent camp, although the white men did not know this at the time.

Here also was a permanent spring of water. That spring is there to this day and in all the hundred years and more since the white men settled there, it has never been known to go dry, even in the worst drought.

Well the natives went into camp and nothing more was seen of them for some time although the settlers kept a sharp look out all the evening. Towards sundown … they saw two warriors emerge from the timber and advance slowly towards them. They would walk a few steps, then stop and stare at the strangers who must surely have been the first white men they had ever seen.

As soon as they saw the natives, Mr Connel said, 'Now we are in for it. Good or bad. Put the billy on, Bill, while I prepare to receive the visitors.'

Eventually after much stopping and staring, they came within twenty yards of the white men, and there they stopped and came no closer. They were both fine stamps of men, broad shouldered and muscular, the shorter of the two being, as far as they could see, a little under six feet. This man, they found out later, was the chief of the tribe. The other was much taller, six feet two or more, and as straight as a rush. They were both armed for war as when on a hunting expedition they carried other weapons beside these, but I will have more to say on that point later.

The boss of the white men, when he saw that the natives would come closer, advanced towards them a few steps and held out his hand. But they both shook their heads, thus indicating they did not understand. He then advanced a little closer, thinking he must try something else. While he was trying to think of something, the two Aboriginals carried on a conversation between themselves in a low tone, while glancing from one of the white men to the other and grinning broadly. Jack Coe said afterwards, he was wondering all the time, which part of his body the hickory spear would strike.

But nothing happened and then Mr Connel suddenly had a bright idea. He walked up to the two and pointing to himself, saying 'John' several times, then turning to where his men stood, interested spectators of the scene, he pointed to them in turn, 'Bill, Jack, George'.

The look on the faces of the two men seemed to indicate that they were beginning to understand and the chief struck himself on the chest and said, 'Yarry,' and, turning to the other black man, said, 'Bungaree.' Having got that far and learnt the names of the men, the boss went and shook hands with each of his men, then turned and again extended his hand to the chief. This time, they understood immediately what was meant and shook hands with the boss and then stepped forward and solemnly shook hands with the other three white men.

All the time this was taking place, the natives kept looking uneasily about them as if prepared to bolt at the slightest sign of danger. At the same time the white men were just as uneasy as to what the blacks might do. But by now the billy had been boiled and the food brought out and each of the whites took a piece of damper and beef and a pint of tea and commenced to eat.

After a time they handed some of the food and tea to the natives and it was amusing to see the look of delight which spread over the two black faces as they started to eat. They seemed to especially enjoy the tea, for after emptying their mugs they passed them back for more with looks of great satisfaction. ...

After sitting for some time in silence the two arose, picked up their weapons and departed in the direction of their camp and thus started a friendship between white men and the black, which was to endure while ever there was a Connel on Inglebah or an Aboriginal in the district. All this just through the common sense of one man, who decided to try decency and kindness, before resorting to violence. ... Of course there were others who did treat them decently and endeavoured to avoid trouble and they were mainly successful, ... [Another example were the two Everett brothers of Guyra, on Ollera Station, who were Christian believers.[3] These brothers went so far as to learn the local language.] But there were others who treated the natives like animals, to be shot on sight. This of course, caused the blacks to retaliate, which resulted in the death of many whites and the extinctions of whole tribes of the Aboriginals.

The Inglebah tribe was never warlike, although there were some bad men in the tribe—a couple who were never satisfied to live in peace with neighbouring tribes, or the white people, and who were mostly trying to stir up trouble.

Later in life, Yarry's name was changed to Jim Yarry Campbell, but Bungaree never changed his name at all—he was not about to please any white authorities! James Dixon was his English name, but he would never answer to it. In the 1920s, Yarry was still alive, and he is remembered as having a long white beard and living in Ingleba. He is said to have had a mild soft voice. He would go for walkabout at times for a couple of days accompanied by his wife, Lizzie, who was very much younger. As an old man, he used to go to the local school and tell the children the Aboriginal stories, the legends that had been handed down from generation to generation.[4]

***

Bidja had seen it all!

Notes

1. The workers' names: The men went by their given names only and may have used someone else's name rather than their own because their lives could be somewhat shifty, so they preferred to be anonymous.
2. Access to *Tales at Old Inglebah*, was kindly granted by the family members of Donald Jamieson of Limbri, New South Wales, in 2012. Jamieson, Donald., 1890-1961. *Tales at old Inglebah* / [Tamworth, N.S.W.] 1987.
3. Everett brothers and other Christian families of New England.
4. King Yarry married Elizabeth Quinn, sister of Granny (Mary) Duval.

Chapter 11

Moving In and Taking Over

From a business plan (the Australian Agricultural Company) to the Church's intervention.

While the British Empire was being extended by adding the colonies in India, Africa, and New Zealand, big businesses, including the Church, influenced New South Wales's New England country—leading to new experiences in the lives of the people there. Invasions, massacres dispossession, including that caused by fledgling settlements, went with these changes.

***

Bidja mourned with his people as they tried to adapt to the many changes affecting their lives. Sometimes his curiosity almost got him into trouble as he crept too close; he wanted to watch what the newcomers were doing, but he fled if the dogs began to alert the white settlers that he was watching from near their simple homes.

The maritime nations had developed ships that could withstand long sea journeys. It was this development that spurred explorers on—Captain James Cook, and other sailors from various nations—to seek the Great South Land, or Terra Australis.

The French were close behind Cook. Their scientists' observations of the British men were scathing: they thought the British held ideas of their own entitlement and superiority. (See the scientific expeditions and observations by the French at that time, SBS TV, https://www.sbs.com.au/language/german/en/podcast-episode/australia-a-french-colony/98q37do99 2022.)

On other parts of the continent, what certainly felt like an invasion had come to the Aboriginal homelands. The newcomers settled down along the coast and hinterland of the land they called New South Wales. Several other white men from overseas lands had stepped onto that land, but none had raised a flag before the British did so at Sydney Cove.

On landing, the British commanders had reasoned like this: they saw no signs of 'civilisation', meaning roads, farmhouses, gardens and so on, so they occupied the land, assuming that if anyone was already there, they would become compliant—and British, because the invaders thought their sovereignty was established automatically by their very occupation of what they saw as an empty land.

At that time, it was generally thought by white people that the white race was superior in every way to dark-skinned races, an outlook that persisted for at least the next 100 years and fundamentally changed the Aborigines' lives as the European settlers became more and more dominant on their country. (Charles Darwin published his ideas on evolution during this period. It was a new way of thinking.)

The two races thought in fundamentally different ways. White men looking for personal prosperity brought the races closer together geographically but, at the same time, drove them further apart in thought. Many changes were caused by the Australian Agricultural Company after it was established on the London Stock Exchange. In 1825, it was granted a million acres on the central New South Wales coast near Port Stephens.

The company's business plan was to produce fine-wool sheep; wool was needed in Britain to make army uniforms for the empire's wars. However, it turned out that the climate and granted land were not suitable for producing fine wool, so other land was sought. Land was ultimately granted on the Liverpool Plains.

This move away from the coast turned out to be successful for the wool-growing enterprise but not so good for the Aborigines, who had already been displaced due to settlement by the first squatters from the Hunter region.

Like the Aboriginal people, the squatters already settled on the plains were not happy about the arrival of the Australian Agricultural Company. Most moved northwards, towards country that was as yet unclaimed, by white reckoning. Congi was the first pastoral property the company took possession of. However, it didn't do all that well there, and when gold was found on Company land—in the Peel River and on its banks—another new enterprise was established, the Peel River Land and Mineral Company. Two land grants were made to this new business not far from the small township of Tamworth, but once again, high-quality wool production was not commercially successful.

Meanwhile, the Aboriginal people were being affected by the changes that the invasion by white men had brought to the north and the south. New Holland (as the land was alternatively named by the Dutch) was being governed from the harbourside township of Sydney by white men who, in turn, were governed by other white people thousands of miles away, across the saltwater, in Britain. Communication between London and Sydney was slow, and there was much confusion as orders and reports went back and forth by sailing ship. This enabled disaffected soldiers of the Sydney area to take the law into their own hands to some extent, so that the governors struggled for control.

The Aborigines of the Central Coast area were effectively displaced when the Australian Agricultural Company's convict shepherds poisoned the waterholes. Many died in agony in the Gloucester region—a massacre so terrible that it was never forgotten. Elsewhere, many were tortured, maimed, blinded, burned or castrated, suffering indescribable brutality, goaded beyond human endurance to become a courageous, hopeless and suicidal people (Harris, p. 140). Any survivors fled into the ranges.

Where was the Church in all this? Some Christian ministers did speak out—often to be mocked in the press. However, there is no evidence that before the Black War in Tasmania, the Church spoke out against Governor Arthur's orders to rid that island of its Indigenous people. Later on, though, the Church became involved in other ways. The authorities wanted to know how many Aborigines there were and how they were faring, and the true measure of how many Aboriginal people there were can be found in the records of blankets that were handed out. This social benefit was overseen by Reverend Threlkeld of Myall Lakes in northern New South Wales. He was the first white man to seriously attempt to learn the Aboriginal language; he had a genuine concern for the people's well-being. (See Waters & Moon, pp. 132–137.)

Aboriginal people lost the freedom to roam on their own land, to catch birds in their nets along the rivers, to carry out their slow-burning land management practices which attracted game to fresh sweet grasses, and to live in peace while living off the fat of the land, taking only what they needed and always leaving food behind for the next traveller. The Aborigines were Australia's first conservationists. They have never plundered the land as white people have, because their concern has been for survival, not for excess or financial gain.

The white people moved back and forth across the land in the corridor, even up to the plateau of Hanging Rock, where gold was found in 1851. After that, the nature of the entire population of New South Wales was fundamentally altered—again.

The white men were not discouraged by their failures; the white population increased both geographically and numerically. In 1851, the discovery of gold was worrying to those in government in New South Wales. They were afraid that convicts would escape to the goldfields, that bushranging activity would increase and that the whole country would get out of control.

The gold rush brought people from many lands to the Nundle and Hanging Rock area. The Aborigines observed the frenzied activity on the river and creeks as in every gully the sweet water was muddied to wash the 'stuff'.

The Church's role in the changes

When the Australian Agricultural Company had built their station near the coast, ministers of religion were brought in and a church was established so that the English newcomers would feel at home and so their children could be baptised and 'proper Christian marriages' and burials could be held.

A reporter from *The Empire* wrote:

In 1853, a meeting was held in Nundle village. There has been talk of building a Church of England church as there has been 'a desire of the miners to promote Christian worship amongst themselves which is a step in the right direction. The goldfields of all places in the world are most likely to estrange the heart from God … It is surprising that of all the creeds, sects, of all the missionaries sent forth, not one individual has been sent to this goldfield to reside among us, to give us the advantages of meeting together for worship and Christian fellowship.' They had collected the sum of seven pounds in two years to support a clergyman—a sum that most thought was paltry. They said that 'the miners would all benefit if they heard two sermons every Sunday.'

Welsh tin miners were known for their beautiful choral voices when they sang in harmony together, as reflected in the following quotation.

They said 'the Welsh Christian influence was heard in harmony—echoing around the hills'.

See Carruthers, J E *Memories of an Australian Ministry* p. 64

Bishop Broughton held several baptisms in the Hanging Rock community—including on a verandah and in someone's tiny sitting room. In New South Wales, it was the practice to gather the children and adults together and baptise them all at once. This was for convenience, because the priest only visited tiny settlements once or twice a year.

From a Christian correspondent in the *Maitland Mercury*, 22 October 1869:

There is a movement on foot to build a dissenting place of worship. Subscriptions are handed over pretty freely. We want, sadly want, some spiritual rigor in this place—the Devil and Mammon have got plenty of honour seven days in the week. God has service, yes service in his honour once a month. Whence go all the Missionary funds? Are they expended on comfort in towns along the coast? Yes, inland districts have not any attraction for preachers of the Cross. Yes, even the dark-skinned idolator has a spiritual guide sent him, but the white brother, the man who is contributing to the commercial prosperity of the country, is left to forget the path that once he may have trod, and a darkness worse than heathen becomes his light.

A simple church was built in Oakenville Creek, Nundle for the use of the Christian leaders, but it was not for the Aboriginal people. For them, Christian ministry took place on reserves, led by missionaries.

In 2017, it was agreed that many tribesmen of the coastal region had been displaced, which had caused great consternation, fear, and 'confusion of the tribes'. Consequently, there still is some argument over which Aboriginal people lived where, as the Birpai, Worimi and Dunghutti people may have blended to some degree over the years. Feelings still run high when the peoples of this part of the coast are discussed. (See *Nineteenth-Century lower New England Aboriginal Resistance* by R. H. Mathews and Chapter 18, Warrigal.)

Notes

- See *Baal Belbora* (Blomfield), pp. 6–7 and maps showing the northern New South Wales massacres.
- A company town was marked out on the western bank of the Peel River opposite Nundle in 1854, but it was never fully occupied.
- The population of Aborigines was dropping due to diseases. Infanticide of female babies was also taking place. The end result was that only a few young women were observed at the camps or when tribes were seen in a mob.
- In 2020, a map was also published showing the extent of massacres in New South Wales, (https://australian.museum/learn/first-nations/unsettled/remembering-massacres/map-of-colonial-frontier-massacres/) indicating the many serious clashes between the white and Aboriginal people. Definition of massacre: 'an event that affected the lives of more than six people' (*Massacres Map [1790–1895]* by Lyndall Ryan of Newcastle University). See also Note 8 below.
- See *Pure Merinos and Others* p. 107 (Pemberton). The churches were somewhat active on the Hanging Rock Diggings; the diggers' families said that they had appreciated the ministry of Reverend E. Williams,

Anglican vicar of Tamworth. Apparently, he would visit the miners in their respective huts and tents. See also Boileau p. 50.

- See *Australia As It Really Is, in Its Life, Scenery, and Adventure.* (Eldershaw, pp. 82-3). 'Here, at the present time, a marked feature amongst all our Aboriginal tribes is the great preponderance of males over females, and expediency would now, of course, suggest the most careful preservation of their female offspring – such, however, is not the practice.'

- Showing the Anaiwan boundary (see map in https://newenglandhistory.blogspot.com/2012/09/anaiwan-notes.html).

- Frontier wars of northwestern New South Wales: See *Massacres of Eastern Australia* (work carried out by Lyndall Ryan). Massacres in the corridor occurred in 1821, 1828, 1832, 1836 and 1839 at Waterloo, Wattenbakh, Mt Mackenzie, Belbora, Bowmans Flat, Gangat, Garibaldi Creek, Stoney Creek, Cogo, Elsenore, Cat Camp, Kunderang, Macleay, Hendersons Creek, Towel Creek, Wabro, Sheep Station, Darkie Point, Myall Creek and Garibaldi Rock. See *Massacres Map (1790–1895)* by Lyndall Ryan of Newcastle University, an electronic interactive map of the many sites investigated in eastern Australia. Note: For Ryan's purposes, she designates a massacre as an event involving at least six people.

- 'Home': See *Pure Merinos and Others* (Pemberton), the story of the Australian Agricultural Company setup at Port Stephens, New South Wales.

- Aboriginal people being referred to as 'heathen' by the reporter at the Maitland Mercury is language that would not be used today.

Chapter 12

Hostilities in the Bush

Relations between the two races in the bush were not good. Several books describing this were written and published in 1840s, although there were pockets where good relations persisted—for example, on the country held by the Everetts, because these brothers learned the local Aboriginal language, which made all the difference to relationships on their holdings. (See the Commissioner's statement in Chapter 38.)

It was a savage encounter

In the 1840s and 1850s, several books were written and published to attract settlers to the land by giving frank accounts of personal experiences that were perhaps coloured by imagination. Frank Eldershaw wrote of his own losses and frightening experiences due to conflicts with the Aboriginal people—though it is doubtful if this account was about Anaiwan people, who, apparently, were usually peaceable. However, when descriptions of events sound so realistic, we risk committing serious misjudgements if we disapprove by superimposing our present-day views when interpreting accounts of what seems to have actually taken place. We should be careful not to propagate attitudes that educated people have historically assumed because of racist views or feelings of superiority due to being modern, educated and supposedly more sophisticated. For example, the description of a trek in the Barnard River valley sounds authentic and not, in fact, a product of imagination; see Eldershaw p. 51:

'It was between the heads of the Barnard and Little Manning Rivers, among the rough and broken ranges of that almost impassable tract of country, that I took …'. One could almost pinpoint his exact location on the New South Wales Parks or Anaiwan boundary map!

A very different encounter

Eldershaw wrote of his decision to immigrate to New South Wales from Britain in 1840 because of *'the sadly waning prospects of family affairs back home'* (ibid, p.5). In 1841, he became a squatter north of Wandsworth, at Manoan (midway between Llangothlin and Ben Lomond, on Western Fall country). What follows is presented as an eyewitness account of his party's experience, written in the language and grammar of the times. It is a vivid first-person account:

> *Towards the close of the autumn of '41, after a beautiful and most prosperous season, we were miserably startled from the unconscious lull of security which long continued impunity from harm invariably produces, by the appalling intelligence that one of my out-stations had been attacked, its three unfortunate occupants brutally massacred, and the sheep, two thousand in number, carried off as spoils, together with whatever stores and implements the station had been provided. Accompanied by three neighbours, I immediately proceeded to reconnoitre the spot of this atrocity. The tracks, camp fires, and numerous gunyahs indicated clearly the recent presence of a tribe of natives numbering, we surmised, at least two hundred. The hut was empty, but we could plainly perceive, by blood and other evidences of deadly struggle, that one at least of the unfortunate fellows had here met his dreadful end. A still further and more minute examination of every track and indication around revealed to our practised eyes, mysteriously but unmistakeably, full evidences of the conduct of the whole catastrophe. The watchman, it was apparent, had been sneaked upon in his hut, and while in the act of turning or in some way attending to a "damper" baking in the ashes, speared in the back. The shepherds had been waylaid on their return with the flocks, and destroyed probably without the chance of an effort for their lives.*

Our subsequent discovery of the bodies tended to verify the accuracy of these observations; we dragged the unfortunate fellows from a neighbouring waterhole, and buried them with such decent rites as our limited means permitted; two of them, the shepherds, were literally riddled with spear-wounds; the watchman had received four spears in his loins, and in addition, the back of the skull - the occipital and posterior face of the sphenoid bones - was completely smashed to fragments by the waddies of these brutal savages.

Possessed of all the information which it was possible thus to obtain, we returned to arrange a party for immediate pursuit. Each of our men was savagely anxious and eager to be chosen for this painfully-imperative task; the thought of their butchered comrades, with sundry vivid reminiscences of personal escapes from a fate as dreadful, made them pant for an opportunity of vengeance on the heads of their wily and dangerous enemies. We made our selection from among them, however, upon other and I hope sounder grounds than could be gathered from the noisiest ebullition of excited feeling. Including my neighbouring friends, we mustered a party of ten, well mounted and accoutred, and taking with us ten days' provisions, we started at daybreak on the following morning in pursuit.

From all appearances the murderous villains must have had at least a five days' start of us; but the broad track of two thousand sheep gave small occasion to halt upon our progress, and the third day's journey brought us evidently very close upon their heels. We had by this time passed eight of their nightly camps, at each of which fresh witnesses to their plunder were abundantly apparent. Well-remembered pass-boxes, the recent property of the murdered men, boots, scraps of paper, torn rags, old sugar bags and other useless refuse of their spoils, were discarded; while the remains of the numerous carcases of sheep, bones, heads, etc., bore ample testimony to the extent of their nightly meals. During the latter part of this day's journey, we perceived with much annoyance that they had headed us more and more for the broken country, near the main dividing range, in the direction of the heads of the south branch of the Clarence, and towards night we were scarcely able to make headway, for the roughness and steepness of the broken ground over which they had passed. Still we struggled on as best we could, anxious to obtain a position close to their this night's camp, fearing from the altered and difficult road they were now pursuing, that they must have observed or in some way suspected our approach. We were compelled to halt, however, without obtaining more substantial evidences of their proximity than could be gathered from the recent sheep-tracks over which we were passing, and which were clearly not many hours old. We chose our camp in the bed of a deep gully at the foot of the mountain over which the Blacks had steered their course. In this selection we were influenced mainly by the desire of concealment, the night being somewhat too chilly to dispense with fires. There was in our immediate neighbourhood also an abundance of pure water, plenty of long but rather too dry grass, for the use of the cattle, and the encircling mountains, thickly covered with scrub and dry timber, afforded us no lack of fuel. Here, then, we arranged our quarters, refreshed our inner man, talked over our plans, and resolved upon the details of the morrow's contemplated attack.

No sooner, however, had the twilight shadows faded and the darkness of a moonless night fairly enshrouded us, than we had reason to apprehend that the spot of our selection would turn out neither one of refuge nor of rest. It was very evident we had been discovered or observed; the affrighted snorts of the horses, an occasional cracking of dead timber, as if being trodden down by some passing foot, the harsh rustling of dry underwood, the startled fluttering of birds, were sounds sufficiently ominous to arouse our utmost vigilance and anxiety.

Our horses were quickly gathered together; each looked to the priming of his gun; the fires were extinguished; watch parties posted; and everything as far as possible prepared to guard against surprise. Hour after hour we waited, however, without attack; the scouts came in, and feeling somewhat ashamed of our apparently groundless apprehensions, we began to think our nerves must have been too much unstrung after our late excitement, we therefore deemed it incumbent to seek some rest preparatory to the labours of the ensuing day. Fixing a regular watch, and advising the utmost caution, we at length betook ourselves to repose. The briefest possible slumber fell to my individual lot, for suddenly an alarm of "fire," and the startling cry of "the Blacks! the Blacks!" effectually dispelled all feeling of drowsiness. For some moments, however, we were utterly unable to perceive or appreciate the exact nature of our hazardous position. A bright and rapidly increasing glare of light, pouring down in circling eddies from the hills, and sweeping the grassy gullies at our feet, surrounded us and effectually excluded every distant object from our observation. In this perplexity two or three heavy spears darting amongst us sufficiently indicated the whereabouts and intention of our agile though invisible foes; we discharged four barrels in their direction, and immediately a yell, the wildest and the most fraught with fear ears ever heard, rang through the burning forest. No time was evidently now to be lost; a moment's delay might for aught we knew prove fatal. By one portion of the party our horses were saddled and all prepared for immediate movement, while the other, with leafy boughs of trees, set vigorously to work to stop the approach of the raging element, which every moment came more near with fierce and rapid sweeps, blinding our eyes to all beyond its livid circle of flame. This at length, but with much difficulty, was accomplished, and lighted by the now extended circle of blazing timber that spread on all sides like a bright horizon round us, we proceeded in search of the late intruders, but in vain, no trace of their existence could be discovered; they had vanished as effectually as if they had never been in the land of the living.

In an incredibly short space of time the whole range of mountains was on fire; miles of long dry grass, thousands of huge trees, and all the dense mass of withered underwood by which they were encompassed, were enveloped in one enormous unapproachable flame; to proceed through this vast burning mass was obviously impossible; retreat, however, seemed equally hazardous no; course apparently was left but to await the coming day and force our way, if practicable, towards where some creek or water-course might reasonably be expected to have intervened to check the spread of this disastrous fire. If no such spot should be discovered, farewell to all prospect of regaining the lost flocks. The case was nearly hopeless; we could not help calculating somewhat, however, upon the peculiar ingenuity of our enemies, nor herein were we much deceived, for when the sun was fairly up we faintly descried through the dense clouds of lurid smoke that almost quenched the light of day, a wavy line of clearer atmosphere, towards which, at imminent hazard from the falling timber that blazed and burst in every direction round us, we urged our anxious way. All tracks of sheep, of course, were lost in this black and dismal spot; but pushing on, we at length descried, to our inexpressible joy, an open mountain spur, divided from us by a rocky creek, running at right angles with our former course, untouched by the ravaging flames and standing out like a bright and beautiful oasis in the black and calcined desert by which it was surrounded. As we approached a wider prospect opened around us; far away in the grassy valleys to our left our sheep were feeding onwards, tended and driven apparently by the Gins and Picannies of the tribe. But what of the Blacks themselves. Where could they be?

We knew too much of their habits not to suspect the approach of mischief, even from this slight appearance of incautious exposure. The question, unhappily, was soon resolved, a shower of spears and boomarangs came flying into our party, four or five of the former striking with deadly aim the unfortunate fellow, who, in charge of the commissariat, was bringing up the rear. On three sides we were beset; each tree appeared to have produced its man, so sudden and startling was their apparition-like approach. Exasperation broke all bounds of prudence and order, and dashing at them, each man as he listed, I soon found myself alone, flying up the scorching hills in wild but profitless pursuit of the quick and snakelike savages, for upon our first discharge they had dispersed in every direction. Searching with reckless haste, I climbed the steep and rugged tracks which wound upwards round the side of the next adjacent mountain, until the ascent became so steep my panting horse could barely stand. No sooner had I fairly halted, than a yell of exultation rang in my ears, and descending towards me from two opposite sides of the mountain, with rapid strides, fierce gleaming eyes, and weapons quivering in their excited hands, a party of these frightful savages were hurriedly approaching. The moment was a fearful one; the almost perpendicular side of the mountain open to my retreat was thickly strewn with large and rugged granite boulders, the deep sand in which they were but partially imbedded, unstable as water, scarce needed the lightest pressure of the foot, the slightest conceivable impulse, to release them from their tottering height, and hurl them thundering into the deep abyss, through which the sparkling waters of the surrounding hills found egress to the plains. Upon the opposite side of this terrific gorge a mass of rock opposed its rugged face to my escape. Destruction seemed inevitable, but any death was preferable to that of butchery at the hands of these insatiate wretches; so with what coolness I could command, and with an aim as steady as circumstances would admit, I discharged one barrel at each mass of my approaching foes, wheeled round my brave old horse, and dashed headlong towards the yawning chasm beneath. At three bounds he was down the mountain, the huge boulders crashing at his heels, the yell of death and disappointed rage still ringing in my ears: the terrific gorge gaping to receive my bruised and lifeless form still rivetted my fascinating gaze; nearing it, until its terrible depths became apparent to my bewildered brain. Involuntarily I closed my eyes; my dizzy senses reeled - I held my failing breath like one falling in a frightful dream from giddy heights, expecting momentarily the fatal crash that should at once annihilate me.

Not so the gallant steed, whose sinewy limbs had borne me thus far scathless; with measured stride and powerful bound, he flew at the terrific gulf, cleared the adjacent rocks, and with a tremendous leap landed me unharmed and safely on the opposite bank. By this time our party had again assembled, and, directed by the infuriated shouts of my savage pursuers, arrived in time to ward off further attack, and to chastise them soundly for their unwonted temerity.

I experienced much difficulty in escaping from the rocky perch whereon my noble horse had landed me, the descent from which was truly hazardous. However, I at length got safely down, and having reached the plains, arranged operations for the night, and taken a slight refreshment we pushed on in the direction of the sheep. Towards evening their tracks led us again in the direction of the mountains, to a gap, or bog, in one of which, for the night's encampment, they were evidently tending. The utmost circumspection here appeared to be imperative; it was obvious to any practised observation that all our steps were closely watched, and their every moment regulated by our own. We determined, therefore, to proceed slowly and cautiously direct towards the gap, into which the sheep, at least, had certainly preceded us, until darkness should permit a change of course without immediate chance of observation. We then proposed taking a circuit from our apparent course, and endeavour to obtain a higher point on one of the adjacent hills, whence we might securely view their force and contemplate operations.

Towards nightfall we descried their fires; the bleating of the sheep and the yelping of their dogs became also distinctly audible. Dismounting at this point, and leaving a strong party in charge of our horses, with strict injunctions to push forward in the event of any skirmish, the remainder of our party crept into the Bush, and taking a wide and ascended circle mounted the jagged rocks which overhung their camp. Here a scene of most astounding wildness was presented to our gaze; a perfect amphitheatre lay beneath us, formed by a mass of perpendicular rocks, whose bare and rugged faces would have afforded scarcely sufficient room for an eagle's nest; except that about midway from the smooth bottom of the glen, on which the camp fires dimly blazed, and the height on which we stood there appeared to be a rough projecting ledge running round nearly the entire of the two opposite curves of this strange and quarry-like spot. A few moments' careful examination revealed to our wondering senses the wily stratagem by which these savage warriors had intended to beguile us into almost inevitable destruction.

The projecting ledge of rock, which was about a hundred feet below us, and apparently about a similar height above the floor of the gap, was thickly thronged with the fighting men of the tribe, each armed powerfully with heavy spears but most of them carrying a boomerang and waddie. Huge stones, also, lay piled about, apparently from their position destined for warlike purposes; and had we but in this instance approached with the incautious haste which usually distinguishes the white man's mode of dealing with these much despised Aborigines, our total destruction could hardly, in all human probability, have been avoided. Hurriedly edging our way towards the mouth of the apparent ascent to the rocky platform, we were startled by the discharge of a gun proceeding from the party below. An ominous stir among the Blacks in the direction of this spot alarmed us for the safety of our friends, and reminded us of the necessity for immediate action.

Pouring in, therefore, upon the eager but unconscious crowd below the contents of ten barrels, a fearful change was effected in their savage glee; a scream of mingled consternation and surprise, a rush in reckless despair towards the only means of escape from their exposed and dangerous elevation; a murderous and tumultuous struggle amongst themselves; their yells of mingled hate and agony, as grappling together in the last grasp of death the foremost of them fell, urged over the ledge's brink by the pressing crowd behind that madly hurried on, into the yawning sepulchre beneath, was all of the horrid scene that the increasing darkness of the night enabled us clearly to perceive.

We had now reloaded, and our party from below pushing forward to the scene of conflict, poured in a deadly volley upon the thronging crowds that lined the rocky entrance to this fatal ledge - back flew the despairing wretches from that dreadful spot - again a volley from our party on the heights dealt frightful havoc in their ranks. The utmost wildness of despair now seized upon them all; some actually dashed themselves in frantic violence to the depths beneath, in utter heedlessness of life. One solitary tree grew in this fatal glen; its topmost limbs reaching almost to the level of their feet; with faint remains of hope, some of the youngest and most active of the tribe sprang at its fragile boughs in vain - few grasped its treacherous aid, where, quivering for a moment on its yielding branches, their latest shrieks of dying agony, mingling with the mass beneath, too plainly told the dreadful fate they sought to shun, but only had anticipated. Sick of the horrid carnage below, I fain would have retired from the dreadful spot, but all my efforts, entreaties, threats, were utterly useless. Shot after shot, with curses wild and deep, the excited fellows launched at their hated foes - their butchered comrades' blood was that night fearfully avenged!

It is by no means my intention to dwell upon the subse[quent] details of this miserable catastrophe; its salutary consequences were, however, sufficiently apparent, not only in the future safety of the Squatter's life and property, but also in the comfort and security of the numerous native tribes that dwell in the mountain ranges of that district. Deeply impressed with a mysterious and superstitious fear of the stupendous power of the white man, they at once renounced all thought but that of serving or conciliating him; and from that day, and in that particular district, scarcely a depredation of any consequence has been committed, and human life has almost invariably obtained that sacred reverence so essential to mutual safety.

On the other hand, the formerly wild and savage Blackfellow, now harmless, tractable, and subdued, *soon gained for himself, first the toleration, then the kind regards of all his white brethren with whom he came in contact; and, as a necessary consequence, those barbarous and inhuman* secret *murders, by poison, or by some violent and remorseless treachery, of which in preceding times I had so frequently heard and read, were happily now abolished.*

With the occasion for fear, the persecution of these roving tribes entirely disappeared, and a good and kindly feeling has grown up on all hands, brought about in some measure, I have no doubt, either by the dreadful and apparently inauspicious commencement, of which the above presents some of the leading features, or of other such affrays probably somewhat similar in their nature, conduct, and result.

Of my flocks in this adventure about seventeen hundred were recovered; and without any further molestation we retraced our steps to those quiet humble roofs, which, by a figure of speech not infrequent even among the dwellers in bark huts and tents, we find ourselves occasionally denominating HOME!

All the black men in northern New South Wales heard of this fearful battle, of those of their families who had died. It was a long time before many of them gave in to the fact that the white man was definitely the victor.

Notes

- *Australia As It Really Is, In Its Life, Scenery & Adventure, With The Character, Habits, And Customs Of Its Aboriginal Inhabitants, And The Prospects And Extent Of Its Gold Fields* F Eldershaw "A Resident And An Eye Witness Of The Facts Recorded" Darton And Co, 1854. pp.6–7

- *Australia as It Really Is* (pp. 63–75). Eldershaw states his reasons for leaving his somewhat aristocratic home and immigrating to Australia. He wrote from the point of view of a homesick young man:

- *THE sadly-waning prospects of family affairs - a miserable necessity for retrenchment - the horrid bore of having at the age of twenty-one to begin to get my own living - and the difficulty of attaining that object in a community so thronged as England with fellow-competitors in the race for life-were among the most important considerations which directed my attention to the subject of Emigration.*

- *In the majority of similar cases ill health is, perhaps, the most fashionable motive to assign, and, indeed, I "enjoyed" enough of this to justify the customary plea; for England moist, foggy, dear Old England! - does not possess precisely the climate best adapted for pulmonary predelictions [sic]; but, if the truth must be told, poverty! unpopular poverty! and the plebeian hope of being able to better my worldly condition, were the real moving causes which urged this important subject seriously upon my attention.*

- (See also *Baal Belbora*, Blomfield, pp. 86–91)

- Two hundred and fifty massacres (frontier wars) have been listed as having occurred on the eastern Australian continent between 1878 and 1930. See interactive map, the work of Lyndall Ryan, Newcastle University https://c21ch.newcastle.edu.au/colonialmassacres/map.php, and R. H. Mathews's account. Mathews's account of his research into the Anaiwan and Banbai, including descriptions of a 'mystic men's language', is interesting as he had begun to compile a vocabulary.

Chapter 13

Aboriginal Vengeance v. Law and Order

As there were several differences in how the two races occupying northern New South Wales thought, clashes were inevitable as neither group was of the mind to retreat. Power was usually with the white men, who had horses and muskets.

Massacres and acts of revenge could occur for personal reasons too.

Possibly the most serious event that caused anger from the Aborigines towards the Europeans was when a white man took an Aboriginal woman for himself. Vengeance could be severe, and swift retaliation was dealt out. Such an offence may have been the catalyst for the event described in 'Raid at the black's camp: The murder of Mr Pain? Nundle 1857', quoted below.

By contrast, here is an observation by an early Catholic missionary to Australia:

A native will never forgive an affront to his woman; indeed, he will make the offending party pay dearly for it—often with his life. The first white men who committed these offences have come to know this. Certainly our travellers will find such strict morals among the natives near the white man's settlements because there the poor blacks are reduced to misery and if overcome by force find no legal redress so that for the sake of survival, they are obliged to swallow their shame for the fear of something worse.

Things are very different with those who live in the bush away from contact with the white man. In the three years of my stay in the interior, I have never seen an unchaste or indecent behaviour among them; on the contrary, I find their behaviour very creditable indeed.

However, when the one white man ventured into the Aboriginal camp at Hanging Rock, he got more than he bargained for:

Although the gold commissioners and their troops were vigilant in the discharge of their duties, nevertheless, deeds of bloody murder and rapine were committed that defied the efforts of police to arrest the perpetrators.

In 1857, a digger was found murdered under the bank of the Peel River, near Foley's old sheep station. Owing to a 'fresh' in the river, some of the debris was removed and Paddy Lee and old Foley the shepherd discovered the body of a murdered man.

Vengeance was dealt out, particularly if gold was stolen:

About three months later, a 'new chum' digger of aristocratic lineage by the name of Pain was found murdered at the blacks' camp on Hanging Rock. The discovery of this murder was brought about by the blacks bringing some gold into Mr McIlveen's store[1] and offering it for sale and stating at the time that they had obtained it fossicking. Some diggers who were present at the time being naturally curious to discover where the blacks had gotten the gold carefully examined it, and one of the diggers recognised amongst some of the specimens of gold several pieces that were very remarkable and known to be the property of Pain, who had been missing for several days.

The diggers arrested several blacks and marched them down to the police camp, handing them over to Constable Paddy Duran. The blacks made a desperate attempt to escape; Paddy shot two of them dead but the third escaped.

At this time, the blacks were very numerous on this part of the country, and as many as seven hundred and fifty were present at the corroboree at Bowling Alley Point. Bungaree was the king of the principal tribe, and shortly after the murder was committed, they all left this part of the Peel River.[2]

Notes

1. This is now called Odgers & McClelland Exchange Stores, Nundle.
2. *The Wallabadah Manuscript* (Telfer and Milliss) gives graphic descriptions of events like this.

Chapter 14

The Maitland Gold Reward

Populations swelled and people moved, sometimes over long distances, responding to exploration and news reports. Even greater changes occurred after gold was discovered in northern New South Wales, for a group of Maitland businessmen launched a reward for a commercial quantity and quality gold found. The reward stood unclaimed for six months.

The Maitland Gold Reward (1852, as described by Pam Brown)

The discovery of gold finds brought fresh hope to the colony. It was struggling, with crops failing in 'the dry.' Hunger was being experienced down in Sydney too. The government at the time didn't want people to migrate simply to go after gold because they were afraid that convicts would 'run amuck' and steal any gold that was found, it would be impossible to keep order in the colony.

But three businessmen wanted to increase the population to enhance business generally in the Hunter Valley. The reward certainly swelled the population as men and families from near and far pressed forwards towards the Hanging Rock 'to make their fortune'—which usually proved to be elusive (or easily lost at the various inns and grog outlets!)

Nevertheless, many people did track through the bush to the north, having landed in Newcastle Harbour, on the mouth of the Hunter River.[1] They were of many nationalities, most of them travelling on foot.

When passing the Teamsters Rest site en route to 'The Rock', they knew they were getting close. They had crossed the Dividing Range at the lowest point (Crawney Pass) and came to a fledgling Nundle village in 1857, tracking first along the Isis River and then the Peel River, keeping the imposing rock monolith, Hanging Rock, on their right-hand side, following a track marked with blazed trees.

Some family groups straggled up to Hanging Rock from the Upper Hunter and the Isis River after the 1860s as drought caused their farms to fail. For example, the Fermor family of Ellerston came up to the tops via the country that later was named as Glenrock Station, Barry Station, and Bellbrook, passing Rota [Glen Almond] on the way. The Fermor family initially came from the township of Sydney, having emigrated from Britain in early 1850s.

Other diggers had arrived from the steep country and escarpment to the east. John and Henry Clarke established a small farm at Bakers Downfall in the 1840s.[2] Their hamlet was on the Cowsby Road near the hill known as Bakers Downfall twenty miles out from Hanging Rock.

The Gold Reward was never claimed, although gold was found in the Limbri area, though not in the required amount nor in good quality. But by February 1852, twenty cradles[3] were operating with some 200 diggers searching for their fortune.

Notes

1. 1830s: In those days, the Hunter River was navigable as far along as Maitland. It could have been from this part of New South Wales, too, the Liverpool Plains, that a steady line of hopefuls streamed northwards towards the new goldfields on the range, hoping to find gold in every little gully and stream, driven by their enthusiasm.

2. Bakers Downfall was named after a convict named Baker who was somewhat of a geologist; 'downfall' is a geological term.
3. Cradles: See 'Gold and How It Is Got', *The Sydney Mail and New South Wales Advertiser*, 28 October 1871. 'The cradle is a small box, so called because it is somewhat shaped like a cradle and is fitted with rockers by which the sidling or rocking motion is given to it'.

Chapter 15

The 'Asiatics'

A change came over the whole district after gold was found—not in abundance, but enough to bring men of many nationalities, some with families, to the Hanging Rock Diggings, as these goldfields were called. But some were not welcomed!

There were newcomers who were Asian men, wearing strange clothes, a long plait at their backs, using a language no one else could understand. In derision, they were called 'Asiatics'. They had unfamiliar habits too, and they smoked. Although they grew lovely fresh vegetables, the Europeans didn't like these men at all. And there seemed to be so many of them on the diggings!

Where the gold rush occurred, populations were swelling and nationalities were mixing; the most numerous newcomers were the Chinese. Around Nundle, their trade and freshly grown vegetables were wanted, but their personal habits, religion and language were definitely seen as threatening by the authorities and by most of the working men.

Derisively called 'yellow men' on the diggings, they were another nationality to add to the mix of peoples. They were mostly young men who'd been sent to the Australian goldfields from Canton Province in China because there was a drought there and people were starving. (Precisely where the Chinese diggers of the Hanging Rock goldfields came from is not known.) Their communities in China followed Confucian philosophy, so they were people who banded together for their communities' welfare. The men who came to the goldfields would have been indentured to the masters of the ships on which they sailed away from China. Their plan was to disembark in New South Wales or Victoria, but those states' governments had made laws to try to stop Asians from joining their populations. This meant they had to sail as far as Robe Harbour in South Australia before they were allowed to disembark. They then walked the 400 miles to the Victorian goldfields carrying their equipment on their backs. (It was an even longer walk to Nundle in New South Wales.) Their plan was to form teams who could work together efficiently; apparently, one group intended, outrageously, to disinter a body from the cemetery, fill it with gold, and ship the embalmed body back to China—or that's how the local story goes.

The Chinese workers really were not wanted by the other inhabitants, who were largely European. They upset their sensibilities by engaging in prostitution and gaming as well as incense-burning and various non-Christian practices.

However, some of the Chinese immigrants became merchants, and they grew vegetables—which were largely responsible for preventing scurvy among the miners.

One local, Victor Fermor (the son of Lilly May Fermor), born in 1915 on the Glenrock Run, said:

The Chinese were everywhere; they did not mine reef gold; they would not go underground. Ah Joy had a shop in Happy Valley. The Chinese worked for gold very carefully (they were thorough). Their water races were very neat, that is, today wherever a water race is found with the sides made carefully of stones placed tightly together you can be confident that Chinese built it. The Chinese made the water work for them. At Wet Creek they worked a race 16 inches deep—the sides of the race were very carefully lined with stones.

I well remember the Chinese graves at Nundle Cemetery. The graves were decorated with a circle of beads threaded on wire. Several graves had marked stones. The graves were eventually vandalised.

The 'Asiatics'

There is a Chinese gravestone hidden from public gaze in a Nundle cottage to this day.)

Chinese diggers had opium dens in Nundle village where the Hills of Gold Motel is today. By 1850 about two thirds of Nundle's population were Chinese.

Victor Fermor said:

The water was vital for gold-getting.

Water races were dug and maintained by individuals who had to have a licence, or Water Right, to do so. It was that person's responsibility to keep the race cleared out and running. Sometimes there would be a coffer dam into which a race fed which would hold surplus water till needed; this would probably be filled during the night, and that way the water pressure was not wasted. A miner was not allowed to stop a stream in any way, so sometimes a race would cross over a stream in a flume; this would be made of a hollow log or iron sheets fixed to a wooded scaffolding. At Wet Creek they worked a race sixteen inches deep—the sides of the race were very carefully lined with stones. (During the early 1900s, the young woman Ethel Brand, mother of Kassie Ninness, was employed to keep the water races' gates open. See Chapter 43.)

Although there was a proposal to bring water to the Hanging Rock Diggings from Callaghans Swamp in a very dry spell, there was no evidence that this ever happened. The rough nature of the land and the great distance involved make it very unlikely. The race would have been dug from Vant's Creek, Ponderosa, to the Two-Mile gap, and would have been six kilometres long. A water race from the Washpool was shorter. Water races were essential infrastructure providing water under pressure for the miners to wash the dirt.

Victor grew up living part-time in the Hanging Rock community, which meant cooperation was needed. If someone was going to town, they never drove past someone without asking if they needed anything from the town. They helped each other. Just as the Chinese worked alongside the Europeans on the Sheba Dams, so too did community groups share their skills and resources to survive. People got together to dig spuds (potatoes) together one day and did some butchering together the next day, working at each other's place in turn.

But things weren't always harmonious, as shown by this article from the *Maitland Mercury*, 6 October 1855, about policing on the goldfields:

> *Oakenville Creek, 1st October, 1855. It is rumoured that a new gold field has been discovered in the neighbourhood of the Crawney Mountains.*
>
> *It is generally understood here that the Government intends to do away with the Commissioner and police force established here. A petition has been drawn up, and signed by two hundred persons, diggers, representing the dangers which they apprehend will occur by the removal of so efficient a force as that presiding over these parts.*
>
> *The Hanging Rock. (From our Correspondent.)*

The police and troops were kept busy on the diggings. Settlement on country was extending out onto the Range. There were to be new settlers; the community was being extended by convicts turned pastoralists, by landed gentry and by Chinese immigrants, as well as by a skeleton staff of police officers attempting to maintain law and order.

Chapter 16

Nathan Burrows: Establishing Runs and Stations

From despised convict to respected pastoralist

In 1849, Nathan Burrows was an ex-convict turned landed gentleman and pastoralist of the Hanging Rock Run.[1] He was the first white man of substance from the tiny Hanging Rock community. He had been transported to Australia from Britain in 1827. He was assigned first to the Australian Agricultural Company at Port Stephens. By 1849, he was a squatter at Hanging Rock. 'Of the local settlers, it was he who first saw the discovery of gold as important for the state and an income possibility for himself. His contact with Tamworth businessman William Cohen led to the publishing of the Maitland Gold Reward, which brought many hopeful persons to the Hanging Rock Diggings.

Nathan Burrows married an Elizabeth Tuckwell.[2,3] He also had a common-law relationship with the Aboriginal woman who was said to have found the gold; the two had brought their find to the Tamworth Bank. Hanging Rock would have been a very small community in 1851 when the gold rush commenced. The Run became the main centre of the farming community. The vegetables Burrows grew there, particularly potatoes, would have been a valuable food source for the growing population as well as providing an income for Burrows. (Irishmen who had arrived from Ireland would have particularly appreciated his potatoes; many had immigrated to Australia to escape a miserable life when the potato famine was decimating the population of Ireland's small farmers, who were starving).

The Hanging Rock Run

When the Run was put up for sale, it was described as follows (*The Empire*, March 1854):

Hanging Rock Station, on the Barnard and Peel Rivers and adjoining the Hanging Rock.

Sale by auction: Mort and Co have received instructions to sell by public auction at their rooms Pitt Street on May 26 at 11 o'clock in 1854.

This valuable station is known as the Hanging Rock Run, the most southern Station in New England, abundantly watered by the Barnard and Peel rivers. The Station contains an area of thirty-six square miles, well-grassed country, fit for either sheep or cattle. One of the boundaries is a creek running into the Peel River (Oakenville Creek) from which an immense quantity of gold and the Head Station is only two miles from the busiest part of the diggings, six miles from the courthouse at Nundle and forty miles from Tamworth.

The improvements consist of a comfortable veranda cottage, detached kitchen, cultivated enclosed garden stocked with vegetables and fruit trees, a stockyard, milking yard with bails and covered calf pen, pigsty, large barn, out-shed for horses, fowl houses, and so on.

There are also cultivation paddocks, of nine acres, and grazing paddock of forty acres with strong three railed fence. On the outstation at the diggings are a butcher's shop and a capital stockyard with gallows for slaughtering.

This splendid property has great value due to its proximity to the good market at the diggings. Adjoining paddocks could be made ready for the plough; the chance of having a lucrative business, wheat, vegetables or garden produce, food for horses, and the fact of a good homestead for store cattle to be slaughtered as required, gives this property a great value. The Hanging Rock Diggings are only in their infancy, requiring labour to develop the hidden riches of this locality.

This description sounds impressive, but it was very rough country! Burrows ran 800 head of cattle and grew potatoes, which he took to Tamworth by dray twice a year.

✶✶✶

A camp of Anaiwan people was secluded in the valley beside the waterway of the Kunderang Creek. Bidja could usually be found among the young men there. He had returned from his walkabout to the coast, told the children all about the great sailing ships he'd seen, the sailors, and all their stuff, which had intrigued him and sparked his curiosity. His hands and mouth had never been still while he told them about what he'd seen.

When the sailors had ventured out from the beach and used their muskets to get animals for food, he'd decided to take off for the camp before he was discovered—he'd learned about the dangers of muskets from his time near the cedar cutters![4]

✶✶✶

The following is one account of the gold discovery, from a local Maitland paper in 1854 and is attributed to Nathan Burrows.

> *The major gold discoveries commenced in August 1851 after Nathan Burrows, a squatter occupying the Hanging Rock country as part of his run, discovered a man in the act of washing for gold with a pint pot at Swamp Oak Creek, which rises at the top of Hanging Rock. The man showed Burrows the gold he had already obtained since he had noticed a few yellow specks at the bottom of his pannikin when washing it after a meal. Burrows went to Tamworth and informed William Cohen, who ran the commercial store, of the discovery.*
>
> *Two days later, Mr Cohen went to Hanging Rock with two other men (Charles Parsons and William Blackburn). In the company of Burrows, they made a close inspection of the area and quickly obtained several ounces of gold. When they returned to Tamworth with the news, the gold rush began immediately. Mining parties were swiftly organised.*

✶✶✶

Bidja saw them. They took some of the dreaded shiny stones to town for an opinion. When Mr Burrows returned, he was excited. So was the black woman with him. Bidja may have ridden with them to Tamworth on the dray that day. He had never been to the dusty new township before. He may have steadied the oxen while Mr Burrows went into the bank to meet his friends.

Bidja found it all very strange—these people were so excited, even though his own people warned of the dangers of the shiny stones.

Notes

1. 'Runs': Areas of country defined by squatters (i.e., people without government permission to occupy land) and eventually leased to them. The government usually lagged behind actual practice when it came to having properly authorised regulations for land use, including leases. Runs were simply taken up, usually for sheep. If a squatter cut out some land for himself in this way, it would have been dangerous as the area was not being policed and might not even have been surveyed—the settlers followed hard on the heels of the explorers. The squatters had no legal rights at all. The authorities were a long way away in Sydney town, and the squatters could hardly be governed from there. They had to work out how to live with the so-called 'Aboriginal threat', so they banded together to protect themselves and their holdings (see 'Massacre on Manoa' by Frank Eldershaw, quoted in Chapter 12).

2. In 1852, a letter from Nathan Burrows to 'a friend' says that 'a black gin that is with one of the white men here and a white woman have got one ounce only, washing with a tin dish—they picked up about ¼ ounce this morning' and that 'a black gin sold £1 worth of gold to the government surveyors and his party …' (*Maitland Mercury*, 1852). The woman mentioned may have been Nathan's common-law wife. Alternatively, the 'black gin' may have been with Elizabeth, Burrows's legal wife. Due to the passage of time, this cannot be determined. Gold finds were such momentous events, so exciting, that reporting could be quite effusively described and contradictory.

3. Concubinage: *Some men lived in concubinage with Aboriginal women (some with white women) in shelters of slab and bark, and slept on rough bedsteads of sheepskins or possum rugs. A bark table or sea chest served every purpose. Smoke from a stone fireplace vented through a hole cut in the slabs and woolpacks hung from the door. Shepherds ate mutton at every meal accompanied by damper (flour and water baked in a fire or fried). A discarded pannikin, filled with clay and topped with mutton fat upon which floated a wick, gave light at night. Bush life reeked of mutton fat and smoke.*

   Even a prosperous squatter contented himself to live in a condition of slab hovels, with hurdles for sheep moving from place to place as each became filthy with heaps of sheep dung and sheep bones. A few British women lived in the bush, and there their children grew up, though some babies died from the harsh conditions. The small graves in old cemeteries indicated where couples endured the worst of sadness. Yet few clergy were available to minister to a growing flock of souls, and no churches or schools existed to instruct the colony's future citizens. (The Great South Land, Mundle, pp. 40, 85)

4. See Telfer and Milliss, The Wallabadah Manuscript: colourful descriptions of life on the stations, bushrangers, early Tamworth and Australian Agricultural Company expansion and droving, including Aborigines' strong opposition and their many defeats. It was a grim and hectic life in the 'wild west' countryside of northern New South Wales in those days.

Chapter 17

A General Practitioner in the 1850s

Bidja saw white men living in squalor in huts with women. The disrespect shown to the women disgusted him. He saw little children die in the filth they lived in. They would be healthier living out in the bush under a gum tree, he thought.

He was puzzled. What was the attraction of those shiny stones? Aborigines had no time for the lumps of gold that sent the white men into a frenzy. He could see that the gold was very important to the white men, as they frantically searched for it and travelled long distances to find it. But he did not understand why. Gold was too soft to be useful—far too soft for making tools!

One afternoon, he saw another stranger ride into the settlement. He had not noticed this man before, and was interested!

Nundle's Dr Jenkins, his gold theft and court case

In 1848, a British doctor, Dr Richard Jenkins, arrived at the Nundle settlement. He had been doctoring in the Hunter Valley; he came over the range into the Peel Valley on horseback. He was a significant man in the Nundle and Tamworth area. He was a 'gentleman': a landowner, educated, and probably perceived to be wealthy, which gave him further status. He thought like a businessman, and he became an employer in the area, all of which made him greatly respected. He served the people there, but his wealth attracted some unwanted attention. The Nundle Courthouse was used for the first time for the trial.

Gold finds and tensions due to the mixture of nationalities made crime on the diggings inevitable. As the population swelled and the community developed, a courthouse became necessary to deal with the inevitable crimes.

Dr Jenkins purchased property and built a substantial inn at Hanging Rock. Only five years later, having sold his properties, he moved to Sydney, and there he became a member of parliament representing the Liverpool Plains constituency, a role he held for more than two years.

He first took up property at Hanging Rock, where he established the settlement's first inn. He offered undercover space there to be rented by the Church and a school. Becoming landowners gave male settlers status in the wider community.

Dr Jenkins had practised as a doctor at Woolomin. He had taken up the pastoral property there and even established a cottage hospital. His surname is memorialised by the street named after him in Nundle. But it was gold that was the most valuable thing in those times. Gold was scarce, and it was hard work to get it. Even tiny nuggets or gold dust had to be guarded with one's life. All local trade was carried out with gold, and miners used their meagre amounts to pay Dr Jenkins. One day he was burgled!

John Shepherd, alias George Riley, was indicted for stealing sixty ounces of gold dust and one valise (travelling bag), the property of Richard Lewis Jenkins of Nundle, on 14 June 1852. Dr Jenkins reported:

On that evening, I was returning from the Hanging Rock Diggings and on my way called at my station, Nundle, and entered into a hut there; I left my horse in charge of a boy, Thomas Davis (aged eight years old). My valise was strapped to the saddle, containing a number of small articles and sixty ounces of gold dust. After a few minutes, I was called out to receive some letters brought by the usual messenger, James Eames. I had been reading them for a few moments when I realised that my valise was gone. This was a great loss to me, I was very angry. I immediately charged three local men with the theft.[1]

Meanwhile, Bidja had seen the robbery. Being Aboriginal, he was not noticed, and being mute, he could not give evidence in the court, not that he would have wanted to. Nevertheless, he was curious to know what all the fuss was about. He looked at the white people with awe as they assembled near the courthouse, some in frock coats and tall hats and others in their work clothes. The doctor was smartly dressed as usual.

Bidja was hungry that afternoon. The weather was drawing in, rain clouds gathering, and there was a smell of snow in the air. He would have a long walk to get back to the camp, where his grandparents would be wondering about him. His strong bond with his grandparents was not unusual. They had cared for him since he was very young, after his mother died, and they had always been very strong in their love for him. The young man would start for the camp soon; it was going to snow on the tops, and his yellow dog was certainly ready to move from behind the boulder where he had been sheltering from the biting wind.

Where did Bidja go that night? Did he curl up with his dog, a dingo pup he'd found starving in a den along the track? They enjoyed each other's company, sharing the tucker; perhaps they made it back to the Aboriginal camp before it snowed?

***

The written record of the trial follows. It illustrates the social levels of the various men. Dr Jenkins was highly respected, being a landowner making him a 'gentleman', an authority figure.

> *But the bag could not be found on the strictest search and was not found in fact till about a month afterwards.*
>
> *When challenged the youth Davis had said at first, 'I know nothing of the matter'; however later he changed his recollections and made a statement in the Tamworth police office: 'Sir I did see my ma and pa with the doctor's valise.' His parents—Davis and his wife—were subsequently apprehended on the charge but were discharged on the grounds that there was no evidence.*
>
> *However, Thomas Brooks, a shepherd in Dr Jenkins employment, spoke up, 'I found the valise on 7 January, on the side of a hill about*

400 yards from the Nundle station. It was only hidden from the view of persons passing by two tussocks of grass; it contained your papers, sir, but no gold was there.'

(The prisoner, who had cross-examined Dr Jenkins at great length, and with considerable ability, did not put a single question to any other witness nor say a word in defence.) The jury retired for ten minutes and returned with a verdict of 'guilty'. The prisoner was sentenced to five years on the roads and the youth Thomas Davis was committed by His Honour to take his trial for perjury at the Circuit Court. In a second court, George Pearce was indicted for feloniously receiving the gold. His honour told the jury, 'If it is that you found the property in the bush, it was still Dr Jenkins' property; and if you took it and used it without making efforts to find the owner, it would undoubtedly be larceny,[2] a serious offence' In reference to that point, they all would remember that he was actually engaged in searching for the valise and contents, at Dr Jenkins' request.

The jury retired for a few minutes and returned with a verdict of guilty. The prisoner was sentenced to five years on the roads and his honour remarked, 'I recommend that the whole sentence be endured, as there was a breach of trust as well as larceny.'

In answer to the court, Dr Jenkins had said, 'Davis was in my employment as a watchman, but he says he was not near the hut when the valise was lost although his wife was in the hut.' The boy Thomas Davis, eight years old, being sworn in had said, 'I did not see the valise Sir when I took hold of your horse. I did not see anyone go near the horse while you were inside.'

But because the chief constable threatened to put handcuffs on him if he would not say that he saw Shepherd take the valise off, the witness did not tell the truth. (Witnesses' behaviour during court proceedings seems to have changed little over time. They still lie when necessary!)

After many more questions were asked, the witness said, 'I saw the prisoner coming back to the house, from the creek, while you were inside, Sir.' His honour examined the witness himself at great length, testing him by his previous depositions.

In the 1850s Bidja was most often with his people, camped on the edges of the Hanging Rock Diggings community or out in the Tuggolo Forest, near the river. He vaguely recalled a story of his people who had trekked over the plateau and down to the river. It was back in warrior Mungengarly's time. He too had been fascinated by the shiny stones.

The courthouse was vacated, the prisoner taken away in handcuffs—but Bidja and his dog had already taken off for the camp; he wasn't interested in the court details. He was just curious about what the white people were actually doing together. What was all the back and forth about? What were the men there saying?

It is unlikely that Dr Jenkins had any personal knowledge of the Aboriginal people who camped at Hanging Rock, but he would undoubtedly have seen them around the diggings or slipping between the trees and bushes when he rode along the track from his inn at Hanging Rock down the steep hill towards his Nundle establishment.

- Historian James Jervis, in a series of articles written in 1955 (see The Farmer and Settler (Sydney, NSW : 7 Apr 1955, p. 21, wrote of Dr Jenkins' expertise in breeding shorthorn cattle and included the following details:

Richard Lewis Jenkins was the son of Richard Jenkins of Newport, Monmouthshire. He arrived as surgeon superintendent on the James Moran *in 1841.*

After arrival he practised medicine at Jerry's Plains for some time. He was active in the community, attending the races, and in August 1843, he and Captain Scovell organised a ball for the gentry of the neighbourhood.

He had left the Jerry's Plains district by 1848 and turned his attention to pastoral pursuits. In 1848 he held Woolomin, Piallamore, and Wombramurra stations on the Liverpool Plains. Later he also owned stations in Queensland.

He established a hospital at Woolomin, however in 1850 placed the following notice in the newspaper: 'The undersigned begs to intimate to the residents of Liverpool Plains and adjoining districts that he has made arrangements to remove from his station to Tamworth, to succeed to the Practice of Dr Haig. In compliance with the wishes of several respectable settlers, a hospital will be established for the conveniences of invalid residents in the interior.—Richard Lewis Jenkins, L.A.C., and member of the Royal College of Surgeons, London. Peel's River, Jan 10, 1850.' (Source, James Moran in 1841)

After the Hanging Rock gold rush of 1852, Richard Lewis established a public house at the junction of Oakenville Creek and the Peel River, Nundle. He purchased gold from prospectors and also sent samples for analysis of the gold.

Richard Jenkins moved to Sydney in 1857 and in the following year was elected to represent the Liverpool Plains seat in the New South Wales Parliament. In Parliament, being an educated man, he argued strongly for the adoption of a system of universal education and the establishment of reform schools for young criminals. He remained in the House only until 1859.

After all the excitement of the trial with the opening of the Nundle Courthouse, village life calmed down, but there were bushrangers around, and everyone was on guard.

Notes

1. https://nundle.com.au/historical-notes/ "Dr Jenkins And The Stolen Gold Dust" *The Maitland Mercury* 9 March 1853

2. Larceny: the 'taking (caption) and carrying away (asportation, removal of) the tangible personal property of another with the intent to permanently deprive the owner of its possession'. (https://en.wikipedia.org/wiki/Larceny)

Chapter 18

Warrigal

In 2014 the Nundle Dunghutti man Warrigal (aged 62) shared a long chat with the author, leaning over his front gate.

His preferred name means 'free'

Dr Jenkins may not have had had any personal knowledge of the Aboriginal people who camped in the Nundle Hanging Rock area. However, he certainly would have been aware of their existence. As Jenkins was an active member of white society, he probably disapproved of Aboriginal people generally, as that was the usual attitude of the white people.

During the period when Dr Jenkins was a member of the Nundle and Hanging Rock populace, it is unlikely that anyone ever sat with an Aboriginal man and really listened to his story. White people of his era just weren't interested. However, by 2018, other Australians had begun to hear Aboriginal voices and really listen to their stories because, like it or not, these stories are all part of the nation's history. In 2014, Warrigal (born Rodney Clarke) told his story to the author. He likes to be known as Warrigal, meaning 'free'. (See Chapter 34, The Clarke Families.)

Warrigal was interviewed 100 years after Dr Jenkins lived on the diggings. His life story provides some vivid pictures of the life and times of the Aboriginal people of the tops because he has such strong memories of the stories his mother and uncles told the boys as they grew up at Hanging Rock in the twentieth century.

Presumably Bidja was somewhere around that day just watching us chatting over the front gate, but I didn't see him!

Warrigal is a Dunghutti man. He was born in Nundle in 1952. The information in this chapter is from his understanding of things and is used with his generous permission. His Clarke family connections came from his father, James (a younger son of Richard Clarke and Sarah Hopkins), and his mother was Nancy Pearl Clarke nee Chapman. At the time of writing, he still lives in the home where he grew up, in Splitters Gully on the outskirts of Nundle village; his two brothers live nearby. His family also lived at Bakers Downfall for some years when he was a child.

The family understands that John Clarke, the English settler who arrived with his brother Henry to join the Hanging Rock community in the 1840s, emigrated to be a farmer; both men brought their wives, and Henry brought several of his children.

John Clarke (1861–1943), Warrigal's grandfather, also had relationships with an Aboriginal woman called Maryann. It is possible that a second Aboriginal woman, nicknamed Friday, also had children with John. Friday may have had children with several white men in the Hanging Rock area during the 1800s, as recorded in *Registered Births, Deaths and Marriages 1788–1905, New South Wales* (owned by P. J. Hackett in 1989) vol. 52, p. 7: 'Richard son of John Clark farmer of Bakers Town near Hay Park and Mary Ann (a black) born 17/9/1852 and baptised 10/9/1853 parish of Tamworth'. There was a full sister to Richard, Elizabeth, perhaps born in 1850. She married a William Murray. Their family tree contains a girl described as a 'Black' and a sister to John's son Richard. These generations continued, and some of the individuals are listed in court reports. This information came from ancestry.com via Pam Brown, Tamworth, who is related to the Clarkes.

James was born on Glenrock Station. 'All the stations had work for Aboriginal men back then.' They were excellent horsemen when working with the livestock and were skilled, reliable and trustworthy, a reputation that they are justly proud of. Sadly, James died from a cattle-mustering accident; Warrigal was very young at the time. (Warrigal's family members have worked hard trying to list the names of his various relatives.)

Today, Warrigal has true local Aboriginal knowledge. He believes that the people of lower New England were of the main group— 'the Dunghutti of the northwest coastal area.' He says a tribe may have contained as few as sixty people, including smaller family groups.

∗∗

Warrigal describes the tribal country around Nundle as if we are looking at it. In his words:

This river [the Peel] is the boundary of the Kamilaroi and the Dunghutti/Anaiwan people. The Kamilaroi were from the south. Two kings fought right up to where Farrer High School is now. They were fighting the Bendemeer people who brought more warriors from the coast, from other tribes, and they battled with the Kamilaroi. This was a very long time ago.

Up in Bendemeer there is a line drawn in a rock. The warriors kept either side of it—that's a battle line; they never came any farther this way [south].

Tribal lands were usually defined by rock outcrops, gullies, marked trees and so on. However, one boundary that was clear to both Aborigines and white settlers was the Peel River. It was a barrier between the large group of Kamilaroi people on the plains to the west and the Anaiwan and/or Dunghutti groups of the ranges.

The languages spoken may have been similar in neighbouring tribes; groups of words or at least some words were apparently understood by both the Kamilaroi and the Anaiwan communities. Spoken language and shared cultural practices may also be recognised as defining boundaries. Warrigal emphatically declares that 'the Aboriginal people of the eastern side of the Peel River never were of the Kamilaroi tribe though obviously there has been some mixing between the tribes over the years.' One example is the Kamilaroi or Anaiwan man Harry Wright and his Dunghutti wife, Sarah (see Chapter 25 and Chapter 31, The Wright Families). This couple went on to form a part of the large Ingleba and Walcha group of Aboriginal people. Warrigal says 'No one around here in Nundle is Kamilaroi!'

Many years ago, each group remained largely within its own territory as each valley held a separate tribe and language, and tribes were basically fearful of each other. They were anxious about being raided to capture women. Their marriage rules were complex and had to be strictly adhered to or sudden death could be the penalty. Trading occurred between tribes; for example, weapons were exchanged for red ochre to be used for face paint. Marriage arrangements could also be made peacefully during corroborees, thus avoiding a fight.

There were many skirmishes between the groups of Aborigines in lower New England; one cause was that, as soon as white settlement began, the Aboriginal people began to starve as their chief food sources were eaten out or cut off by flocks of sheep guarded by shepherds or by rough wooden fences or dry-stone walls. When Aboriginal people's netting traps for marsupials, and the marsupials' habitual tracks, were destroyed by sheep belonging to squatters' flocks or by convict shepherds, the Aboriginal people no longer had any control over those animals and their movements, which meant their food supply was seriously disrupted.

∗∗∗

Warrigal tells a Dreamtime story about the origin of the gold of the Peel and Oakenville waterways:

In the myth, Oakenville Creek is the Valley of Golden Tears, but it starts with the rainbow serpent.

Everything was flat and there were no mountains, so the rainbow serpent and the sea serpent said, 'We'll make some valleys and rivers.'

So they set off over many hundreds of years.

When they came back, the sea serpent was lying out in the sun.

'What have you been doing?' the rainbow serpent said. 'I've been busy all this time and you're just lying around.' (The problem was that the saltwater was spoiling the freshwater because there were no rivers and valleys to keep the waters separated).

They got into an argument, and finally the rainbow serpent killed the sea serpent and the valley there is the mouth ('nuttal'—Nundle—means mouth) and the hills around are the teeth of the rainbow serpent. The tail runs all the way down the Peel River, New South Wales—it is the mountain range.

After that, the rainbow serpent looked around, and he could see that all the rivers from the sea had stopped flowing inland along this area, so he set out and made a mountain range the full length of [eastern] Australia to stop the water from the sea flowing inland. Then all the inland lakes dried up … and that's what you got.

Our people believed that the gold of Oakenville Creek is the blood running down into the creek from the tops after the sea serpent was killed. It is how we used to think and tell the children.

We used to go there [Bakers Downfall] a lot, with Dad and all the uncles, catching eels and that, at Cowsby. There was a big lagoon there full of cumbungi [bulrushes] and eels. We used to go when I was little, and we used to walk barefooted and catch eels with our toes. I love them, they're good when eaten! You can boil them in milk, or you can soak them overnight in salt and vinegar, anything to soften the meat. It's pretty tough—or you can take a long slice off and barbeque it, or cut it into sections like an oxtail and stew it. They used to get them and salt them and then smoke them up the chimney and you've got eels all through the winter. We ate a lot of kangaroo, rabbit, wild duck, fish, and even wombat too.

He also said, 'I remember when we were kids, we had to get out in front of the class and recite all these stupid things, and everyone laughed at us. We hated school. It was pretty tough being the only Aboriginal family in the school and community.' This was in the early 1960s. He feels the humiliation to this day.

On weekends Warrigal and the other kids would walk up to Hanging Rock through the bush to visit the families there. They would go to Bakers Downfall too.

During our interview, Warrigal described some of the traditional practices, such as how to catch a wombat for tucker (food):

You put a piccaninny down the hole. When he finds the wombat, he knocks on the roof of the burrow with a rock. Then the men dig down and pull the wombat out through the hole, and they can spear 'im. That was out on the New Guinea tops [Barry Station top country]. That's what it was called back then. There were ovens made from hollowed-out ant bed there too. Some can still be found out in the bush—if you know where to look.

Some call the ovens 'fondas' (see Chapter 19, The Crafting of the Stone Axe).

Warrigal is a very private man. His greatest pleasure is to 'go walkabout' for six months each year. He goes to Queensland where it is warmer than in chilly Nundle; he catches up with his family members there.

A further understanding about the tribes and language of lower New England is that of Patricia Bartholomew-Locke, who believes that her grandmother always spoke the Nganyaywana language when Anaiwan friends came to visit. 'They would sit out on the verandah and chatter away. They didn't speak it in the house,' she said. (See Appendix 2, A Language Lost in Time.) This language was the Anaiwan cultural connection to their country—the place of their birth.

Notes

❖ See *Papers of Robert Hamilton Mathews, 1866-1984* [manuscript] https://catalogue.nla.gov.au/catalog/1186177

❖ R. H. Mathews was a surveyor and something of an anthropologist. For the Birpai, Anaiwan and Dunghutti, the Great Eastern Ranges became a last refuge and a base for desperate resistance to the loss of their traditional lands and way of life. For twenty-five years, they fought an intermittent guerrilla war, emerging from the rugged ranges and gorges in planned sorties to scare off sheep and fight the shepherds and stockmen encroaching on their land. Reprisals were severe and indiscriminate—more than twenty massacres of Aboriginal people occurred throughout the Hastings, Macleay and Manning ranges over that period, usually including the deaths of women and children.

- ❖ On occasion, the landscape bears the names of some of the slain; in spite of efforts to deny and forget, some brave leaders are still remembered. Garibaldi—an imposing character—fought valiantly from the ranges in what is now called the Oxley Wild Rivers National Park but was killed with all of his family group as they slept, in a dawn massacre. Garibaldi Rock towers above the site where he died.
- ❖ Aboriginal resistance was brought to an end by the 1860s. (See the Great Eastern Ranges Ltd website, https://ger.org.au/)
- ❖ In 1903, Mathews noted that 'the remnants of the Anaiwan tribe are scattered over the southern half of what is known as "the tableland of New England" including Macdonald River, Walcha, Uralla and Bendemeer, Armidale, Hillgrove and other places'. Apparently, Mathews sat in the Anaiwan camps listening, and learned some Anaiwan vocabulary. He discerned that there were two other languages that were spoken among the people there—Banbai and a 'mystic language that was only spoken by men during initiation ceremonies'.
- ❖ This record by Mathews should settle for all time the current confusion about the identity of the tribes of lower New England. (Source: *The Languages of the New England Aborigines, New South Wales* vol. 42, American Philosophical Society, 1903, pp. 249–263.)
- ❖ Note: The Clarke brothers, John and Henry, from London, came and settled as farmers at Bakers Downfall, twenty years before James and Mary (Granny) Duval lived in the area.
- ❖ Bread-making: See *Dark Emu, Black Seeds* (Pascoe).

Hi Sue,

What a spectactular axe! Definitely an Aboriginal edge-ground axe, made from a volcanic or metamorphosed volcanic stone. The axe was first made by 'pecking', or 'hammer-dressing'. This involved hitting the surface with another stone over and over again, eventually shaping it by attrition. Then the cutting edge was ground onto one edge. It is highly polished, and I suspect that was done by rubbing with leather or similar; some of the polish may have resulted from the materials is was used on.

It doesn't look as if it was heavily resharpened. It would have had a handle originally. My guess is that it was originally made somewhere in the wider Nundle region, as that type of stone occurs around there.

There is a major axe quarry a Moore Creek, but your stone doesn't look quite right for that, and the manufacturing technique is different. Axes like this date up to 40,000 years ago in Northern Australia, but most of them from around here date to the last 5000 years. My guess would be that your axe is from sometime in that later time-span.

Thanks for sharing!

Cheers,

—Mark

Dr Mark Moore

Senior Lecturer

Archaeology & Palaeoanthropology

Higher Degree Research Coordinator

School of Humanities

University of New England

Chapter 19

The Crafting of the Stone Axe

Another aspect of Aboriginal culture was the crafting of stone tools.

In 1991, a pastoralist on the Barnard River found an axe head. This stone tool was found on Anaiwan country. Archaeologist Dr Mark Moore at the University of New England confirmed that it was made in lower New England, specifically the Nundle and Hanging Rock district, which is Anaiwan country.

BARNARD RIVER STONE AXE–era 3000 BC

Stone axe head

The axe may establish that the twentieth- and twenty-first-century Aboriginal people of Nundle and Hanging Rock are Anaiwan, not Kamilaroi as usually claimed by authorities. To be identified incorrectly is offensive to the Aboriginal people. White people usually feel the same way about their ethnicity or nationality.

The axe head's story began around 5,000 years ago, and the circumstances may have been somewhat as follows. This story of the crafting of the stone axe, or Woljha's story, is fiction, but is based on cultural understanding.

***

One day when crossing a creek on the annual walkabout to the beach, a man saw a dark stone, a small heavy rock. He thought, I could shape that into an axe head. That man was Woljha (Eagle). He had seen the rock in the gravel, wet and shiny. He was pleased by its weight in his hand. He knew that it had the right balance for a fighting axe.

So, during the warm times, when the family were in the camp at the coast, Woljha worked on that stone, chipping away at it, crafting it into an axe head. His son was watching. He saw the little chips of the stone fall onto the earth and get lost among the grass, and he noticed when his father put the stone aside and slept briefly, before waking and taking it up and commencing again to work its shape. He knew that much, much later, his father would grind the cutting end. Then the stone would be ready for polishing and being attached to a handle.

Woljha's family could not travel fast. His wife had a shortened leg, which meant she had a limp and found it hard to keep up. When her two children were small, she'd had to walk with the baby girl at the breast and the little boy perched on her shoulders, which had made her life hard, but she knew nothing different. It was her job to prepare vegetables for the family to eat.

For days and days, Woljha's son watched him work the rock. One day his mother told him to take food to his father, but that day his father was short-tempered—he wanted meat; he was tired of the steamed vegetables his wife had prepared for him. On a hot day soon after that, Woljha brought in a kangaroo on his shoulder and tossed it onto the cooking fire. They ate well that evening.

After even more days, and much chipping, eventually Woljha was satisfied with the axe head—it had the right shape. He then used the big flat rocks nearby to grind the cutting edge smooth. That work took him a very long time—he needed to get it right! Finally, he polished the cutting edge by rubbing it with leather. The son watched and absorbed his father's persistence and patience. Working the stone took his father many, many days.

For the axe handle, Woljha used a stick he had found and carved. He took the sticky resin from the grass trees, moulded it into a ball with his fingers, then roughly worked the sap around the wood to fasten the two items together, binding them firmly with woven grasses and sinews from the kangaroo's legs.

To cook a kangaroo, Woljha would throw it onto the fire after the long leg bones were broken. A cut was made along either side of the breastbone so the meat cooked evenly. The tail would usually be cut from the animal's rump and cooked separately, a tender piece that was enjoyed by the children once their teeth were strong.

So they could make fires, some glowing embers would be carried very carefully in a thick hollow reed with a little dried grass placed in the top; occasionally a gentle breath would be blown to keep the embers alive. It was Woljha's son's job to keep the coals alive, for days on end. The child was helping his father, and at the same time he was learning about his culture and gaining the skills he would need when he was a man.

One evening at sundown, they were down near the river. After they had eaten, the family lay down together, Woljha with the young boy at their fire with their dogs, and the mother with the girl child some distance from the men, at their own fire. They usually made small fires—big ones were far too destructive!

The next morning, Woljha felt the sap. Was it still soft, or firm enough to work with? He was pleased when he found that the join had hardened. He had set the handle well, and it had dried thoroughly.

He stuck the axe in the belt of possum skin that he wore around his hips. It would certainly come in handy! Woljha's next job was to make a youth-sized spear for his son, who had now reached the age to have a man's weapon of his own; the making of the axe had taken a very long time. But he was in no hurry! Woljha was pleased that his son had been so interested—even helpful—in the making of the axe.

The next day, the family made their way further up the riverbank to find a warmer place to make a camp; it was getting too cold down in the valley. However, after several days, Woljha and his wife became ill with an awful skin disease. They had fever, and after five wretched days, they both died.

The two children were strong enough to roll their mother's body in her possum-skin cloak and get her up into a tree out of the way of marauding dingoes; they didn't know what else to do. They piled rocks and stones over their father's body to keep the dingoes away. It took them all day. They were terribly sad, and they hardly knew how to deal with what had happened to them. The boy took up their father's things—his long spear and his precious stone axe—and together they trudged away, leaving the desperate sadness behind them but also locked deep in their hearts. The special spear the boy's father had promised him would never be made.

The children wondered if they were really alone. Would they find some kin further along the valley by the river? Would they find a relative who would help them deal with their terrible loss, their sorry business?[1]

Just when they were starting to think about giving up, the children found some people a little further along the river—just around the next bend! The two children were very quiet, overwhelmed by the burden of their sadness. The adults took care of them, showing they understood.

***

On another hot day, in another time, a family group was camped in a different spot beside the same river, just resting under the casuarinas, with the children playing around, paddling at the river edge, and chasing the water dragons. The group had been climbing up into the ranges. They had been walking for two days, going steadily up the mountain from their camps down on the beach, for the weather was getting cooler. They had walked a long way the day before, having left the coast far behind them. They had reached the tops of the mountain range where other, larger, family groups were to remain for a time. The clan's annual inland trek was over for now. But this group, led by Mungengarly's son, had kept moving. They were going to travel even further, down through the valley and onto the flat country. Mungengarly's son wanted to get down to the Big River to the west (which was much, much later called the Peel River) with his mob, for he'd heard that there were shiny stones in the water there, which was something that excited him. He was an ambitious young man. The Elders had heard stories about shiny stones too, but they thought they were something dangerous, to be avoided. They said that shiny stones were only to be used in sorcery between them and other tribes.

One day, along the track, their precious stone axe head was lost. The handle had broken, the sinews had rotted, and the bindings had split. They had been hurrying, and the women and children were tired and slow, but Mungengarly's son wanted to reach the valley, where they would be a little protected from the fierce Kamilaroi people, who would be watching out for them. Travelling could be dangerous for him and his mob—but he was excited when he thought of the shiny stones he would find! One penalty for all the haste was that the stone axe head got dropped while the children trudged along behind the adults. But, on the bright side, the season was changing—the bush fruits getting ripe. His people knew where to find them.

There was another view of how the axe head was lost. One afternoon, when the sun was high in the sky, the whole group was resting in the shade, dozing, except one small restless boy, who was playing with his mother's special stone. He let it drop into the long grass at the foot of a tall eucalypt, curled himself up until he was comfortable and dropped off to sleep. When he woke up, he forgot to pick up the stone. Next day, the group moved on. That evening in the clear sky there were moving lights like bright spots in the darkness.

The next day it was hot and windy, which brought a bushfire to the riverbank where the group had rested. The flash that came in the storm that night caught the tall eucalypt at its base. The fire burned for days, and the special stone became covered by the burning debris. When the rains came, fresh tussock grass grew, covering the place.

***

A great many seasons passed. The stone travelled through eons, in deep time. One day, it was picked up. It was lying beside the path of a young Anaiwan woman. She happened to notice the unusual shape in the grasses along the track. She was heavy with the child in her belly, and although the stone axe had no handle, it would help her scrape the fatty tissue from the possum hides that she had been keeping to make into a covering for the baby. It would be needed soon, and the nights were getting cold. Soon, her people would set out on their annual walkabout over to the coast, where there would be plenty of fresh fish and pipis for them to feast on. The hot sun would be high in the sky, not weak like it was down here near the river. They would be warm there. The older children would swim, and the little ones would play in the cool water and on the sparkly white sand. The children's skins would be as glossy as obsidian from all their playing in the saltwater and feasting on oysters and fat reef fish. With their bodies plumped up with good health and their white teeth gleaming, they would be flashing broad smiles all round. She was looking forward to it all.

Despite this, she was anxious. Could she make it over the mountains this year? And the baby might come during the walk. How would she manage giving birth alone? She had no grandmother there to encourage her, to help her by bringing some herbs or a drink of water.

Luckily, though, she felt the first labour pains not long after the family started walking, and she met an elderly woman—one too weak to climb the mountain—who stayed with her, encouraging her until the baby came.

***

It was at another time, and in another place altogether, that a pastoralist working his grader on the rough track above his family's house saw an unusual black stone among the spoil. He stopped the grader, got down and picked it up. When he'd wiped off the dust and dirt, he thought, Wow. I've got to take this home to show my wife.

Notes

- Aboriginal Sorry Business is observed according to the closeness of the relationships and the status in the community of the person who died. A period of serious grieving may continue for some time, and people may have travelled for some days to attend. (In Papua New Guinea, a death in a village is celebrated by the related women each covering herself with pipe clay and wearing a very large necklace made of tiny seeds threaded on a string. Wailing and singing goes on for days and nights, and very little food is taken during the ceremonial period.)

- The settler Frank Eldershaw described Aborigines' cooking:

The only attempt of a cooking apparatus that I have ever seen has been a kind of steaming oven made of stones or clay, sometimes scooped out of the ground and sometimes raised a little above it. In this oven they approach their closest effect of boiling food, which is mostly made use of for the preparation of the strong edible roots or vegetables which they gather wild from the ground. The process of steaming vegetables is simple: the oven being open at the top is fully heated by the largest fire the dimensions will admit; when ready, the roots to be cooked are put together with a quantity of green leaves thrown in, and the aperture is then partially built up, through which water is then poured in onto the burning stones or clay beneath; this hole is then closed up with wet clay until the so-called vegetables are thought to be 'done'. This is the most elaborate attempt at cookery in which they indulge.

The circumstances of these roots, if not so prepared, will take the skin off their mouths from their exceeding pungency that may perhaps point out the strong necessity which has driven them to this unusual exercise of this ingenuity … Aboriginal's ovens as being made of stones and clay where food, usually vegetables, were piled inside on top of a smoking fire and the food steamed. (Australia as It Really Is, Eldershaw, p. 91)

- ❖ Time, deep time: Aboriginal people had no concept or word for time passing until their lives began to be measured by the white people's clocks. The only natural time measure is the sun and the seasons changing. Also, the Aboriginal people of northwestern New South Wales understand the weather as six seasons per year, not four.

Chapter 20

Bushrangers and Rogues: Bakers Downfall

In northwestern New South Wales, the population had become more varied. White people and Aborigines were learning to tolerate each other, but at the diggings, not much had changed.

However, as gold was found, local villains began to make themselves felt. Over the years, some men of dubious character travelled in the bush, on the lookout for someone's treasures, items that person could be relieved of. Bushrangers had arrived—which was just what the government had not wanted to happen! Settlers in isolated homes became afraid—particularly the women and children.

The evidence of the bushrangers' presence—the stories—can be found at the tiny settlement of Bakers Downfall.

***

Some way out from the Hanging Rock settlement, Bidja held the horse ready. They all knew the rider would come that day and that he would need a fresh horse. The one he was on would be blowing hard.

Bidja knew that Thunderbolt had a few head of cattle secreted nearby—he'd heard the cows calling their calves who had strayed deeper into the bush.

Thunderbolt was a local hero, a bushranger, and the community admired him from a distance. No one knew his real name, but he commanded respect at the camps. He was wanted by the traps. The locals said of him, 'he would bring in the firewood for anyone who'd give him a feed.' He'd robbed some isolated farms and stolen guns and flour where he could get it, slashing the bottom of the flour sacks to avoid getting any that might have had arsenic added to poison the Aborigines when they stole flour.

Fred Ward didn't settle round the fire with them that night; he would not stay and relax there. Mrs Clarke would give him some warm food. He would change his horse; he always kept spare horses nearby. The settlement known as Bakers Downfall on Cowsby Road (Nundle Forest Way) was one place where he felt a little safe from the traps.

He tossed down a pannikin of rum, and then he was on his way. He never stopped anywhere for long—he was a fugitive from the law. He pulled the dark-skinned girl, Friday, up behind him.

Ward—Thunderbolt—was used to interacting with individuals in the corridor, like the John Clarke family at Bakers Downfall. He never stayed on the west side—he always returned to the east side of the range.

***

Who was the dark-skinned young woman? Was she the Maryann who had children with John Clarke? The white men sometimes spoke of her at their campfires as 'Friday.' Was she an Anaiwan or Birpai woman, or even Dunghutti? Was she kin to the Bartholomews, Fermors, Partridges or Clarkes? Today, 150 years later, no one really knows.

Thunderbolt was the most successful Australian bushranger, if bushranging longevity is the benchmark, as his exploits went on across northern New South Wales for six-and-a-half years, until he was shot near Uralla in 1870. With his death, the New South Wales bushranging epidemic of the 1860s officially ended.

The discovery of gold gave bushrangers access to great wealth that was portable and easily converted to cash. Their task was assisted by the isolated location of the goldfields and a police force decimated by troopers abandoning their duties to join the gold rush.

During our conversation, Warrigal said, 'We had photos of Thunderbolt and of Joey Monkin and others, but the big photos were stolen when we were kids.'

Chapter 21

Two Strong Men Wrote

The Gold Commissioner wrote to his wife, whom he was missing.

The second strong man was an Aboriginal student, who 150 years later wrote about the same general area from a different viewpoint after he had looked for stories of his family's experience, particularly any that resulted from the terrible disruption of colonisation.[1]

The Commissioner's letter might have read like this.

Police Barracks, Nundle

23 August 1885

My dear,

It is so hot here today.

The diggers are restless, it is being said that the Chinese intend to disinter some of the bodies of the diggers' mates, fill them with their gold and then ship the terrible burdens back to China. The other diggers are furious at the prospect.

Bushrangers too have been troublesome—another tense situation, particularly as I am short of police—thefts at outlying homesteads mostly—food and valuables taken—but no one has been killed—yet! I know that the Governor brothers are around here. The whole population is afraid of them—they have a savage reputation!

It has been terribly hot here for weeks. I hope that it rains this afternoon as that might calm everyone down somewhat. My police here are too few to quell a riot—many of them have absconded after gold. There is little that I can do. I do miss your calming presence. Our 'road' had become a deeply rutted dry clay mess. A dray-load of Mr Burrow's potatoes went over the side last week—hopefully some of the lads can gather some of the vegetables that have not been damaged—we don't have food to waste here in the diggings, as you know. The river is very low now, which makes the diggers restless—and feed is short for the livestock, the animals are hungry.

I hope that the children are learning their numbers with Miss Carol—is she strong enough to keep them in line, do you think?

The Escort is about to leave—good pieces of gold have been found this past week. Two officers will ride along with side arms. I hope it gets through to Tamworth without getting the attention of bushrangers.

Take care my dear—I will join you as soon as my relief arrives—I am feeling weary these days—

Your loving husband,

Steven George

What happened in Nundle that hot day has not been recorded. However, perhaps the rains did fall and the diggings quietened down. There was great relief when the gold escort arrived at its destination sooner than expected!

Bidja, peeping over the sill, watched the Commissioner writing his letter. He wondered what the marks on the paper were. Would he ever understand these white men?

***

A hundred and fifty years after the Commissioner wrote to his wife that day, and in the same general area (lower New England) a man—a young Aboriginal student—searched for his family members' stories. He wrote up his conclusions and published them. His book is called *Surviving New England*, and his name is Callum Clayton-Dixon; he is a grandson of Anaiwan man King Bungaree (James Dixon). He is convinced that nothing good ever came from the colonisation of his country by the white men.

One incident Callum retold that illustrates the fraught environment occurring up on the range was when a mob of 7,000 sheep being driven across the tops and forested valleys from the Australian Agricultural Company estate on the Peel River had to be driven back across to be shorn. On the way back, the shepherd was attacked and brutally killed, and 100 head of sheep were driven off. This severe action illustrated the level of anger held by the tribesmen, who resented the use of their country by the settlers. It was the large mobs of sheep that were responsible for the starvation the Aborigines experienced as every blade of grass was nibbled very close to the ground, so that little vegetation ever grew back to replace it; indigenous food animals like wombats and wallaroos did not graze there any more. In spite of the fact that the Company overseers had purchased a dozen muskets and buckshot to protect themselves, the shepherds became so worried by the Aboriginal warriors' attacks that they refused to take that route across the range ever after. (Ninety head were returned to the Company subsequently, but all the shepherds had lost heart for crossing the range via the corridor during future seasons.) Interactions between the Aboriginal men and the white men were becoming too savage for graziers to carry on their usual pastoral activities. It was violently vengeful Aboriginal men against ambitious white men. This continued for thirty years, until the settlers outnumbered the Aborigines in the uplands.

✳✳✳

Obviously Bidja heard all about the drastic encounter—down at the camp, the people would discuss its meaning for them. Around that time, they'd also heard that there were some different white people living in the range country—recently arrived people who had very mysterious ideas, different from those of the big squatters and settlers with their vast mobs of sheep! These families were known later as missionaries. They worked in dangerous and sometimes violent situations, unwanted and resented by both the Aboriginal warriors and the squatters or Company people, who were usually suspicious of 'do-gooders'.

As Bidja sat under the casuarina that day, he saw people he hadn't seen before. They didn't look like the diggers. They had a baby with them, who was crying. There were flies on her face. The father brushed his fingers gently over her face, and she stopped crying. When he saw that small, gentle action, Bidja realised that these people were not like his people.

***

Note

1. *Surviving New England: A history of Aboriginal resistance and resilience through the first forty years of the colonial apocalypse,* by Callum Clayton-Dixon, Anaiwan Language, Revival Program, Armidale NSW, 2019; and *Remembering the Myall Creek Massacre,* by Jane Lydon and Lyndall Ryan (eds), Sydney, NewSouth Books, 2018.

Chapter 22

Missionaries Worked under Tension

The young Englishman was thinking, How will I ever make contact with the blacks? Will any of us ever be able to explain about our God to these savage black men? He was worried for the safety of his wife and child. Culturally, the two peoples were so very different, and his group had no language, no words to use, yet. That would definitely help, the missionary thought to himself. His child was crying—there were flies on her face! He tenderly brushed them away. He was unaware that that one simple gesture established a soft attitude in the heart of an onlooker, creating a bridge to the foreign culture amid which he hoped to work. He continued to puzzle about the understandings of the black men and their culture. What did it all mean?

He could see that some things the Aborigines did were harmful, but in other things, particularly when the men held their young children, he saw actions that were good. The missionaries wanted to find ways to show the difference between good culture and harmful culture. They had decided to use the Bible words, 'foster the good but refuse the bad or harmful acts'. The Bible told him, 'By their fruits you will know them'.

He knew that if questioned, a black man might defend his culture by affirming that God showed his people what foods were good for them and what fruits might be poisonous, that his people could distinguish between the kindness and violent rage that the missionary saw in their behaviours as they interacted in the camp, and that they knew how to respect their elders—all of which they understood without having to think. However, the missionary had a completely different God to model—the Biblical God, who is personal, loving and full of forgiveness and kindness. He knew that the Biblical God was the only Creator, a Living God distinct from nature and the created world—the Biblical God was not the spirit of a rock or a tree! The Bible's words implied that a common language would be needed for understanding to develop with the black men. They understood that when a person was violated, the wrong had to be punished. The thoughts went round and round in his head. Would he ever be able to talk with these people? It was going to be a huge challenge for him to learn how to say what he wanted.

It was 1842. In European culture at that time there was a deep interest in Charles Darwin's new idea that people and animals evolved from 'primitive' to 'advanced'. It fascinated many intellectuals, who thought it meant that without any personal intervention we all could become 'better' or 'improved' without having to do as God said. It was very attractive to white people's thinking.

***

The young father turned his thoughts over and over while he watched his daughter curl up and fall asleep in the sun. Bidja was still watching the men from the shadows of the casuarina trees.

***

In 2016, it was noted that missionaries had established individual centres of ministry at Ingleba, Pindari, Kyogle, Tingha and Summervale, and that from these centres, a strong Christian witness evolved as they served each other. (See Waters & Moon, pp. 54–59; those writers were somewhat sceptical that any progress had been made.)

However, there were missionaries such as Sister Ruby Hyde—a dedicated white woman who managed the Colebrook Children's Home in South Australia in 1952— of whom it was said "she simply wanted a future for these children with hope in it rather than despair..." (*One Blood*, Harris p. 562). Perhaps she could see little hope for them in the future unless God Himself intervened, changing their thinking. She prayed that He would honour His promise—his words that were given to all people on earth. (Jeremiah 29:11). Another faithful Christian woman, Margaret Morgan in Western Australia, said,

> *"My Aboriginal friends today are glad they were not left 'as they are' and that they were given a chance through education to express themselves in a white-dominated society"* ... *for Aborigines were 'a minority in their own country'.* (*One Blood,* Harris, p. 558)

***

Various men also made a difference to Aborigines' lives. A missionary of northwestern New South Wales, Lancelot Threlkeld, was a veteran of Lake Macquarie Mission, and he was called the Aborigines' Advocate. He reported to the government that '200–300 blacks were trapped in a swamp and slain by Major Nunn and his men'[1] and that Nunn was boasting that he was 'popping off all the blacks as well as other threats', which illustrated how some white men were treating the Aboriginal people. There is hardly a comparison between this behaviour and that of someone like Threlkeld! He really did make a difference.

Elsewhere on the continent, Reverend Murray Siefert began influencing Aboriginal culture; as tribal fighting was reduced, Aboriginal families became larger as more babies were raised. The missionaries have been blamed for a loss of Aboriginal culture, but it is important to note that it was they who noted the injustices. They noticed the dispossession of Aboriginal land and reported it. Outside the missions, Aborigines were being shot, tortured and sexually exploited by those who would deny them their very humanity. Missionaries sincerely tried to convey a message of love and selflessness, but their message was clouded by members of a so-called Christian nation in experiences that contradicted the Gospel and prejudiced the Aboriginal people against the religion of the white settlers. (See Harris's summary on the *Australians Together* website.)[2]

In the twenty-first century, some Aboriginal people have expressed deep appreciation that they no longer have to live in their old ways. One might realise while looking over beautiful Aboriginal artwork that the troubled heart can be healed. See the 2016 Bible Society publication *Our Mob, God's Story*, in which Aboriginal people's individual faith experiences and enjoyment of the love of a caring God are richly expressed.

Notes

1. https://en.wikipedia.org/wiki/List_of_massacres_of_Indigenous_Australians
2. https://australianstogether.org.au/discover-and-learn/our-history/early-settlers/

Chapter 23

A Journalist Reported

Way across the great saltwater, they read it in the newspaper

Note: this is an imaginary article showing the kind of news the English were reading.

***

One day during the nineteenth century, when English people picked up their *Times* newspaper, they read of certain doings back in Australia. In the paper that day, it was even claimed that Aborigines were cannibals - 'such was the level of their primitive state' - which was untrue, but the thought fascinated Londoners.

One of the articles they read might have gone like this.

15 June 1856

On Wednesday last, a large corrobboree was held by the Blacks on the banks of the Peel River north of Nundle town. The excited crowd was observed from a concealed position; the blacks were all rushing around in formation, wearing little else but paint. Much noise was made with the knocking of sticks together in a recognisable rhythm. A low chanting rose and fell in a cadence. There were men and young boys all decorated upon their bodies. No women or girls could be seen—the writer believes that they could take no part in a corroboree for it was chiefly for men, though perhaps during a ceremony, a young wife might be captured! Female voices could be heard some distance away echoing the men's singing in higher cadences.

The position I was in was dangerous—it was forbidden for a white man to witness a corroboree—and the light was fading. Being in some fear for my life, I crept away from the celebrations, no more informed about the event than earlier. It had been an exciting afternoon—but the evening would be more so, I believed, to anyone intrepid enough to venture forth towards the bora ground.

I followed a well-worn path back towards Nundle, where I wrote up my piece.

Our Correspondent John Smith

***

Chapter 24

The End of the Dancing

The last big corroboree on the Peel River country included people from the nearby ranges. It was after 1857, by whitefella time.

The white population built up again during the 1880s with fresh gold finds and workings, but further along the Peel, near Bowling Alley Point, it was a different story altogether.

The story in this chapter is based on a newspaper report.

The tribes were really resenting the inroads that settlers were making into land that had been theirs from time immemorial. Grass for the animals, the marsupials, especially the possums they depended on for fat, was being eaten by the strange creatures called sheep. The fish traps they had so carefully woven from narrow strips of pandanus leaf were being knocked down by the bigger new creatures called cattle, and some of the long-used waterholes had been spoiled by the settlers' beasts. Poison that white shepherds put into the waterholes had killed many of their people, particularly in the area around Gangat (now Gloucester).

King Bungaree (named James Dixon), the leader of the Anaiwan people, who usually stayed on the tops well above Nundle, which was becoming an established village, sent out the word that there was to be a meeting on the land that the settlers called Bowling Alley Point, on the bank of the river they called Peel. Bungaree shared the leadership with Yarry (Jim Campbell), an older man.

Tribes came from north, east and west, the largest group being Kamilaroi people from as far west and northwest as the water known by the settlers as the Darling River.

It was going to be a hot day, and the people were excited, especially the youngsters who hadn't been to such a gathering before. Some of the older boys had been ceremonially marked as men now; they had endured the initiation and had been separated from the group along with the older men of the Anaiwan tribe, in the high valley where the sweet water ran down to the river. They were anxious about what was to follow for them today. Their faces and bodies had been painted to get them ready for the ceremony. The dancing would go on or for several nights during the big gathering. The youths had already spent some weeks away from their mothers and sisters and other women. The young women were excited and nervous too, for they might be taken by a husband from another group that day.

White people were not allowed to watch any of the ceremonies or the dancing of the corroboree, which was going to tell the story of the white people's intrusion into their lands, where their food supplies were now really restricted. The tribes had tried to adjust, but it was becoming impossible! The men were feeling threatened, and they wanted to take revenge. Unless Bungaree and the other Elders could calm the fighting men down, there was going to be serious bloodshed soon, for sure!

Weapons, red ochre, flints, axes and grinding stones could be exchanged today; a big gathering of people was a good time to extend trade into distant parts of the country. Such gatherings also gave youths the chance to get wives, though they had to observe the complex marriage rules of their own tribes to do so. The dancing ground—the bora—had been prepared for days, clouds of dust being raised as the men checked the secret space. No woman was allowed to go there. (No vegetation would ever again grow on a bora ground; as of 2019, no one knows the reasons for this.)

At this time the black men were very numerous in this part of the country, and as many as 700 of them were present at one corroboree at Bowling Alley Point. Bungaree was king of the principal tribe at that time. (Tamworth Observer, August 1857)

It is believed that this ceremony took place on the western side of the Peel River on Anaiwan country—the foothills of the range—maybe near Bowling Alley Point. It may have been the last large corroboree in north-western New South Wales.

Someone must have watched from a hillside in the distance that day, for an article appeared in the Sydney paper.

***

After the dancing, the people fell into sound sleep. They were exhausted from all the excitement of the preceding days.

Later that evening, back in the camp on the river bank, Bidja was seen.

In the gentle evening light, Bidja had silently observed the single white reporter, who had been watching the dancing from behind a tree. No one else had realised that the reporter was there, and no one had seen him leave.

At the next time of the new moon, a meeting was held of the people in the area the settlers called the Barnard River forest. Bidja made sure he was there too. At sunset, while watching the dancing, he noticed a fine-looking young woman who shyly glanced his way from time to time. He thought she was beautiful. Their courtship would be very private. Marriages could only happen according to strict customary marriage rules that were very complex. He didn't know if he could marry her, because he didn't yet know her clan connections or her skin name.

They slipped away at dusk together, with Bidja walking a little ahead, keeping to the rules of courting; they walked up the hill between the rocks and trees. That evening, no one saw them disappear into the distance, into the mist that curled around the peaks of the ranges and the stunted eucalyptus trees.

The people of that camp never saw the couple again.

However, before long, Bidja learned that he had lost his lovely girlfriend to a much older man who already had two wives but wanted a younger one. Bidja couldn't fight for her because the man held a superior position to Bidja in the tribe. So, reluctantly, he turned away from his camp, and he and his yellow dog roamed together over the country on walkabout.

He tramped onward, exploring country, but always getting permission to enter another's homelands. He never forgot that there was a wrong that he alone must address—eventually!

Timeline of Events in Northwestern New South Wales, 1818–1923

This consists of family events and details from several sources, combined to give a fuller picture of the people of lower New England and the many events of their lives.

1818: John Oxley explores north of Tamworth and eastwards to the coast with fellow explorers Innes, Dawson and Dangar.

c. 1820: Maryann, child of Milbona and Corumba, born at Rimbanda (Kentucky).

1822–23: The Agricultural Company is floated in the United Kingdom, acquires 40,000 acres land grant at Port Stephens, New South Wales, and establishes various crops and fine-wool sheep, but these enterprises are unsuitable for the allocated country and climate.

1823: Cunningham explores the Hunter Valley to Liverpool Plains.

1825: Dangar, the first settler on New England country, explores for the Australian Agricultural Company to the central coast.

1825–1838: Massacres at certain sites inland from Port Stephens.

1826: John Duval, later called a Beardie, arrives. A convict from Britain shipped to Sydney, he is apparently unrelated to the Duval family featured in this book. He is assigned to Captain Dumaresq on the Tilbuster stock run. (He helped aspiring settlers to select land for pastoral property at Armidale.)

1832: Major Mitchell 'discovers' Peel River.

1833: Australian Agricultural Company land on Liverpool Plains in the Tamworth area is exchanged for a holding at Port Stephens.

1833: The Australian Agricultural Company moves all its fine-wool sheep to a new land grant on Liverpool Plains, and the squatters already there are displaced and go further north, to Wolka, for example.

1834: Australian Agricultural Company town established on Company lease on Peel River, opposite Nundle village.

1835: Massacre at Wattenbakh.

1835: Clashes on the Darling River.

1836: John Schofield takes up Woolomin Station (the properties changed hands a good deal, perhaps due to drought). The Schofield brothers arrive in Nundle village.

1837: Nundle is gazetted as a town to service the local pastoral properties and provide access to Tamworth.

1838: Maurice Quinn arrives at Rimbanda, having been shipped out from Ireland.

1838: Myall Creek Massacre of Kamilaroi people near Bingara.

1839: Waterloo Creek Massacre, Inverell district.

1841: James Duval Sr sails from France to the township of Sydney on SS *Lady Kennaway*, meeting Margaret Mullane onboard. (He married her in Sydney in 1842.)

1841: Wombramurra changes hands from Mr Armitage to Dr Jenkins. (It was sold again in 1846.)

1842: Maryann Quinn's child, Mary Elizabeth (Granny Duval) born at Winterbourne Station in 1842. (Her siblings, James, Bodella (Jessie), Hugh, Mariah and Patrick, were also born in the 1840s.)

1842: James Duval Jr born in Sydney. (His brother John and sister Margaret Jane were born in 1843 and 1845, also in Sydney.)

1842: John and Henry Clarke arrive from Britain as settlers. They have walked from Newcastle (Coaltown) and Port Macquarie settlement to Bakers Downfall, Hanging Rock.

1847: Settlers are granted long-term leases calculated on the supposed carrying capacity of their selections.

1850: Nundle's population reaches 800: about 300 were European and 500 were Chinese.

1851–1852: First gold finds in New England, at Limbri district and in the watercourses and gullies feeding into the Peel River at Oakenville Creek on the western side of the range.

1853–1859: Peel River Land and Mineral Company established in Britain. (This was subsequently called the 'South Sea Bubble' as it was a failure financially.)

1855: First allotments sold in Nundle.

1860: Massacre at Kunderang Station in Eastern Fall country.

1863: Adam Bartholomew born in the Moonbi area.

1870: James Duval moves to the Tamworth district with his wife, Mary Elizabeth, and their several children. (He acquired work with the Australian Agricultural Company on Cann's Plains as a shearer and later moved with his family to Duncans Creek; he also worked at Foley's Folly as a carpenter.)

1874: Nundle town is laid out on the east bank of the Peel River.

1882: The worst year of tension between blacks and white men in northwestern New South Wales.

1885: Death of young James Duval.

1890: Adam Bartholomew marries Annie Duval at Nundle. She is nineteen. (Their first child John was born at Barnard River on Barry Station, also called Glenrock.)

1923: Death of Granny Duval at Gloucester, New South Wales.

1991: Stone tool found above the Barnard River. (In 2017, it was attested as being at least 5,000 years old and from the Nundle district by Dr Mark Moore at the University of New England.)

See also *Indigenous Australian Timeline 1500–1900* from the Australian Museum, Sydney. Material from that timeline is used here, with additional comments, by kind permission of the Australian Museum.

IMAGE ALBUM FOR THE STORY OF GRANNY DUVAL

Jessie's daughter Sarah - often visited by Granny-Barrington

Doc Woods

Mariah Dixon (nee Quinn)
sister of Granny Duval

THE STORY OF GRANNY DUVAL

Cedar cutters could be violent against Aborigines

Top End pastor baptising Aboriginal child with love. Pic courtesy of Carmel Sears

Butchering you Know sketch by Col Mundy Slaughterhouse Creek, Myall Creek

Strong resistance by blacks, but ineffective - they didn't have horses and guns!

Aboriginal tribe in the New England granite country, c. 1860.
This early photo depicts the Aboriginal inhabitants as a natural and integrated part of the landscape, a sight now absent from the New England countryside. Despite appearances, the Aboriginal people in this area have retained close links with the landscape through their sense of relationship to place.

Granny Mary Duval Elder in later life
Ingleba, Hanging Rock, Gloucester 1842-1923

James Duval and his wife Mary Elizabeth

Maurice Quinn with Maryann
c1840 at *Rimbanda* NSW

Harry Wright and wife Sarah,
two most respected Aborigines
of New England

THE STORY OF GRANNY DUVAL

Adam Bartholemew
boundary rider

Hanging Rock school children of 1902
(Lily May front row)

Annie Bartholomew wife of Adam
nee (Hannah) Duval

James (Quinn) Morris

Sarah Morris (nee Betts)
wife of James Morris

Lady Hannah Mary Fermor
proud grandma

Lily May Fermor (nee Bartholomew)
midwife, generous grandmother
and loved gardener

Ada Lesley (nee Bartholomew)
daughter of Annie and Adam.

Auntie Meg Bartholomew

James Bartholomew, black tracker, much loved in the family.

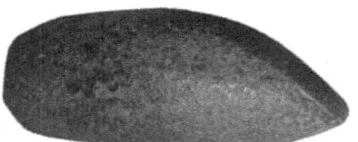
Stone axe head found above Barnard river in 1990

Ted Clarke
in his World War 1 uniform

Several Aboriginal family members have advised the books content L to R Judy Quinn, Elaine Bartholomew, Hope Strudwick, Trish Locke, Faye Griffiths

Victor Fermor - born 1915
boundary rider and story teller

THE STORY OF GRANNY DUVAL

Nundle Village 1891 (etching)

Hanging Rock hospitality at the heifer station with locals mixing socially.
(etching)

Panic at the heifer station, the Traps are coming!
(etching)

Sunday Church
Oakenville Creek, Nundle, 1854
(etching)

(etching)

Chinese diggers using a cradle to separate soil, gravel and gold flakes.

(etching)

Bulletin Cartoon *White Australia* attitudes and fears of Asiatics.

Part Two

These New England Families and Individuals Made a Difference

Part 2 chronicles the stories of many of the families of the Nundle and Hanging Rock area and especially the significant Aboriginal women, including Granny Duval, who helped shape their community since the white men came. It also considers other historians who have researched this, with personal accounts, anecdotes and memories precious to the families, and oral history of significant events that occurred.

Chapter 25

The Black Matriarchs

They were the women who took control; it became personal.

The Black Matriarchs were tribal women of the nineteenth century, Aboriginal women who successfully straddled two generations and two cultures, living in both the Indigenous world and on the edge of the British settler culture.

The five matriarchs became the heads of a very large community in New England who were respected in both the Aboriginal and white societies and still are. The author adds Granny Mary Duval to the list of five.[1]

Their story of the matriarchs is not one of loss but one of cultural survival. The special quality the women had in common was their particular capacity as mothers.

Aboriginal women always worked hard as equal members of their tribe, but with white settlement this work expanded to include work on the pastoral stations.

The trend towards having work and some rations commenced following the establishment of the pastoral stations in northwestern New South Wales from the early 1826, providing work, but no pay, to the Aborigines of the camps nearby. Able Indigenous women also were wanted for stockwork. The habit of 'employing' Aborigines without pay on pastoral stations became unlawful, particularly in central Australia, and was sometimes called 'nigger farming'. It was outlawed from the 1960s onward.

During the early part of the nineteenth century, for the Aboriginal people, the patterns of their lives were changing radically, particularly for the men of the tribe, whose status had traditionally been that of the warriors and leaders of their people. This meant some of the men became 'broken' during the changes; they experienced lost status, lost purpose, lost language, lost country, lost authority among the tribe and lost expectations for their own lives.

The Aboriginal women rose to power as the men's authority and dignity were inevitably reduced. Much of the traditional cultural kinship system was destroyed, and the culture that accompanied it was almost destroyed too. It was only kept alive by women's efforts, particularly those of the Grannies, the women who took a leading role in maintaining continuity amid cultural change. They retained their cultural habit of communal living. The five women were termed matriarchs by Patsy Cohen because of their remarkable ability to straddle the two generations while keeping the family identities strong. Their strength as mothers was exceptional. (See Cohen and Somerville, pp. 108–137.)

They adapted, apparently successfully, to white men's ways in clothing, food and drink, language, housing and relationships. Some of them who were exposed to Christian teaching passed Christian values on to their children and grandchildren. In the long run, these adult women and their men became well respected amongst the white settlers of the New England tablelands, particularly around Walcha.

The big changes that turned their lives upside down happened to all the Aboriginal families. They occurred because Aboriginal country had been taken up by white settlers, and this directly affected the Aboriginal people's traditional food supply. New ideas such as 'settling down' were encountered in northwestern New South Wales; settlers of 'good character' were allowed to take up land parcels. European diseases had already taken many Indigenous lives, and many more fell to the dubious comforts of alcohol. Some settlers and their servants lost their lives as they tried to protect their 'assets' in the bush. Confrontations between Aboriginal and white people largely ceased in 1844 and peace came to the valleys of New England.

Introducing the matriarchs

Five particular women are described in *Ingelba and the Five Black Matriarchs* (Cohen and Somerville). They were not necessarily closely related by blood; their common factor was that they lived in the Walcha and Ingleba district, so they had a relationship with one another through their association with their cultural places. They also spoke the same language (see Appendix 2 *Language Lost in Time*).

The author believes that Mary Quinn (Granny Duval) could have been listed as a sixth matriarch. She was of the same generation. Her sister Mariah is one of the five.

Maryann and Maurice Quinn's daughter Mary Elizabeth became Granny Duval as an older, respected woman of the Nundle district, since she had married James Duval at Walcha in 1863 and in later life was caring for her own children and grandchildren in the Hanging Rock and Nundle area.

Granny Duval was a Black Matriarch who moved away from Ingleba, going south to the Hanging Rock area, and her connection with her sisters and brother James was somewhat weakened by the distance.

Mary Elizabeth had the athletic prowess of the Aboriginal people of that time and was a competent horsewoman. It was she who was connected by family and blood to the Ingleba group of Aboriginals; her brother James Morris (Quinn) was there and probably her other siblings too—Mariah, Hugh, Jessie and John.

Her husband James Duval was a man from the town, and as a white man raising a family of his own, he had to find work. His parents' influence must have been very different from that of parents of the Ingleba group, who seem to have been stable and deeply caring adults.

At Rimbanda, Mary's grandparents Corumba and Milbona may have still been nearby in 1860; perhaps they lived in the camp, where meagre rations and the occasional blanket were handed out in exchange for some work about the place.

(Ancestry.com lists further children of Milbona and Corumba and may well be correct.)

In the *Bullcorronda/Mt Yarrowyck Report* of the Registrar of Native Title, New South Wales, by Waters & Moon are records of the story of the many New England Aboriginal families, one group of which were related back to Maryann Quinn; this group 'were missing' when the report was being written up in 2016 (pp. 117–118).

There was quite a debate by the Aboriginal people of Hanging Rock about just who was related to Granny Duval; she was their ancestral grandmother.

The oral history[2] about these particular people and the issue of their identity, their surnames, is found in a conversation between Margaret Somerville and Lulu Kim and Patsy Cohen (Cohen and Somerville, pp. 112–113, 130). It was thought—in oral memory—that Maurice Quinn was the father of these children; this was mentioned, for example, in answer to the question 'Who was Granny Morris?', which led to the following answer: 'Mariah was their grandmother. She wasn't their mother. Quinns I think her name might; I can't think, but old Granny Mariah … she was very old; yeah and she was very old, poor old soul. Would she have been related to Lulu? … Old Grandfather Morris; that was her sis … brother. They were brother and sister.' This was a statement about Granny Sarah Morris and her relationship with the rest of the family, with the Quinn children; trying to work the relationships out, out loud.

The photo of young Mariah kept by most family members probably indicates that she was part of this family. Her black serge dress shows the clothes that the Aboriginal women were expected to wear by the white people—the women's dress of the day.

Maurice's children with Maryann, according to Ancestry.com, were Mariah, Mary, Bodella (called Jessie), James, John, Hugh and Patrick. Since it is known that Ancestry's records are not always reliable, there is room for error there. But someone has put the data there—someone who knew about the family?

The five Black Matriarchs that Patsy remembered are as follows:

- Granny Mariah: a daughter of Maryann Quinn who married James Dixon (Bungaree) at Woolbrook; born in the 1840s; date of death unknown; 'she was the oldest of the lot'
- Granny Louisa Mackenzie: from Texas, Queensland; born 1850; died in 1954
- Granny Sarah Wright nee Mahoney: lived mostly round Nowendoc, Nymboida, Wollomombi and Callaghans Swamp; born 1834; died 1938
- Granny Widders: full sister of Granny Sarah Wright
- Granny Sarah Morris: married James Quinn (Morris); brother of Mary Elizabeth Duval nee Quinn and James, son of Maryann Quinn.

The sixth matriarch, whose important story is told in this book, is Granny Mary Duval nee Quinn.

Kin networks were not written down because to write a family tree confines it to that piece of paper, whereas when the tree is conveyed verbally, it goes on; it is more like concentric circles.[3] Limited literacy may have been another reason for mistrusting a written record. A verbally reported list will have some people missing because to the speaker at the time, those they leave out are not important to the story.

The matriarchs' story is not one of loss, but of physical and cultural survival. Their lives happened just within living memory—Cohen and Somerville recorded the stories in 1990.

The five women Cohen remembered were distinctive because of three factors: they straddled two cultures; their men's status was destroyed after contact; and their location was at the farthest extent of the memory of Cohen's culture.

Granny Mary Duval

She could be distinguished by the topknot that she usually wore on her head, crocheted perhaps.

The author believes that Mary Elizabeth Duval nee Quinn also qualified as a Black Matriarch. Although she and her family moved away from

Ingleba, she satisfied the definition of matriarch because she too was an exceptional mother who straddled the two cultures.

> *The most important relationship that a maternal grandmother had was with her granddaughter. It has been suggested that this was the critical relationship for the transmission of traditional women's knowledge. We were told that in former times 'much knowledge was passed from women to their granddaughters during the period of isolation at menstruation.'* (Ellis and Barwick chapter in Brock, p. 21)
>
> *[These women did in fact] pass on the knowledge, skills, and beliefs that were essential elements in their culture.* (Cohen and Somerville, p. 110)

These women were respected for their strength and love for all their children; they raised large strong families. It was Granny Mary Duval's sister Mariah Quinn (daughter of Maryann and Maurice Quinn) who married King Bungaree, while her sister Elizabeth married Yarry (Jim Campbell). These women were capable at handling livestock, as were their men, who were in demand to work on the local properties. Back then nobody knew about the effect that this 'nutrient-free diet' would have on Aboriginal people's metabolisms. *"The five matriarchs were the heads of a very large New England community and were highly respected in the Aboriginal and white societies."* (Wright-Burgess, p.30) The story of these women is one of cultural survival.

See *Ingelba and the Five Black Matriarchs* (Cohen and Somerville) and the *Bullcorronda/Mt Yarrowyck Report* of the Native Title Office (2016), which show the lineage of these women, most of whom are genealogically related back to Maryann Quinn who was born in around 1820 (pp. 117–118).

Granny Mariah

Granny Mariah (from Woolbrook): Very little was known about her. People can remember her, but there are no stories about her life. She was the oldest of the five matriarchs. A photo of her was found in Grace's trunk where she kept her treasures. Mariah had three children—Emma, Walter and Mary. She is linked genealogically with the Greens, Towneys,

Millers, Dixons, and Yarrys. Patsy recalled visiting Mariah as a young woman. (Cohen and Somerville, pp. 114–120)

Granny Louisa McKenzie

Granny Louisa McKenzie (1850–1954) was from Texas, Queensland, but she lived between Woolbrook and Armidale. She was referred to by several names, as is the Aboriginal custom, but 'Louisa was her given name'. She had seven children yet was in hospital only once in her life when she was hit by a car. Nancy, her daughter, said about Granny:

'I was curious about her; she told me that her mother was a full-blooded Aborigine and that she was given away, as they gave away young girls to men of the tribes that they're friendly with, and she got herself pregnant to a white man. That's how she ended up being half-caste; she broke all the rules. They travelled from station to station, but she always dragged a bush around so that they couldn't track her … Years ago when they were on a station, they took the name of the station owner, and they'd give them a name; what her Aboriginal name was, I never knew. When she was over sixty, she could never get a pension as she had no papers, no registration of her birth, or parents … Poor old thing.

I remember her as poor, stubborn, independent, and rough; she spoke the lingo—when she lost her temper it just rolled out of her. She used to do the washing and ironing at the Minto Hotel … They just had big coppers and they'd boil up the sheets and pillerslips—lovely fresh smell—when you bring them in they're lovely. I used to go and help her hang them out and sometimes to iron—and iron them with no electricity! She wore big long skirts right down to the ground. They'd wash and iron them just the same, and you'd get into bed with them (p. 118).

She used to walk from Tilbuster to here when she was in her eighties. Under her long skirts, she had a dilly bag made of an old flour bag; she would carry her money and special little pipe—no one could touch it. But if she was drunk, she'd fight with you! She could be really aggressive. She'd hit you.'

'Ma Louisa taught me many things (her mother would never have given her that name). I gotta be very wary of men, and I must respect a bora ground and never go near; the men would never talk about it. She taught me to never let a man touch my clothes or my hair particularly when I had me monthlies. To be careful of mussing, whenever I cut my hair, it was sacred, and watch out for any mussing—magic performed using hair; mussing is a magic power; it isn't singing, you know.' Ma Louisa died here in 1954. (Cohen and Somerville; spoken by Nancy Tighe, recorded by Margaret Somerville, and used with author's kind permission)

Granny Sarah Wright

Granny Sarah Wright[4] lived for 104 years from 1834 to 1938. Her family name was Marny (Mahoney). After she married, she had eight children and she raised at least two more. She walked on her toes—she had a shortened leg, always covered up with her long skirt. She never had any shoes. Her children got a good education at …? The men were working the cattle with horses. Out at Niangala, she would cook for twenty men. When the men were out looking for the bushrangers, her husband (up at Nowendoc) said, 'if anybody comes here, give them a feed, feed him.' She was never frightened of the bushrangers.

'With Granny Wright, we had the best; she was a wonderful cook!' Harry Wright and his Sarah (Wright).

Granny Wright came from Nymboida and married Harry Wright. They spent their time travelling around in the Ingleba district. (Harry was an orphan child, perhaps of the Kamilaroi people, who apparently was raised on Callaghans Swamp Station. If that's where he was born, then it is likely that he was Anaiwan rather than Kamilaroi. Harry had had some Christian upbringing apparently, and he passed his love of the Bible stories on to Sarah; she then taught the stories to their children.)

Harry and Sarah Granny Wright had eight children, and she reared several of her brother's children after his wife became ill. 'She'd always tell you about herself … she told us she lived around here in Armidale and out there at Ingleba and all them places.' She was brought up here. 'We knew all the Wrights out there; the Wright people would look after us, the Armidale people, and there were good to Aboriginals. 'ere ... other people out in the country that looked after us; you could go and camp on their property and do anything at that time around' (recalled by Lulu Kim).

Margaret asked, 'Did she ever speak the language? Can you speak any of the language?'

'No not a word. When I was going away to work, the children were all sick. She sent for 'im (Doc Woods[5]); that was the time I was sick too. She was there talking away to him all the time and she was talking to him in the language. When he went away, she said to the girls, "You've got a white sickness." That was in Callaghans Swamp and Branga Plains.'

'To this day I can remember all her cooking, cause she used to make ... She had a hamper and big ovens; she used to cook bread in them big iron camp ovens. She had two to make her bread in. I used to make yeast for her. We used to boil the yeast; she showed me how much to use ... the yeast weeds. Herbs they used. Hops they called them. She showed me you had to put so much in the saucepan and put boiling water on it.'

'It's a funny thing while ever we were down there chasing the bushrangers (the Breelong Black[6]/the Governors) Granny was feeding one of them back there because Grandfather said that "if anybody comes here, give them a feed, feed them." I suppose he was dark. Well, she's never been frightened cause the bushrangers were around that time and she was never frightened. No, she gave them a feed, or any old tramp that went past, a feed. She used to do that up at Nowendoc.'

Granny Wright became senile as her death approached. 'We used to have to watch her. She would scramble out of her bed and sneak off up to Nivessons, where she worked for them many years. We all loved her; we were terribly sad when she died' (recollections by Lulu Kim). (Cohen and Somerville)

Two more women were considered matriarchs—Granny Sarah Morris and Granny Jessie Widders. They were more closely related to the Aboriginal people of Nundle and Hanging Rock than Granny Louisa; her husband James was full brother to Mary Quinn, Granny Duval.

These recollections were as far back as Patsy's oral memory could reach.

Granny Jessie Widders

Jessie Widders nee Mahoney. Nancy Widders said of Jessie nee Marny:

'she was only a short little woman; she came from down Nyangala way. As I grew up, I became more conscious of being Aboriginal; she was a lovely person, my Granny. I used to be with her while mum went out and did the washing.' Maude Cutmore added, 'I knew her when they all were at Walcha … They all used to come over at showtime. The people used to crowd there for two or three days at the show. There were sideshows and a boxing tent and horses doing tricks. The Aboriginal people would walk from Kempsey and Bellbrook. They'd start a fortnight early and camp along the way and there'd be a lot of them together. Some would ride horses, some in sulkies and buggies, and some on bikes. When they got there, they'd stop down at the dump. They'd put up a big tent!

'I never ever heard my mother and father growl!' (Cohen and Somerville)

Notes

1. Gone but not forgotten: Along with the five Black Matriarchs of Ingleba, Mary Quinn is included in the *Bullcorronda/Mt Yarrowyck Report* (p. 117). She is acknowledged as the head of the lower New England Anaiwan group, born in 1842 on Winterbourne; she was a tribal woman, a sister of Maryann, who was born in 1820 on Kentucky (Rimbanda Station) country.

2. Oral memories were passed from grandmother to grandchild. 'Oral societies function in the present, sloughing off memories that no longer have present relevance' (Ong, 1982). Therefore, it can be inappropriate

to create precise generation listing from oral memories alone; it leads to genealogical confusion!

3. Kin networks: see *Broken Circles* (Haebich). "This major work reveals the dark heart of the history of the Stolen Generations in Australia. It shows that, from the earliest times of European colonization, Aboriginal Australians experienced the trauma of loss and separation, as their children were abducted, enslaved, institutionalized, and culturally remodeled. Providing a moving and comprehensive account of this tragic history…" (see https://catalogue.nla.gov.au/catalog/2141650)

4. The Wright families of New England sprang from Harry and Sarah Wright. She reared ten children, including her own eight. One was policeman James Bartholomew (see the Bartholomew family story, Chapter 29). James was loved by all the children.

5. Doc Woods: see Chapter 39.

6. The Breelong Blacks: see Appendix 5.

Chapter 26

Two Felons: Maurice Quinn and James Duval

This chapter is about Maurice Quinn and (arriving twenty years later) James Duval—both had an eye for a pretty girl. Both men would become 'believers' in the Aboriginal cultural sense. Both were labourers.

In 1836, the Irish people were starving; this was caused by the great potato famine. The tubers rotted in the ground, and many people starved. Maurice Quinn broke into a cottage and stole several items.

He was caught, arraigned, and sentenced 'for the term of his natural life'; he arrived in Australia on 9 March 1837, an Irish transportee from Britain. His ship was SS *Calcutta*; his offence, burglary and robbery; his year of birth, 1810; his description: hazel eyes, ruddy complexion and dark brown hair. He could be identified by a scar in the right inner corner eyebrow and was five feet five inches tall. His ticket of leave was granted on 10 September 1845, no. 1663. He was sentenced 'to remain in the district of Maitland'; presumably the Maitland administrative district extended to include Bendemeer. His conditional pardon was granted in July 1850.[1]

He was assigned[2] to work under the oversight of Mr Stitt of Rimbanda Station.

∗∗∗

Maurice Quinn walked alongside a mounted officer all the way to Rimbanda Station. He had recently been put ashore at the new penal colony settlement of Port Macquarie, where Bidja had seen him with a group of others just off the ship, seasick, exhausted, pale and weak-legged.

He was suffering the effects of being down in the ship's hold, hardly ever seeing the sun, chained to other prisoners, hungry and seasick. He had been off-loaded at Port Macquarie and had shambled all the way to Rimbanda, tethered to the stirrup of the officers' horse for the whole 150 miles. (Bidja kept up, silently slipping in and out between the trees, always just watching.) Maurice had become badly sunburnt and had used animal fat to soften the pain, but it stank. Later, he realised why some of the gins smelt so bad! Maurice was to be an assigned man, supplied in response to a request for labour.

At Rimbanda, Maurice worked closely with others; he was trusted. Mrs Stitt treated them well. Maurice formed a deep relationship with a tribal woman, Maryann. They had seven children together; Mary Elizabeth was their second child. Maurice worked there for over thirty-five years. (It was their daughter Jessie who ran away, terrified, from Ingleba to settle at Barrington.)

The Aboriginal women got some food from Mrs Stitt in return for working with the animals, in the garden or in the house. Maryann may have been one of them.

When he met her at Rimbanda Station in 1839, Maryann had developed into the beauty that attracted Maurice Quinn. She was nineteen. There would be no demonstration of affection between the two—Aboriginal culture did not allow such behaviour. If walking in the bush together, she would have insisted that he walk a little ahead of her. Otherwise, he would not have 'had his way' with her at all; her brothers would have slaughtered him without ceremony. There would certainly have been a customary marriage and observing the rules, being respectful towards the Elders.[3] She had grown up 'on country' and was strong and healthy; she knew how to survive in the bush away from the tribe, which she proceeded to do as she and Maurice became parents. Maurice fathered at least seven children with Maryann; he lived on Rimbanda for thirty years.

At Rimbanda, the Aborigines, as well as the 'strays'—runaway convicts—and Bidja, camped down in the creek bed. They shared their few threadbare blankets and food. Mrs Stitt made sure they had a meal of sorts every day. She was a caring woman. The talk at the fire at night would have been in the slang English of Sydney town, the Irish of Dublin, and the Anaiwan language. Occasionally Mr Stitt added his northern English dialect to the mix of languages as he gave directions for work the next day! The convict workers apparently made no attempt to escape—they knew they were safe at Rimbanda, on the country there.

This is how Maurice died. On 18 September 1869, one day out in the paddock, a sudden storm came up, and he was struck by lightning. He died there, a crumpled heap on the ground under a tree. It was reported in the press that a black woman and the manager's wife searched for him. The report said the anguish of the black woman's grief was terrible to hear. It is assumed that she was Maryann Quinn, the mother of Maurice's seven children, all of whom were growing up on Ingleba. He had been sixty years old. He was buried where he fell. (A memorial has now been erected to his memory on Rimbanda Station.)

***

All the time Bidja was steadily observing the goings-on with the white men.

***

Twenty years later than Maurice, in 1860, James Duval, aged seventeen, found his way on foot to Rimbanda Station. He staggered onto Rimbanda country hungry and footsore, having fled from the Walcha property where he'd been kept for six months. The management of Branga Plains had obtained a chain gang of men to work on the place. James stood it as long as he could, then he left his brother John behind and walked the thirty miles from the Walcha area. The traps[4] (police) were after him.

James was a white youth. He was lonely, hungry and fearful, but he had matured during his exploits, having left his life in Sydney Town well behind him.[5]

He had struck out alone after fleeing the cold, brutality and hunger of Branga Plains, where he'd been one of a working party with his younger brother, John. He ran (avoiding the traps) and arrived at Rimbanda country, where he met Maurice and Maryann. One of their daughters was Mary Elizabeth, who had been born at Winterbourne Station in 1842. She was nineteen when she and James met and married.

On arrival, he'd hunkered down with the Aborigines at their camp in a dry creek bed. They were tolerant, although some were a little suspicious of the young white man. The camp was a stone's throw from the sheds and rough homestead. A few Aboriginal men from there did work at the station, mostly stockwork—mustering and handling the animals—work for which they were skilled.

James Duval Jr[6] appears to have peacefully navigated the Aboriginal taboos about white men consorting with a black woman, for James and Mary Elizabeth Quinn, granddaughter of Milbona and Corumba, were married on 24 August 1862 in Walcha, New England, in the Roman Catholic Church. On the certificate, James is shown as a labourer, she as a 'half-caste Aborigine' and her father as Maurice Quinn. They'd been living in the Walcha area. She signed with a cross, so presumably she had had little education.

Mary appears to have kept herself well clear of the camp men, especially when they were drinking their rum. Since the 1830s, men of all types had been moving onto the plateau above the Liverpool Plains and lower New England. Escaped convicts were always on the make around the place. James and Maurice had both seen that there was a serious threat to young Mary's wellbeing when the stockmen 'were in their cups', as they frequently were, and would want to sexually exploit her.

James's family had a chequered past—his parents were not to be admired; they let their children down. His father, John Duval, had been a sailor on the SS *Lady Kennaway*, and had married a Margaret Mullane in Sydney. They had four children. It appears John committed a gruesome murder in Sydney in 1844; both adults were imprisoned in Darlinghurst Gaol from the late 1840s until their deaths. They were no strangers to trouble, as the *Sydney Herald* reported in March 1852 under the title 'Horrible Depravity':

> *It will be remembered that on Monday last James Duval (Sr) was brought before Mr Dowling as a rogue and vagabond, having been found by Sergeant Brigden sleeping on the market wharf surrounded by his four infant children, his eldest being under ten years of age; in compassion to the children, Mr Dowling discharged the man from*

custody with an admonition, merely [sic] … On Thursday the wife, Margaret Duval, was brought before his worship, having been found lying in Hunter Street in a beastly state of intoxication, with three of the children.

The following details have been sourced from family records.

After the murder in 1844, the children were taken into care of the state and held at the Randwick Asylum for Destitute Children. The two girls were taken to the Female Factory in Parramatta. With their parents jailed, the four children were, in effect, orphans and on their own.

Growing up on the streets of Sydney, the Duval children would have been well on the way to becoming 'larrikins'[7], which was the term given to rough-living young people of Sydney, many of whom were orphans and tough youths and were getting into lots of trouble. They had the ability to get themselves out of trouble without adult help. As a result, they became fiercely independent.

'Currency kids'[8] were not trusted by the adults who had arrived from across the seas by sailing ship. These kids spoke quite differently. They had their own gang language. They were usually bigger and stronger than the settlers' children and could usually stand up for themselves. Australian-born children received some education, as shown by the fact that in Sydney and Parramatta, more than 80% of the men and 75% of the women signed their own name on the marriage register. The boys usually excelled in sports, and contests were organised between 'currency' and 'sterling' boys in foot races and bareknuckle boxing. Literacy was much lower in the rural areas where schooling was not as available.

The following story of how James and his brother John made their way from Sydney town to Walcha in 1860 was written using jail records and newspaper information.

***

James and John were always hungry. If they couldn't steal some food, perhaps they could get some work so they could get money, even a penny. They kept their eyes peeled for a fresh loaf cooling on a window ledge. Eventually they spied one, and it was gone in a flash!

The two Duval youths had escaped from the Randwick lockup, and had been hanging around the cottages at the bottom of George Street in the township of Sydney for five nights. They had a better chance of 'making a strike' and cadging some food around there - stale bread, mostly. Being petty thieves, they were getting into trouble, and one day the traps caught up with them.

This time they were incarcerated for six months, but then, an order came for some free labour. A gang of ten boys were marched 180 miles north to Branga Plains, a pastoral property managed by the Catholic Church. The manager had written to request a gang of prisoners to do the labouring on the property, and James and John were included. The boys were to become free labourers!

They walked in chains the whole distance to Branga Plains; the soldier escorts were mounted. The rough track took them from Sydney Town to Parramatta. Then they were led northwards up the Great North Road, the new route that was being carved out of the Sydney sandstone and the bush with convict labour, following the river valleys towards where Broke Village and Wollombi are today. From there, their escorts marched them through the Hunter Valley towards the ranges in the north. They struggled up the mountains at Crawney Pass, the lowest point, where ox-drawn wagons and horsemen could make it up; the ridge at the top is called the Nundle Spur. Many followed this track, including prospective goldminers heading for Hanging Rock, men looking for land to raise sheep and cattle, and settlers and manager–stockmen driving other men's livestock across the range. The work gang continued on, following the Nundle Spur along the tops to the new township of Wolka (now Walcha).

***

In the 1860s, a great many travellers made for the plateau country to the north, where gold was still being found, though not in the gold-rush quantities that had been found earlier. Since the 1830s, men of all types had been moving onto the Liverpool Plains, having crossed over the ranges towards the lush grasses and rolling foothills of New England. On the plains near the growing township of Tamworth, squatters selected land that looked good and settled down until they were pushed off when the Australian

Agricultural Company grants were made. The government at first tried to discourage settlers because there were far more convicts than settlers. The authorities were afraid that the convicts might abscond—which they did, in considerable numbers. Some became bushrangers.

✳✳✳

James was miserable. His feet were blistered and bleeding because the boots they'd given him were too small. Every step had been agony. Eventually, he had thrown them away. It was a relief when they finally arrived at Branga Plains. They settled down in the barracks, having been given only a crust of bread and a mug of tea before bed.

The next day, James's life as a felon on a country holding began in earnest. How he hated it! They were worked hard, and he was always hungry. It was freezing at night, much colder than Sydney. He endured it for six months, but one night after the evening muster, he escaped. Leaving his brother John behind, he struck out alone.

The alarm was raised in the morning and word went out that 'James Duval, number 476' was on the loose. He was said to be dangerous and 'not to be approached or sheltered.'

James was just seventeen. He pushed along on his own, going northwards, putting as much distance between himself and the traps as he could, following the bridle track through the range and plateau country areas known then as Ingleba, Aberbaldie, Surveyors Creek and Congi, keeping well away from trouble.

He was cold and alone. At night, when he heard dingoes howl, he shuddered in fear. He barely slept, such was his terror and his hunger. By daylight, he kept on, miserably, along the just-discernible track heading north, staying away from homes or settlements.

✳✳✳

Bidja resumed his walkabout. He had been shadowing the tired young white man, slipping in and out of the trees, observing the youth as he limped heavily along. He had felt sad for him; he was obviously tired and footsore. After a while, Bidja had left him.

✳✳✳

James suddenly felt sad. Something had changed. Something was missing … had someone really been there? He was so tired that he wasn't sure what he'd seen.

Further along the track, late one afternoon, James noticed patches of smouldering grasses.

He did not realise that there was a blacks' camp just over the hill. The clansmen had set fire to the dry grasses late in the afternoon[9] so that in the warmer time, there would be fresh sweet grass to bring the kangaroos and wallabies in to feed, making them easy to catch. The burning foliage was long and thick, blocking the sun from the new shoots, close to the earth, that the fire would uncover. The damp night air would extinguish the fire before it blew up and became dangerous.

That evening, the men of the tribe had lit the fires and then gone off to hunt for an animal for everyone's tucker. When they returned with a kangaroo, they found that a baby had been born that day, and the mother was very weak. The Grannies had taken charge, caring for the mother, and the new baby was given to another young mother for feeding.

The men put the kangaroo onto the hot coals of the cooking fire. The hair quickly burned away, and before too long, everyone had a chunk of hot tender meat to enjoy. The especially nutritious fat from around the kidney was given to the sick mother.

The warm food calmed the excited children. Soon everyone was curled up with their dogs around their small fires. As the camp fell into silence, the reedy cry of the new baby was heard, registering that the mother's spirit had passed from her. All the women started making heart-wrenching wails of grief, for the mother had been a much-loved member of their clan.

On the other side of the hill, James was curled in a ball on the damp cold earth; he had no fire. He smelled the roasting meat on the breeze and wished he had the courage to go and ask the blacks for some food. It was torture to be so hungry! He could hear them somewhere close by, but something terrible must have happened, as there was suddenly a lot of wailing and noise.

At sunrise the next day, James continued to follow the barely discernible track in the grass. He didn't come across the blacks. In the late afternoon, he found himself near a homestead. It was Rimbanda. He had walked for twenty-five miles.

James became one of the group that camped near the shed the settlers had built. They worked as labourers and stockmen. Work and food were shared. James had grown and matured while fleeing from Branga Plains, having left his childhood behind in Sydney.

Before long, he made friends with a lovely young woman in the camp: Mary Elizabeth Quinn. He knew that he wanted her for himself.

***

When James Duval and Mary Quinn married in 1862, they were not going to be settlers or squatters. They were not immigrants, either, as they were both Australian born. They had twelve children in all. Perhaps it is surprising that James turned out to be so responsible—was it Mary's influence? He was obviously a young man with strength of character.

***

In later years, having moved with his growing family to Hanging Rock, James got work as shearer's mate on Goonoo Goonoo Station, then called Cann's Plains, not too far away. He became interested in shearing and woolpacking. He was keen to learn all about sheep and the work of farming them.

At smoko, he would give a thought to his family. Mary was a gentle and caring mother; he knew that she would put into practice all that her mother had taught her. He remembered that Mary had been happiest living on Winterbourne Station and at Ingleba, where she had all her relatives, her community, nearby, especially the other children she was so fond of, children who were growing up in the impoverished conditions (by white standards) that resulted when Aborigines tried to make a go of living in two different worlds.

James worried about Mary's safety. The camp where they'd made a first home was near the settlement of Walcha. By the time the family moved down to the Nundle district, they had five children. Then another baby, named Hannah, was born. It was this child who carried on the family's name as Bartholomew. Hannah was usually known as 'Annie'.

∗∗∗

Eventually, James found a little work at the Foley's Folly settlement, and perhaps his son worked with his father at carpentering there. James's various jobs over twelve years were as follows.

In 1869 and 1870, he was a shearer at Goonoo Goonoo Station (according to the electoral roll).

For 1870–1873, no record remains.

In 1874 and 1875, James was listed as a builder at Foley's Folly, Hanging Rock.

In the census records of that time, James Duval is listed as living at Duncans Creek, east of Woolomin.

In 1881 and 1882, James and his family were still living at Foley's Folly, where he'd found work. His family had grown to seven children. Foley's Folly was a small community that vanished completely in the 1950s when the forestry department bulldozed the area and planted radiata pines for commercial harvesting.

During 1885, James became seriously ill after a fall at Foley's Folly. He was taken to Sydney for treatment, but he died in 1886 of congestive heart failure. He was only forty-two. He was buried at Rookwood Cemetery in Sydney. Sadly, the family could never visit his grave as it was too far away.

It was James and Mary Duval's daughter Annie who carried this Aboriginal family story down to the Bartholomews. Annie, or Hannah[10], grew up in the Hanging Rock community, where she received some schooling, but the family sometimes lived down in the valley of Glenrock Station.

Wording of the Duvals' marriage certificate:

Usual occupation: James, labourer; Mary, half-caste Aboriginal, [her] father's name being Maurice Quinn

Usual place of residence: Walcha.
Roman Catholic Church

[The note on the marriage certificate: Signed, James Duval [and] Mary X her mark. Witnesses: William [illegible] [and] Eliza Hamilton]

The couple were to have thirteen children in all. Their first baby, James, died. Mary was rearing her children at the diggings and camps.

Notes

1. Minor crimes called for transportation, but major crimes called for a hanging.
2. Convict labour was sought by station managers; it saved money, and often, an officer came with the workers to keep them in line.
3. Culture, disputes, and marriage rules: The process of the law was one of political negotiation that involved everyone in the community. When there was a dispute, the Elders met to discuss the punishments: their word was law. Offences regarded as unlawful included the unauthorised killing of a person, sacrilege, incest, adultery, theft, unauthorised assault, insult, and neglect of kinship obligations. Punishments could range from making compensation over an agreed period of time to having to face a squad of spearmen while armed with only a shield and that person's ability to protect himself. Disputes between Aboriginal groups were settled by negotiation, ritual punishment or formal battles. Settling disputes under Aboriginal law was part of the purpose of the great gatherings of Aboriginal people; other purposes were to trade, to hold Bunya nut and shellfish feasts (this was how the middens of shells were formed), to arrange marriages and to perform ceremonies (Ginibi, R. L., *Aboriginal traditional and customary law*, Law Text Culture, 1, 1994, 8-12.).
4. Traps: derogatory colonial word for the police.
5. Children of James and Mary (Granny) Duval (1862–1900s): After her first baby, James died, first four Duval children were named Kate, Elizabeth, John and Ada. The others were Louisa, Margaret, Hannah, Mary, Agnes, Catherine, Claude and Francis (not in birth order; thanks

to the Holmes family for these details). Six Duval children were registered at Armidale, and the others were registered at Tamworth.

6. James Duval Sr (James's father) was a free man. He was French by birth, a sailor, and had been born in Brest, Brittany. He sailed to Australia on SS *Lady Kennaway*. He apparently met Margaret Mullane en route. She may have been a convicted woman on that same ship. Margaret is listed as a 'bootmaker'. James Sr came from a community in Brest. She and James Duval Sr had married at St Mary's Church in the township of Sydney in July 1842. A further record about James Duval's sister young Margaret Jane says she died in an orphanage at age of three.

7. Larrikins: In the 1840s in Sydney, the young larrikins loitered around the doors of Sydney theatres and made a point of molesting any man who wore a respectable black hat by tugging it down over his eyes. Known by their hats (made from the indigenous cabbage-tree palm), the street loiterers were called the 'Cabbage-Tree Mob.' In their skylarking, they were early nationalists, the spiritual ancestors of rowdy larrikins at the big cricket grounds in the 1970s. (Melissa Bellanta, Larrikins: A History, St Lucia, University of Queensland Press, 2012)

8. Currency kids: They were the type of people Governor Macquarie wrote to the Home Secretary in Britain about: 'Such people would be the most useful in developing the country—the practical people, who knew how to survive even thrive in the Australian bush!' They were battlers, a term used to describe the settlers who were to become the backbone of the Australian nation. According to Governor Macquarie, they would become 'the yeomen of Australia'.

9. Firestick farming was practised by Aboriginal people to encourage new growth after the winter grasses had dried up. Marsupials would be attracted to the young grasses, would creep in and would be there for the people to catch for food. The grass fires were always kept small; the evening mist would control them.

10. Aboriginal habits with names: People are often given nicknames, and children were often called something other than their first names. For example, Hannah Duval was known as Annie, rarely as Hannah.

Chapter 27

The Toffs and Two Orphan Boys

Bidja noticed that the boys were just like him! He was still observing—taking it all in.

***

Certain 'toffs' had a significant influence for good. Their attitudes contrasted hugely with those of various other white people whose influence was harmful in the extreme. Rear Admiral Phillip King and Mrs Parker King reared two orphaned Aboriginal boys. One, Harry Wright, ultimately became the head of a large, interconnected Aboriginal family group.[1] The other, Tommy Dumaresq, wasn't related to the families featured in this book at all.

Rear Admiral Phillip Parker King was a member of parliament and was the superintendent of the Australian Agricultural Company at Port Stephens and at Stroud. It was written of him that he championed the cause of the Aborigine.

Two generations of boys were fostered by Mrs Parker King and her son until their family moved to Parramatta. It was believed that Harry was born in about 1843 in Tamworth. It is thought that he came from the Callaghans Swamp Run, which was an Australian Agricultural Company property, so he was probably Anaiwan. People said he was taught the ways of a gentleman.

Mrs Parker King saw to the boys' religious instruction, and they attended church services regularly, including family prayers. Mrs King left young Harry and Tommy in the care of her son, Phillip Jr, when she went to live at Parramatta with her husband when he entered parliament.

✳✳✳

Bidja, in the shadows, watched as the horses were saddled and the stores fastened on the packhorse. Two officers were in the party. Farewells were shouted, then the group slowly trotted away from the homestead.

They were planning to travel through the lush hinterland to survey country further up the valleys towards Hanging Rock. They would survey the very steep road from Gloucester to Nowendoc, straight up Hungry Hill[2]. They hoped to establish a large sheep station in the Nowendoc area for 8,000 sheep and eighty head of cattle.

Bidja saw young Harry ride off with the officers and the one who was called 'boss'. He wished he could go with them.

✳✳✳

As Harry grew up, he took on significant responsibilities and joined Philip Gidley King when the latter took over the running of Goonoo Goonoo Station (another Australian Agricultural Company property) after 1853. (It was country that James Duval would work on as a shearer's mate fifteen years later.) Harry most enjoyed being outdoors on horseback.

As an adult, Harry became a valuable and skilled handler of livestock. He married Sarah Mahoney of Wollomombi, a Dunghutti woman, who was born in 1859. They went on to have nine children and rear several other youngsters. Sarah learned a great deal from her husband and taught the children Bible songs and stories. Her youngsters went on to live settled, responsible and productive lives. Sarah was much-loved across the whole community.

The second Aboriginal so-called 'orphan' was Tommy Dumaresq, born at Port Stephens on New South Wales's coast. Mrs Parker King wrote about him for her family[3], saying, 'When a teenager, "Tommy" attached himself to Sir Edward Parry. As an adult he straddled two very different cultures

… he was generally about the stables. He was intelligent and active'. Later, he 'was about the butler's pantry'.

'Later still,' Mrs Parker King wrote, 'he and his gin went to Mrs Dumaresq's farm with her. His gin—or Nanny—was taught needlework, how to dress herself properly, and many other useful things.'

The adults tried to teach them both to read, particularly Watts's First Catechism, but they weren't successful. Nevertheless, Tommy and Nanny always attended family prayers.

Tommy also stayed in touch with his Aboriginal culture. They stayed with Mrs Dumaresq for two years, but on returning home with her, they asked for some leave to go to the bush and live as wildly as their tribe. They returned after a few weeks, appearing clean and decent (by the European standards of the time), and went straight to their various duties.

Their reason for going bush, they said, was that 'other natives would kill them if they didn't leave the Dumaresq household every now and then to be with their own people.' Tommy's relatives kept the Dumaresq family in fish in exchange for some tea and sugar. Tommy continued to care for his mother while she was in the tribe and he was living with the white family.

Later, Mrs Parker King wrote about Tommy Dumaresq, that

'he never conquered the difficulty of learning to read, but acquired such an insight into the Christian religion as gradually to influence his conduct.'

Tommy very much wanted to remain with the family.

He never managed to learn to read, but when their butler left, Mrs Parker King gave Tommy his job and for three years he was more than adequate for their family. He was given a red livery of his own.

His conduct was so good and he was so regular in church attendance and church cleaning, which showed the depth of his religious feeling that she asked Mr Gore the vicar to baptise him. He consented to train him and conferred baptism on him because he showed that he understood the meaning, the gravity, of the Rite.

Sadly, soon after this, he was encouraged to visit a public house and partake. He came out tipsy and lay all night in damp grass, and the outcome was a serious lung infection. He was ill for eighteen months, then finally succumbed. Mrs Parker King wrote:

His sorrow, for having got drunk, was very great and he asked, if he had said any bad words during that time or spoken disrespectfully to any of us.

The family cared for him. He recovered to some extent and then went back to the coast where they hoped his health would improve. But Tommy died, assured in his spirit that he went with the faith of Christ in his heart.

He was always appreciative of what the family did for him:

On being asked by Mr. Cowper, why he hoped to go to Heaven; he replied: 'because Jesus Christ died for sinners.'

He was buried in the Churchyard at Stroud by the Rev. William Cowper - and there will he rest till the morning of the Resurrection when we trust he will be among those whom no man can number

These two Aboriginal youths, 'rescued' by the King and Parry families, were both reared listening to the Christian message. They took it to themselves individually and, in the case of Harry Wright, carried the blessings and comfort of that divine relationship into the lives of their own family members … for Harry chose Sarah, who followed his guidance when she taught their own children, as well as those of others, of the love of the Saviour Jesus Christ.

Notes

1. Monica Wright-Burgess wrote: 'The owners of these [seven] Runs used Aborigines as stockmen and cattle and sheep drovers as they knew the country well and were excellent horsemen. Harry was one of the best of them, he was considered a leading authority on livestock, due in part to his upbringing by the King family.' (Wright-Burgess, *The Wright Story*, pp. 9, used by the author's kind permission). For further detail about Harry (who was also called Henry), see the 1989 interview

with his granddaughter Annie Whilamena Kelly born Shay Kelly, Dunghutti woman.

2. The well-defined route indicated part of the way. It turned eastwards, crossing the Port Stephens Line. It was the route that most foot traffic followed from the coast at Port Macquarie up to the range and beyond to Tamworth. In February 2, 1836, the route was described as follows: *'The distance from the nearest point of the Port Stephens location to Liverpool Plains is about eighty miles, and the country intervening offers facilities for the formation of a road, which is now in progress. The Peel line between Callaghans Swamp and the Port Stephens road on the east, also the branch road northerly along the main range, has long been abandoned and is now scarcely distinguishable; but the Nundle spur and its northerly trend by way of Ingleba are still in use although largely suspended by the railway.'* (from an expired website https://thelatestold.news › tag › walcha)

3. Wright-Burgess, p. 7

Chapter 28

Foley's Folly

On the Hanging Rock Diggings, gold had been discovered, and the Hanging Rock Diggings gold rush commenced. Thousands of eager men arrived from all over the world to try their luck.

Brigadoon-like, the Hanging Rock goldfield in 1866 had two hotels and a population of 150. The hamlet that came to be called Foley's Folly was located near Quack-a-Naka, or Quackanaki, not far from the Hanging Rock village.

Diggers on the goldfields were a mixed bunch. As at any other settlement, there were men from twenty different nations on the Hanging Rock Diggings. Those who were gentlemen took responsibility for leadership in the community. Officially, when a man owned land, he was classed as a gentleman; these were the only men who got to vote.

It was these men who applied for a school in 1878; Hanging Rock Provisional School functioned in rented premises. A chapel building for the Primitive Methodist community was also organised by Mr Bond and cost 2/6 ('two and six', two pounds and sixpence) per month in rent. The boys used to annoy the teacher by hiding in the bushes, sneaking across and ringing the bell, then hiding when he came out to find out who it was. The punishment was a severe caning.

The Gentlemen's Roll—the electoral roll in 1869—listed the names of Messers Bond, Boyd, Cooper, Crawley, Daplin, Dell, Dennet, Emblem, Goldring, Harrison, Haney, King, Lambert, Lowe, McDivett, Mulchay,

Page, Robinson, Shea, Snedden, Stevens, Thomas, Travenna, Vant, Wallis, Watts, Wingate and Woodley.

These miners were the leaders of the community; they requested a better postal service and established the store at Foley's Folly. They had also invested funds in, and put a lot of energy into, the Wheal Prosper Company mine, where stone was brought to the surface for crushing via a 435-foot-deep shaft. However, whenever there was a drought, activity stopped, as water was required to drive the crushing plant.

Was there actually a man named Foley mining in the area? It seems there was: Foley's surname is listed in the goldminers' records of the Hanging Rock goldfield between 1875 and 1880.

Initially, Mr Foley's miner's lease was judged to be of little value, and he gave up and sold it to Mr Bond. But later, there were good gold finds at Foley's Folly.

In 1868, the *Maitland Mercury* newspaper ran an article describing *the diggers' discomfort as they must navigate the track up to The Rock their complaint being that as the Commissioner Mr Addington does not live on the gold-fields but rather lives at Armidale—he seldom ever comes here … which is a great loss to the people … as the government continues to receive great quantities of gold from this field … our roads are in a deplorable and dangerous state and the whole distance from here to the Hanging Rock and to the Peel river too … are bad—because no one is here to look after us.*

There was nothing but a steep bridle track between Hanging Rock and Nundle village at the time.

The diggers were also angry that the authorities would not let them work a particular 'lead' (good site for gold). The lead in question apparently was located right under the constable's hut—a building they thought would be blown down the next time they had a really big storm. It made no sense at all to the diggers to be prevented from looking there for gold.

In another article in the *Maitland Mercury*, the writer bemoans that 'not one shilling has been spent on our roads or anything else. The people of Nundle and Hanging Rock have a right to say they have been neglected'.

As Mr Bond, a leader in the community, was goldmining between 1876 and 1880 at Foley's Folly, it may well have been his cabin that James Duval was building in 1874, when the Duval family's address is shown in postal records as Foley's Folly.

The numbers at Foley's Folly were growing in the mid-1850s, with over 500 Foley's Folly letters passing through the Post Office each week. This indicates the population level at the time.

The homes, mine heads and machinery of Foley's Folly were bulldozed when the New South Wales government started planting cypress pines in the 1950s. Old-timers can go there today (as at 2016) but almost nothing can be found of the hive of activity that existed in the 1870s and 1880s. Foley's Folly has vanished, like Brigadoon, into the mists of time. Abandoned ironmongery survives here and there among the pine trees.

Chapter 29

The Bartholomews

Who was Adam Bartholomew, and where did he come from?

Apparently, his father had the same name and came from Hanging Rock. The surname appears on the electoral roll from 1857 to 1879 in Queensland. Was this man Adam's father? Was this the Adam who married Annie Duval? Did he come from the Chatham Islands in New Zealand?

One birth certificate says that Adam's son Edward was born at Barry Station and that Adam himself was born at Muswellbrook; however, another source shows Adam G. Bartholomew was born in Moonbi around 1863 and was variously known as Edward, Edmund, Adam or Teddy. On Patricia Bartholomew's family chart, by the New South Wales Native Title office lists Adam as having been born at Moonbi.

Perhaps Adam Bartholomew had been eyeing off young Hannah (Annie) for some time as she ran down the track to school each day, her hair ribbons flying in the wind. She was nineteen when they married in the Victoria Hotel at Nundle in 1890 with the rites of the Wesleyan Church.

Adam signed his marriage certificate with an X, so it appears he was not well schooled. His death certificate tells us more about him than any other source. He worked as a labourer and a boundary rider. He was the father or stepfather of Ina, John, Lilly May, Ada, Frederick, Florence, James, Edward, Annie, Elizabeth, Mabel, Sarah and Malcolm Roy. The four youngest (including Ina) were Ted Clarke's children with Annie, but all grew up named Bartholomew. Adam worked on properties in the area between Barnard River and the Upper Hunter district. His and Annie's first child was born at Barry Station in 1892.

There were nine children from Adam and Annie Bartholomew's marriage, plus four others from Annie's relationship with Edward Clarke.

Three of Adam and Annie's girls, Ina, Annie and Lilly May, were enrolled at the new Hanging Rock School (established in 1880). Lilly was a good student at eight—she had already received some schooling from her mother while they were living at Glenrock, twenty miles away.

When the community at Hanging Rock began buzzing with the news of the latest gold find, Adam decided his horse sense and stockwork experience were worth more in a steady job than wasted in looking for gold. Getting down into the mud looking for flakes of gold was not his way to provide for his family of seven children. He left all that to his mates.

Adam was a boundary rider. His work, for the most part, consisted of regularly riding around the fences to check that they were in good order, blocking up any panels that were broken, putting out strangers (other properties' stock that had strayed onto the run) and generally doing all he could to keep his master's stock in and everybody else's out.

His wife, Annie, may have stayed behind in the Hanging Rock settlement sometimes, especially after the school was opened, while he went off to find work. Their family records show that they lived on Barry Station too.

His granddaughter, Muriel Wall, said in 1990 that she remembered him as 'a big man with a big voice' sitting on a big chestnut horse, looking down at her and booming, 'Do you know who I am, girl?' She was about six at the time.

Muriel's mother Annie (Adam and Annie's daughter) and her siblings sometimes lived at Glenrock Station in the Upper Hunter Valley, near Barry Station. Muriel's siblings were Millie, Victor, Ada, Arthur and Margaret.

When Adam worked as a boundary rider, he not only looked after the livestock on properties but also checked the condition of the dog fence. It was the longest fence in the world and traced a crooked line from Jimbour, in Queensland's southeast, to the Great Australian Bight. Without the men and women who maintained it, wild dogs would have brought sheep farming to its knees.

Boundary riding was a lonely life; the men were out in the bush for months at a time. Adam may have met up with the local mail deliverer from time to time to get his mail, perhaps a well-aged loaf of bread, and, of course, some rum.

***

Adam Bartholomew commanded a real presence. His black gelding stood silently, waiting for him to make a move.

He'd found the fence holed earlier that morning—wombats again. He'd mended it only recently, on his last run along the fence. There was evidence of dogs having got through to the sheep. They had made a real mess of the ewes and lambs. It was definitely not the season for lambing! The neighbour's rams had been in again. That meant the fence must have been holed earlier in the year too.

The weather had been so bad that they had left the ewes, which were heavy in wool and lamb, in the sheltered gully, hoping they would make it. But wild dogs had found their way through the dog fence thanks to a burrowing wombat, determined to keep going on his old track.

Adam knew of some Aboriginals who had cleverly invented a way to trap wombats when they tried to break through a fence—they dug a hole and set up a hinged gate like a seesaw. When the wombat stepped onto the lowered end, the board flipped, dropping the wombat quickly into the hole so it could be dispatched. The ears could be handed in to the officer at Nundle for a payment. Wombat meat was not usually eaten by the Aborigines. However, if you were hungry enough …

Adam patched up the fence as best he could. That bitter day, he used his knife to dispatch the suffering ewes that had been mauled. He couldn't do anything for the surviving lambs. They wouldn't see the night out; the foxes would see to that.

He noticed a heifer down in calving. She was more valuable than the sheep. Obviously, the bulls from next door had visited! She was much too young to be calving, especially in this weather.

Adam dismounted and went to the exhausted heifer. The calf was half out and obviously dead. He helped her by pulling the calf, and eventually stood her up and pushed her up the track a bit to where there were a few cows clustered in some shelter.

He looked at the fence again. He hoped it would hold until he could come back and do a better job.

He rode the two hours back to the boundary riders' hut and was pleased to unsaddle the horse and cover him with a bag. After lighting a fire, he soon had rum in his hand and was making a billy of hot tea with lots of sugar to cheer him up. It had been a typical winter's day for him. He thought the boss should run only cattle there as there were too many dingoes—they didn't give the sheep a chance. The dog fence was not giving the stock the protection it was meant to. The sheep produced nice fine wool out here, but they lost so many it was a terrible waste. But he could only do as he was told. He wasn't the manager.

On another occasion, at the end of a hot summer's day, Adam rode the dog fence back up the mountain towards Hanging Rock, feeling satisfied with the past month's work. He planned to stop off for a spell at Granny Duval's little inn near the dog fence and catch up with her over a cold drink. Granny Duval was his mother-in-law. She would have news of the latest baby. Adam had been devastated when little Frederick had died in 1899 at just two years old. The new baby's name was to be James.

Granny Duval was a midwife. She had the women's skills that many Aboriginal women had—know-how that was especially needed during childbirth. The isolation many women experienced was pretty frightening for them, especially when the child was their first.

On rare occasions, Granny might be called out to assist a white woman, though they usually preferred to go to the hospital in Tamworth when their babies were due. Adam wondered if it shamed the white women to call on an Aboriginal woman for help.

It turned out Baby James had arrived the night before. Adam couldn't wait to get home and meet his new child. Like most men, he had hoped for another son—and enjoying a hot bath, with the tub in front of the kitchen fire, was a luxury he couldn't have out bush.

Poem: The Boundary Rider

A vivid description of a stock-fence worker's day by Thomas William Heney—poetry from 100 years ago!

The bridle reins hang loose in the hold of his lean left hand;
As the tether gives, the horse bends browsing down to the sand,
On the pommel the right hand rests with a smoking briar black,
Whose thin rings rise and break as he gazes from the track.
Already the sun is aslope, high still in a pale hot sky,
The afternoon is fierce, in its glare the wide plains lie
Empty as heaven and silent, smit with a vast despair,
The face of a Titan bound, for whom is no hope nor care.
Hoar are its leagues of bush, and tawny brown is its soil,
In that immensity lost are human effort and toil,
A few scattered sheep in the scrub hardly themselves to be seen;
One man in the wilderness lone; beside, a primaeval scene.
Firm and upright in saddle as a soldier upon parade,
Yet graceful too is his seat, for Nature this horseman made;
From childhood a fearless rider, now like a centaur he.
And half his strength is gone when he jumps from the saddle-tree.
Back from his sweat-wet hair his felt is carelessly placed,
Handkerchief at his throat, sagging shirt round a lank firm waist;
True to the set of strong loins the belted moleskins are tight,
Plain from forehead to stirrup a virile vigour in sight.
Yet scarce more than a boy, but the long blaze not more sure
Has left on the countenance spare a hue that shall ever endure,
Than the life of the plains has set reliance and courage there,
Constancy, manliness frank in a young face debonair.
He should be no less who rides for ever each spacious bound,
Better than human speech he knows the desert around.

He journeys from dawn to dusk, and always he rides alone,
The hue of the wilderness takes, as his mind its monotone.
He hears the infrequent cries, shrieking or hoarse and slow,
Sheep bleating, the minah's scream, the monologue of the crow;
He rides in a manless land, and in leagues of the salt bush plain,
Seeks day after day for change, and seeks it ever in vain.
In his hands his life each morn as he swings to his leathern seat,
Woe to him if he falls where as water the plain sucks heat,
Alone in a vast still tomb, cruel and loth to spare,
Death waits for each sense and slays whilst the doomed wretch feels despair.

(Public domain)

Adam's death

While Adam was away working at Glenrock Station (or Glenmore) in 1921, he died at Moonan Brook. He was dismounted and digging a stone from his horse's hoof when he was bitten by a brown snake.

He tried to go on but didn't make it. There was no one to see what happened or race back to the homestead for help…

He was buried at Moonan Cemetery, aged only about fifty-eight. The death was registered at Scone, New South Wales.

His death certificate records that he died from heart disease; this was perhaps exacerbated by the snake bite. It reads:

1821, 28 December

New South Wales Death Certificate

'Glenmore' Moonan Flat

Upper Hunter Shire

ADAM BARTHOLOMEW—farm hand Male, about 58 years.

Cause of Death—Heart Disease—inquest unnecessary. Scone Coroner—R. Lockhead

Buried—1921, 29 December, Moonan Brook

Born—Moonbi NSW

Married—Nundle, aged 26 years. Wife—Annie Duval

Family Members at the time of his death—John 29; Lily M 28; Ada 26; Florrie 22; James 21; Annie 18; Elizabeth 15; 1 male deceased

In Adam Bartholomew's community, an inflamed throat occurred frequently and led to heart disease in adults. It is still a very serious condition for Aboriginal people, both children and adults.

***

Uncle Jimmy Bartholomew was Adam's uncle. He was in the native police; he operated from Glen Innes.

James Bartholomew rode a big grey gelding. He was popular with his family. He patrolled the bush around Walcha. One day he was out searching for two boys who had stolen some food from a settler's house.

The two boys were hiding behind a rocky outcrop made of the rounded granite stones of the tableland. They had been hungry that day. They'd heard the horse walking slowly as it carefully avoided the rocks.

Jimmy spied them from a distance. When he came closer he called out, 'You boys get away from here. Go where our people are.' He turned the big gelding as if on a sixpence and thundered away in the opposite direction.

It was difficult when a native policeman had to hunt down and charge a miscreant from his own clan. James felt conflicted between doing his job and his loyalty to his own kin.

When the boys peeped out from their hiding place, they saw the dust being raised by the pounding hooves of Uncle Jimmy's horse as he cantered away. They were safe from the law that day.

Chapter 30

The Fermors

Drought had its grip on Upper Hunter country. Struggling families began to move up onto the range towards the goldfields. Maybe they would do a bit better there?

> *Early in 1866 groups were seen travelling along a dusty track of New England … first came some bullocks or horse drawn drays, with occasionally a tilted cart containing the younger members of the family; then followed spare bullocks, horses, brood mares, foals, milch cows, a female or two on side saddles and some thriving "corn stalks" … Some of these parties forcibly remind an observer of scenes described in the Old Testament, when patriarchs moved in search of fresh pastures accompanied by their families from Old New England.* (R. B. Walker)

Bidja watched the family trudge along the Nundle Spur towards the Hanging Rock settlement.

John, the father of the group, thought there should be work there for him. They were another white family coming to swell the numbers at Hanging Rock, the nearby gold diggings. The Aborigines were already outnumbered.

John's wife was Hannah Mary nee Taylor from the extensive Taylor family of the Scone and Pages Creek district. John and Hannah had experienced deep sadness: their first three babies had died, and were buried back on Belltrees at Scone.

***

Some other family members may have identified as Aboriginal, but the known family origins came about when Mary and James Duval's daughter Annie (Hannah) married Adam Bartholomew and when Annie and Adam's daughter Lilly May married Bill Fermor.

***

There were eight mouths to provide for. John was a good horseman and hoped to get work as a boundary rider, maybe with the Australian Agricultural Company on the Peel River Estate.

Bidja wondered who they were and what they would be doing on the Diggings.

***

The Fermors in New South Wales had aristocratic lineage, but that did not protect them from the trials of living in the new colony. (Cullin (ed), *The Hunters Head Ellerston 1829–1979*)

> *Sir Edward Fermor—brewer—of Hastings, Sussex England [...];*
> *was born in 1817 and died in 1871.*
>
> *1855. His son Henry with his wife Elizabeth, nee Isaacs, set sail aboard 'Nimrod' for Sydney Town. They were the first family of that name to emigrate to Australia. They brought with them five small daughters: Amelia, Catherine, Ellen, and twins Henrietta and Elizabeth. Henry's motivation seems to have been to live and work in Sydney where a close relative owned the Australia Hotel in Lower George Street. They would have a roof over their heads in the building, Henry was to be manager of the hotel with a promise of a secure livelihood. Having a somewhat aristocratic lineage did not protect them from the trials of life in the colony!*
>
> *1855. Their son John was born and baptised at St Phillips George Street in June 1856. (Years passed—ultimately five Taylors married*

five Fermors) (from Gae Maunder, a Nundle resident used with permission).

Elizabeth Isaacs had a brother living on the land outside Scone in the Hunter Valley. In 1856, Henry and Elizabeth packed up their family and moved northwards—to the bush.

Their son John was raised on Ellerston Station (which in more recent years became Kerry Packer's property).

He was employed as soon as he was old enough to work. He had no formal education—as an adult, when he applied for a Provisional School to be provided for his children, he put an X beside his name. This deficiency seemed to push him to try to get schooling for his children Charles and Hannah (1891), who were the first pupils. At this stage, the children were riding twelve miles on their ponies from Pages Creek to school during the winter months, when snow fell regularly. The school operated for only three months due to falling attendance. William Willis, the teacher, wrote in August that 'the lack of a floor in the classroom allowed dampness to soak at a distance of four feet from the walls on the inside'.

For the next seven years, the children were educated in a room at Stilton offered by Thomas and Ellen Taylor. Charles and Hannah were John's children from Pages Creek school. Ferdinand Tilse (the nephew of John Tilse, who married Catherine Fermor) enrolled his children William, Ferdinand and Leopold. Thomas and Ellen's children were Horace, Frank, Lilly, Thomas and Ellen. Also at the school were children from the school at Hunters Vale, in the Collins's house.

In 1882, John had married Hannah Mary Taylor, the daughter of Hannah McMahon and Henry Taylor. The neighbours and fellow farm-hands from Ellerston Station joined in the celebrations. They were married at St Matthew's Church Gundy, opposite the Gundy Store. They lived in Ellerston or Belltrees for the next ten years, the period when three of their babies sadly died.

The House-to-House school merged with Ellerston Provisional School in June 1891.

In 1895, Sir John Fermor's family were living at 'Wilderness' at Scone, and in 1898 he moved his family back to Ellerston and applied for a public school with his younger brother Horace. Together they provided six children, the Taylors six, and James Pinkerton another six. John was still trying to get schooling for his children—perhaps he was deeply aware of his own shortcomings.

In 1901, John Edward Henry Fermor (born 1855) had inherited 200 English pounds from a great aunt, Emma Stone—a sizeable sum in those days! In 1905, John moved his family to Hanging Rock and to Goonoo Goonoo Station near Nundle, where John was employed as a station hand, living in an old house at Middlebrook. His children were Charles, Hannah, John Edward William (known as 'J. E. W.'), Ellen, Adelaide and Gertrude.

John had the reputation of being a fine shooter and maker of leather goods. The community nearby had plenty of work for him and for his young adult children. His eyesight deteriorated, but he could still make splendid plaited whips and reins after the leather had been trimmed by his grandson Ron (who much later married Margaret Bartholomew—Marge Fermor). John and Hannah raised their granddaughter Kathleen and grandson Ron. Marge Fermor (see Chapter 44) remembered Hannah as being 'loving and caring—but very tough'. When John collapsed in 1942, the cause of death was recorded as myocarditis. His passing was certified by his family members Hannah, Frank and Victor, and a Mr Clarke, and Reverend McLean, Church of England—Hanging Rock and Nundle. He was buried in Nundle Cemetery, but there is no headstone.

Hannah died of heart failure at Tamworth Base Hospital in April 1922. She was buried beside John. The death was certified by her grandson, Hunter John Fermor.

Hannah's daughter Lilly May was loved by everyone—she was especially known for the lovely flowers that she grew. She usually brought some down to the village when there was a funeral on! It was Hannah, Mary and Sir John who helped raise some of the Bartholomew children.

Victor Fermor, the son of Lilly May Fermor (his siblings were Muriel, Arthur, Ada and Margaret), told the author, 'We grew up at Glenrock or Barry Station. I had some primary schooling till I was fourteen—then I went to work-boundary riding.'[1]

In the nineteenth century, the selectors of the Upper Hunter—the Pinkertons, Aslins and Fermors—experienced financial difficulties, especially during drought times. Their land was often too small or unsuitable to keep their flocks of sheep and their families thriving. On the whole, the squatters and settlers had bigger farms and were wealthier and became the 'bank' for hard-pressed selectors. When a selector was going broke, they were handy to take the unproductive land off the selector. These selectors were the people who migrated up towards Hanging Rock—perhaps, initially, in response to the lure of gold. For example, Frank Amore Fermor had selected land near Moonan Brook when he was twenty-seven. When Mr H. L. White inspected Frank's holding at the 1886 monthly appraisal[2] he found his 'paddocks to be in bad order'; presumably that portion ended up as part of 'Belltrees' at Scone. The squatters believed that the land was rightfully theirs. Selectors used new legal processes to buy land and were left to try to farm their small unproductive parcels of land. There were strong disagreements between squatters and selectors. The squatters remained the most powerful and wealthy landowners.

None of this tension over land ownership would have involved any Aboriginal people. The white men involved would have been too busy opposing each other! Status among the white men would have been significant at this time, but the concept of Aborigines owning land would never have been considered, except by the missionaries, who watched them being denuded of their country, their homeland, and reported it to the authorities.

Adelaide Fermor married into the Pacey family—connected by Hope Strudwick and possibly to 'Richie' Clarke.

There were jobs on all the stations for men of the Upper Hunter district. It is said that at some stage during the 1920s, men from the Tamworth district, Kamilaroi men, were taken across the range to work the livestock on these Upper Hunter properties, which might account for the confusion over Aboriginal identities. (Warrigal was not confused over this.)

The Fermors had a connection to the English aristocracy. When the author met Ada Lesley in her Hanging Rock home in 1988, Ada was fascinated by the historical connection to the ancient Fermor family in

Hampshire, England. The Sir John Fermor Primary School has a fine reputation as an educational establishment—but it was the 'Sir' aspect that so fascinated Ada. Perhaps there was hope in that small community that some of the family's heritage properties might have passed along to local families. Certainly one Fermor did own Glen Almond for some years, but no further advantage came to this community as far as I know. The school website includes pictures of the establishment and a Fermor newsletter.[3] Some Fermor reunions have been held in New South Wales.

The Australian-born woman Gertrude Fermor married John Edward Bartholomew, who was Ada and Lilly May's brother. One of their children, Ethel, married an Alan Brand, which began the line of the Brand families of lower New England—of these their daughter Kathleen—known as Kassie—see *Bush Kids The Welfare Missed*; Chapter 49.

Notes

1. The author interviewed Victor's sister Muriel in her home in Nundle. Muriel spoke of how when she was a young girl in the humble home on Glenrock, a rider on a big horse rode up to the cottage gate. He was big man, she a small child. He bellowed down to her, 'Do you know who I am, girl?' She was a little scared. Her mother came to see what was going on and knew at once. He was Muriel's grandfather, her mother Lilly May Fermor's father—Adam Bartholomew, on his way to his boundary rider job at a property along the road at Moonan Brook.
2. Squatter Mr White's regular responsibility was to inspect how well the selectors were managing their small portions of land. A selector's section of land could be resumed if he didn't manage it well.
3. https://www.fermorschool.org.uk/

Chapter 31

The Wright Families

The Wrights of Walcha and Armidale were one extended family whose presence enhanced the large community of Aboriginal people living on Anaiwan country. This information is used with the generous permission of Monica Wright-Burgess, author of *The Wright Story*.

***

In 1830s, Harry, an Aboriginal youngster, was taken under the wing of Rear Admiral P. G. King, away near the coast. The Wrights were the children of Harry Wright and Sarah nee Mahoney of Ingleba Station. In 2016, there are many Wright and Morris families in the New England district. (See Chapter 27, The Toffs.)

The Wright men became quite a cattle dynasty in New England—they were well liked members of the New England community. The author had the privilege of spending some time with Monica Wright-Burgess. Just listening to her talking about her family and her growing-up experiences instilled in me a respect for her people, who had not had the privileges I had experienced. She had a different way of seeing things; it deepened my views. I was quite charmed by the sweetness in her character. It has been a privilege to know her and her husband.

The Wright families of Ingleba sprang from Harry Wright and his Dunghutti wife Sarah Mahoney. Harry was an orphan, thought to have been born either in Tamworth, as a son of the Kamilaroi people, or at Callaghans Swamp. It is more likely that he was Anaiwan.

Sarah's birth surname may actually have been Betts or Burton, not Mahoney. She is remembered as having been born in Wollomombi.

Chapter 32

The Morrises, and the Morris Name Change

The Morris families may have had two distinct lines—one descended from baby Maryann and a second line descended from an English settler of the district.[1]

It is believed that the Morris family line described in this chapter sprang from James Morris and his wife, Sarah Woods. James's rightful surname was Quinn, as he was the son of Maurice and Maryann, but he changed his surname to Morris— the community consensus is that he did this because it sounded right to him! That is, it sounded like Maurice. The Morris families became extensive in the Ingleba and Uralla-Walcha districts. The men were fine stockmen and well respected. They worked on properties including Tia River, Callaghans Swamp, Cooplacurripa, Gongi, Branga Plains, Nowendoc, Giro, Yarrowyck and others in the mountainous New England region. It is believed that James was the child of Maryann and the full brother of Granny Duval. His mother is reported to have died in 1929 in Armidale when she was about seventy years old.[2]

The Wright Story (Wright-Burgess) describes this family's story in more detail, including their family tree.

But why did James Quinn change his surname to Morris? Perhaps this was what happened?

***

The people were gathered for the first census. Bidja was there that day, looking on, absorbing all the activity going on around him.

There was much confusion—the clerk was struggling to write down the people's names correctly. He was angry—everyone was talking at once! — but he did his best. He asked the name of the next man's father and wrote down what he thought he heard. The clerk and soldiers went to cool off. Everyone's tempers had been getting hot. The women were tired of standing around in the heat. Their long black serge dresses were uncomfortable — clothing that the white people said they must wear. The children were fractious—they wanted to go and play. Their mothers were cranky.

Bidja wondered what it all meant. His name was not recorded; no one had noticed him. But he was always watching the goings-on around the Rock; he didn't miss much!

***

It's unlikely the clerk knew about the phonetic spelling that was used by the scientists who were exploring the country. Aboriginal words were too long and complicated to write down carefully. It's unlikely anyone present realised that they were recording the words of the Nganyaywana (Anaiwan) language—an extremely complex tongue that was described much later as 'the language lost in time' spoken by the 'Eneewin' nation (see Appendix 2). There may have been no intent behind the surname change to Morris. It is believed in the family that it just was the combination of poor literacy, very long complicated, hard-to-spell Aboriginal names.

The information on the origins of the Morris families of New England is taken from *The Wright Story* (Wright-Burgess, pp. 27–30) and is used by gracious permission.

> *Sarah Betts was born around 1859 at Wollomombi. She married James Morris (Granny Duval's brother) from Ingleba in about 1881.*
>
> *Sarah Betts and Jessie Mahoney (Marney) were sisters. Some accounts say that they were the daughters of an Aboriginal woman named Sarah, who was from around Hillgrove Station. Her surname is said to come from her European father. She is usually referred to as*

'Sarah Betts', but has also been listed in the records as Sarah Burton and Sarah Clark. (this surname confusion is not unusual).

Sarah Betts and James Morris had ten known children. It may have been her daughter, Elizabeth, who married King Yarry Campbell. Their children included Sarah Morris, who married Frank Archibald at Nymboida. He was the grandson of Bob King (see Bullcorronda/Mt Yarrowyck Report, pp. 104–105).

Another daughter, Vera Morris, married Jack Widders around 1914 in Walcha. She was the aunt of Steve Widders, who has been a consultant for this work, particularly about cultural issues. Steve officially opened the memorial that was erected in Nundle village in 2016 to nine 'missing' local families and their men who enlisted for World War One: thirteen men—from a very small community—all of whom identified as Anaiwan.

Their other Morris children were James, Joseph, Jane, Russell, Henry, Ruby and Richard. The family connections here may be inaccurate![2,3]

Notes

1. Sorting through the given names: Frequently, given names were repeated across generations. This makes it a challenge to trace family members accurately. It is as if you started with layers of jigsaw puzzles on top of each other, with pieces missing from each layer. It becomes confusing sorting out which piece (name) goes in which layer (where and when).

2. Their children all grew up together in the Hanging Rock or Nundle communities. The bonds between them are still strong today. Hope Strudwick's amazing collection of family records, including some very old photos, has been greatly appreciated as I tried to collate all this information in my own mind and record it—hopefully accurately—so that these Aboriginal people's stories, the memories of them, are not lost. They were the 'Old People' whose identities I was seeking back in 1986.

3. Reading between the lines, these family members would all have known each other—their community relationships were relaxed, so the children all grew up in one large extended group. The Grannies

provided a steady influence. Children did not necessarily 'go home' at night—many would just bunk-down wherever they were when they finished playing and fall asleep. 'It takes a village to raise a child' certainly applied in Hanging Rock. These Grannies made sure that each child had a hot meal at the end of the day. The children were reared in a community, not in a series of families. As the community's life evolved, some of the children's mothers were employed away from home. Their families had to survive, so it was up to other adults to keep an eye on all the children all the time. See *Ingelba and The Five Black Matriarchs* (Cohen and Somerville).

Chapter 33

The Lesley Family

Young Thomas 'Snow' Lesley, along with Bert, his brother, came from New Zealand to join the Hanging Rock community in the 1930s. Pretty soon Ada, Lilly May Fermor's daughter, attracted his attention. She was fifteen. Ada and Snow went on to have nine children: Barry, Pamela, Robert, Daphne, Judith, Mervyn, Colin, Ian and Kevin; the family lived on the Hanging Rock plateau, over towards the property called The Wendron.

Although she had such a large family to raise, Ada followed her mother's gardening interests and grew beautiful flowers. Ada was fascinated by the Fermor story, particularly their English ancestry, which included connections with Queen Caroline, and the possible peerage that should—perhaps—have passed to John, the eldest Fermor son.[1]

Along with her own nine, Ada took on three more children, whose mother, Thelma, had died tragically. What Ada did is the Aboriginal woman's way; the women of this family were exceptional mothers! Thelma's children were named Wayne, Geoffrey and Neil. Marge Fermor nee Bartholomew raised Thelma's two other boys, Peter and Charlie.

Snow Lesley was quite a carpenter. He built a new house for his large family at the corner of Barry Road and the track to the Lookout. The community of Hanging Rock in the 1950s was very large, with all these family groups, many of them cousins, all growing up together: Clarkes,

Brands, Duvals, Fermors, Lesleys, Partridges, Bartholomews and more. There were other families too: Paceys, Hawkins and Hoads.

Note

1. Ada's British family connections intrigued her—especially a story about the Queen's ladies-in-waiting! (One of the Queens of England had a lady-in-waiting who was a Fermor.)

Chapter 34

The Clarke Families

There always were several families of Clarkes, who had notoriety in the Hanging Rock area.

They were descended from two English brothers who arrived in the area in the early 1830s, John (aged forty-seven, died in 1859) and Henry, both born in London. Henry brought his wife and seven children out with him.

In this family, too, names could be somewhat variable.

More than a mystery with many different names, Emma, Selina or Emily Stringer (or Sheelah, Toogood, Kirk, Rotherham, or Robinson) was married twice. She died in 1964 aged ninety and is buried in Nundle Cemetery. She had six children. She was married first to a John Clarke and then to a Phillip Stringer. A former Hanging Rock resident clearly recalled that 'Granny Stringer used to sit on the bank at the side of the road smoking her pipe.' Apparently Granny was quite a character and well known in the community. (from the author's friend Fay Inman)

An Aboriginal woman sometimes referred to as Friday or Maryann may have been the grandmother of Ted Clarke's four children. The author understands that Ted had four children with Annie Bartholomew (a fact remembered by Ted's grandson George Partridge, told to him when he was a small boy. 'They were always known as Bartholomew.') These family connections are likely to be correct.

In summary, there were two generations of John Clarkes, one of whom had two children with a woman described as 'a black'. The two were Elizabeth, born 1850, and Richard, baptised 1852 in Tamworth. Richard married Sarah Hopkins in 1878 in Scone, New South Wales (her parents were Myra Crawford and John Hopkins). (Pauline Webby, New Zealand; thank you, Pauline.)

From an 1865 letter (held in the Department of Education archives in Sydney):

The applicant Mr E. Clark is a hard working, honest, sober and industrious man and he has a wife and six small children depending on him for support. To my mind he has not had any other means of supporting his family for many months than by shooting kangaroos. Also I found he is a sober man. — D.W., School Inspector.

✳✳✳

Up at The Rock that day, it was freezing. Bidja watched the man as he went out to get a kangaroo. The man usually cut bark for roofing, but no one had asked him for any for some time now.

The man had three children at the school. They loved going to school—but their father was embarrassed, as he couldn't find the two shillings he owed to the schoolmaster.

✳✳✳

It is believed that these Clarkes of Hanging Rock lived at Bakers Downfall. The original John Clarke came to Australia from London in 1840. The generations appear to have been as follows:

Generation 1: John Clarke and his wife Emma Selina Kirk (also known with surnames Robinson and Rotherham)

Generation 2: John Clarke Junior, Emma's son, who later lived at Bakers Downfall

Generation 3: Richard and Elizabeth Clarke, John Jnr's children; Richard was baptised at Tamworth 1852, and his mother was listed on the baptism document as 'Maryann, a black'

Generation 4: James (the youngest) and Ted Clarke, two of perhaps six children of Richard and his wife Sarah Hopkins (her name from the marriage certificate); Ted had four children, possibly with Annie Bartholomew nee Duval and was also married to Gerty Fermor

Generation 5: Rodney 'Warrigal' Clarke of Nundle, son of James and Nancy Pearl/White/Chapman (also of Aboriginal heritage)

Generation 6: Children of Ted Clarke and the children of Rodney 'Warrigal' Clarke

Another adult in this family tree was William Stringer. Most of these people's births were recorded as occurring at Bakers Downfall.

They were living rough. So many children died with throat infections at that time. The small graves may be those of children.

***

Bidja was out and about on an even colder day.

Mr Clarke was really encouraged when the inspector came to his family's humble home and told him his debt had been wiped. He was so grateful! When he went out again that day, everyone noticed that he had a spring in his step.

Watching, Bidja had a soft spot in his heart for Uncle Ted.

***

Four children were always unsure about their identity—on their father's side—they knew their mother was Annie, of course.

Sadly, Warrigal's father, James Clarke, was killed in a mustering accident at the riverside when Warrigal was young.

Chapter 35

The Partridge Families

This chapter is dedicated to the memory of Stephen Partridge, 24 May 1963 to 24 May 2022. He provided family knowledge that is much appreciated. The Nundle community has lost a generous, capable and innovative man. He will be missed.

✱✱✱

The generations of the Partridge family moved up to the plateau country of lower New England in the 1940s and settled near Hanging Rock. It was a large family, and they were not well off. Their mother Mabel did a splendid job of raising the children. These were hard times for the whole community at the Rock. (See 'What creature did Bobby see down at the cherry trees that day?', *Port Macquarie Historical Society Chronicle*, 5 January 2001, see Appendix 6 below).

Who was Stephen G. Partridge, and how did his family come to be living at Bakers Downfall?

He came from England, where his great-grandfather was born in the late 1600s. When he arrived in New South Wales, he was a young man, just twenty-one. He had arrived in the colony by sailing ship, the *General Hewitt*. His story had begun in 1793, when he was baptised at Cookham, in Somersetshire. He had grown up to be a healthy and personable young man, well-educated and able to take responsibility. His life had contrasted with those of the convicts who waited in the rotting hulks moored in Plymouth harbour awaiting transportation to New South Wales. He had become a soldier, and his job now was to escort the convicts on the ship *General Hewitt*, bound for the colony of New South Wales. They barely managed to get there, arriving in 1821 after a difficult voyage.

It appears he accompanied the surveyor John Oxley 'on expeditions of service into the interior'. Corporal Partridge was a practical and skilled young man who was able to work as a carpenter, sawyer and lumber yard supervisor. He became a Superintendent of Convicts when Governor Macquarie became concerned about increasing numbers of escapes.

A more distant site of settlement was found at the mouth of the Hastings river; this new settlement was to replace Newcastle as a place 'of punishment for refractory convicts'. The new settlement, Port Macquarie, became a more respectable town than Newcastle. For young Partridge, this colonial appointment meant a handsome salary of £100. He was to be the third-in-command in establishing the new settlement.

The *Port Macquarie Historical Society Chronicle*, vol. 1, lists five generations of the Stephen Partridge story. Free settlement was established in 1830; Governor Darling granted a spirit licence for a public house and meeting place for Port Macquarie, for which Mr Partridge applied. A description of him exists as 'industrious, steady, well-conducted and well-meaning' combined with comments that 'he fed his stock with government corn … and other similar practices', which slightly ameliorated the claims of misconduct being made against him at the time. However, he rose above the accusations and complaints and, having gained some support, he was granted the licence in 1830. But this was not a successful phase of his life. He was to live with his family on the premises. Mr Partridge had married twice and now had five children to support.

He seems to have been something of an entrepreneur—obviously a man with initiative, ability and drive. The fact that the law permitted loose interpretations of the events that he was involved in led to some criticism and to changes in the law—though he was never charged—and he attracted several glowing testimonials. When he resigned from the position he was described 'an active and zealous officer who had the respect and good will of the prisoner population to an extraordinary degree.'

***

Out and about that day, it was Bidja who first noticed one of Partridges' Aboriginal house servants carrying ground corn out in a bucket for his animals. Partridge kept pigs and chooks in a shed down behind the public house.

It was newcomers to the Port who dobbed him in to the authorities—they resented the privileges that Partridge had acquired over time in the community. Privilege has always been a matter of who you know.

***

New settlers were arriving in the township in numbers, so a surveyor was appointed to establish a town plan; this removed a lot of Partridge's property, which, naturally, he was not happy about! A marked division was occurring between the existing establishment and the newcomers, who were critical of people like Stephen Partridge, who had had a considerable hand in developing the community of Port Macquarie. Partridge had established some personal status in the township as he was considered to be the most 'considerable dealer in the settlement.'

His third wife was a young Irish convict who had been assigned to his household. His children needed care as his second wife had died. The new couple had six more children.

In 1835, he became a police constable, and in 1836 he became a Superintendent of Convicts once again. At the census of 1841, his household is shown as including nine males and six females.

The colony was developing; land was being acquired for families determined to settle in the district.

Stephen Partridge died at eighty-six, having spent fifty-six years in the colony working under six different commandants. He was a minor but important official who saw Port Macquarie become a free-trading port, despite the decline of the economy and the variable weather, which challenged the new settlers. In an altercation with a surveyor one day, Partridge declared that he would never change his way of working, or his habits: 'I care for nobody' was shouted. He is buried at Port Macquarie. His much younger wife, Julia, died in 1889.

***

One day, someone was watching to see what Partridge was getting up to.

Bidja saw someone come to the poultry shed with a bucket of corn for the chickens there. Partridge was up to his old tricks, stealing from the Government—a serious complaint would be made forthwith, they would make sure of it!

Officer Partridge was hauled up before the court. He'd been seen doing something covert, but his popularity was such that he was not charged. It was a huge relief for him and his family.

***

Stephen's son Joseph Partridge, born 1823, was married in Armidale in 1846 and died in Walcha in 1898 aged seventy-five. Nothing is known about him and his family—except that they were 'battlers'.

Port Macquarie Historical Society Chronicle, vol. 1, no. 5, lists fourteen generations of the Partridge family, commencing in Britain in about 1697, with five generations prior to the story of Stephen Partridge, born 1793, then nine generations, including at least one full-blood Aboriginal woman, Milbona and Corumba's daughter, born in 1820 at Rimbanda. This part of the family includes a French sailor; John Duval, an English currency kid, born in Australia; and an Irish convict, Maurice Quinn.

How and when did the Partridge family migrate to the Hanging Rock area? How did George Stephen Partridge, the father of George, who was born in Tamworth 1940, make a living?

The Partridge men of the 1870s were excellent horsemen and cattle handlers. During the 1900s, the men found work on Glenrock; they had to be able to ride skilfully and shoe a horse if necessary, and some were even farriers by experience.

In 1878, several Partridges were soldiers and settlers in the corridor, at Port Macquarie and at Bakers Downfall. The family became merged with the Clarkes when Annie Bartholomew nee Duval had four children with Ted Clarke of Hanging Rock; their four children were always known as Bartholomew.

Mabel Bartholomew was born in 1907 at Niangala. She was the daughter of Annie Bartholomew nee Duval and Edward Clarke, and is of this Quinn/Duval family line. She married George Partridge Sr.

The Partridge youngsters who grew up at Bakers Downfall were good, humble people who found work where they could get it. They were battlers. 'Dad was just a labourer,' said George. Their mother, Mabel Bartholomew, was much-loved and respected. She reared a large family - many to feed - up under Hanging Rock. This is the known connection between the Duval/Bartholomews, the Partridge family, and the Clarkes of Hanging Rock.

Subsequent generations of Partridges grew up in the ranges, at Walcha, Hanging Rock, and Nundle. Some of the men found work on Upper Hunter valley stations in the early twentieth century. They were skilled young men, handy people to have working on a pastoral property.

The Partridges certainly left their mark wherever they settled!

★★★

Bidja would certainly have been aware of the large Partridge family who were all growing up together at the Rock.

One time, he watched the kids playing with a jalopy, until it landed—for the last time—in the blackberry bushes! It is believed to be still there.

★★★

Chapter 36

These Went to War; Being Aboriginal in Australia

In 1914, war was declared. Word came from Britain-on the wireless; so war came to the tiny the Hanging Rock Diggings settlement too.

***

There was tension in the air—Bidja was aware that something serious was occurring. The lives of the young Aboriginal men there were about to be changed.

***

The following was their experience—it was life as they knew it.

There were many eras when denial described Aboriginal experience generally.

Eras of denial spanned 1883 to 1900, to 1938, to 1951 and to 2022. Aboriginal people had no citizenship rights. Most Aborigines were confined on reserves, and starvation was the rule for any troublemakers. They had no 'voice' (their ATSIC Voice was cancelled). The official expectation was that they must become like everyone else (i.e., white and 'respectable'), but they were not treated like everyone else! They were denied land ownership and citizenship. They were often denied access to the same health care as others and were usually denied the same education.[1,2,3]

In spite of all that at least fourteen Anaiwan men of lower New England enlisted for service in World Wars One and Two, but were denied the respect and benefits that should have stemmed from that war service.

The men were, as far as the author could ascertain:

1914-1918 FIRST WORLD WAR
- Richard CLARKE 1880-AIF No-163270
- Henry (Harry)CLARKE 1883 AlF
- Edward CLARKE 1885 AIF) AIF=Australian Imperial Force

1939-1945 SECOND WORLD WAR
1. Malcolm Roy BARTHOLOMEW
2. John Edward Henry BARTHOLOMEW-1916 NX 106570
3. Frederick BARTHOLOMEW
4. Malcolm CLARKE 1904 (or Dick Clarke)
5. James CLARKE-1901 -Hanging Rock -NX 40183
6. Leslie Frances DUVAL-1915-Quirindi-NX 96744
7. John Raymond DUVAL
8. Oscar DUVAL.
9. Victor FERMOR
10. Arthur FERMOR
11. Horace FERMOR

Christian leaders formed the Aborigines Advancement League in 1957, but their polite pleas were ignored.

These Christian leaders all had written previously in 1938, but were ignored: Reverend Doug Nichols, William Cooper and Jack Patten.

To manage the reserves, government authorities created the Aborigines' Protection Board—but it was the savage management of the Board they needed protection from! The Board existed from 1883 to 1951.

From 1951 to 1962, in spite of doing war service, most Aborigines were ordered to adhere to the assimilation policy of the Australian government, which it was designed to keep the population white and was very restrictive. It led to the removal of non-white children from their mothers.

In recent years, First Nations people have been respected in Australia if:

- They are sports stars, such as footballers.
- They are musical stars, like Harold Blair, Uncle Archie Roach, and the many others.
- They are theatrical stars, like Uncle Jack Charles, Gurramul and others, who have entertainment value.
- They have recorded some war service in more recent times.

It is not spoken of, but there have only ever been two alternatives open to First Nations Australians: to become like the rest of us, or to remain as a race apart—that is, separate.

Notes

1. See First Australians (video), SBS and Screen Australia https://www.sbs.com.au/ondemand/tv-series/first-australians;
2. The Australian Wars (video), SBS and NITV https://www.sbs.com.au/ondemand/tv-series/the-australian-wars/extras;
3. Stan Grant's video Black Like Me, ABC TV, 19 September 2022 https://www.abc.net.au/news/2020-07-13/stan-grant-black-lives-matter-four-corners/12429206.

Chapter 37

The Historian Professor Margaret Somerville

Several individuals have made a difference to my understanding and to the continuity and truths of the stories of the Aboriginal people of the past. Several respected Aboriginal people have commented as part of the recorded stories, too.

This entire record has been enhanced by these historians. They have provided authority. It really helps to have a professional eye (and ear) cast over the recorded text as this author makes no claims to be a historian!

One helpful historian was Margaret Somerville, whose writing made a great deal of difference to the author, who commenced this journey in 1986 almost completely ignorant.

In the 1990s, Margaret Somerville was a young woman studying at the University of New England at Armidale. She was particularly interested in the Aboriginal people of the Walcha and Ingleba area. She struck up a friendship with Patsy Cohen, and between them they met other Anaiwan women of the Ingleba reserve and recorded some of what they collectively remembered about the Black Matriarchs, whose lives extended to just within Patsy's memory. Their collaboration resulted in the book *Ingelba and The Five Black Matriarchs* (Cohen and Somerville). Somerville's sensitive questioning and careful listening provided a wealth of insight into Aboriginal life around the turn of the twentieth century and how these strong women adapted to their new reality. Her work provided a bridge between two very different ways of living and hugely increased my own understanding of Anaiwan lives and culture. Permission to quote from Cohen and Somerville's work has kindly been granted.

Early in my research, Jillian Oppenheimer OAM provided geographical and geological perspectives overlaid with historical understandings of truth-telling and a 'memories' perspective. These have been valuable.

Chapter 38

Commissioner Macdonald

Bidja sneaked up to the window that morning and peeped over the sill. The important white man was writing at his desk. Bidja was puzzled: what was he doing?

The Commissioner of Crown Lands did his job responsibly. He reported as was his duty.

***

His letter was in answer to an official query (see Chapter 21) that he had made in writing the previous year, in 1841; his reply was sent from the Nundle Police Barracks.

He cared about the Aborigines' welfare, so he wrote from his own point of view (as did the Aboriginal student Callum Dixon much later, in 2016, when he wrote *Surviving New England*).

The Commissioner's letter could have been originally published in the *Sydney Herald*, as indiscriminate reprisals almost entirely ceased![1]

From *Governor's Despatches* vol. 40, England:

1 July 1842. Sir,

Referring to your circular 1 July 1841, reporting on the points. and aspects of Aboriginal Tribes, more especially to notes of 25 August 1840—

I do myself the honour of acquainting you, for His Excellency the Governor that although during the past year some hostile attacks were made by Aborigines on the Stations of Mr MacKenzie, Mr Garden and Mr Gill near the wild and mountainous country of the Eastern Falls of the Tableland, in which two shepherds were slain and a considerable number of sheep destroyed and driven off, yet when it is considered that the district has extended its limits so rapidly to the northward, since the location of the large tract of country adjacent to Moreton Bay—and that consequently the Squatters have encroached upon the hunting grounds of tribes hitherto holding no intercourse with Europeans, these aggressions appear to be much less extensive than might have been anticipated, and trivial when compared with those of previous years and I am induced to attribute this in a great measure to the growth of a more just, humane and tolerant spirit influencing the growth and conduct of the Settlers in the intercourse with the Aboriginal Sons of The Soil and to the more general growth of good feeling, I look forward for future beneficial results.

Observing the Aborigines' ceremony—the bora initiating the young men … it seems to me that they number five or six hundred. (1842)

With respect to any change in the 'Social condition' of the Aborigines, I am not, I regret enabled to hold out much prospect of any general improvement—for from the widely scattered state of the Tribes—their distrust and fear of each other—their constant feuds, the diversity of their dialects, and our almost entire ignorance of them, I realise that there is only a very remote probability of affecting any radical change in their moral or social condition as a people, yet it must be conceded that nevertheless individual instances of their aptitude and capacity for social improvement not uncommonly occur. And I would more particularly in this district mention, as a most praiseworthy example of beneficial influence and policy, of a kind tolerant and judicious treatment of the natives by Settlers, the case of Messers Everett and Halked—these gentlemen have succeeded by kindness and perseverance in inducing a small Tribe frequenting the tract of country contiguous to their Station of Wandsworth, to remain almost constantly upon it—the young men being employed in varying capacities, not only as stockmen and shepherds, but as Domestic servants also in the house; and although these gentlemen have settled only four years in the district, and stations in their neighbourhood have been attacked on various occasions by the Natives, yet no outrage of any kind has ever been attempted on them.

I would also beg further to instance these gentlemen as affording the only solitary example of any attempt of having been made to study and acquire the Aboriginal dialects of the districts.

In conclusion I am happy to have it in my power to assert with confidence that the outrages formerly so frequent in the Colonies, from Shepherds and Stockmen taking the Law into their own hands and making indiscriminate reprisals on the natives for cattle scattered and flocks driven off have in this district entirely ceased. And taking into consideration the good feeling that is gaining ground in the colony, on the subject of Aborigines—the protection afforded them both by the Border Police, the Increase in Magistrates, and the great interest taken in the welfare and improvement by the local Government, I am induced to hope that my next report on this most important subject ... will have satisfactory evidence of progress having been made.

[To] The Honourable Colonial Secretary

I have the honour as Commissioner of Crown Lands to be your most obt. servant G J Macdonald JP

Note

1. "1842 REPORT ON N.E. ABORIGINES Settlers Commended" [republished in the *Guyra Argus (NSW : 1902 - 1954)* 9 December 1954: 4.] <http://nla.gov.au/nla.news-article173251728>.

Chapter 39

Uncle Joe 'Doc' Woods

It is doubtful that 'Doc' Woods ever met with the Commissioner of Lands. Woods was a much respected member of the Indigenous community of lower New England. He was very much one of the tribe—a healer and a carer.

***

Doc Woods and Bidja were mates. They understood each other completely because they lived in similar mystical worlds—although many white people called that make-believe. The Aboriginal people understood both aspects of their lives perfectly. They had dreaming stories and songlines that celebrated the unexplainable aspects of the peoples' lives—things that were too complicated for the very basic whitefellas to comprehend. The whitefellas were wild men, who came to Nundle with gold dust in their pouches then poured the rum into themselves until they fell down dead drunk in the mud of the track.

Bidja and Doc Woods had much in common. Wherever they went, they blessed the people!

***

Uncle Joe 'Doc' Woods was a trusted 'medicine man', certainly a Cleverman—one who was called on in times of need by the Aboriginal people. He was no charlatan, and he demanded no payment for his services. He would usually use the Anaiwan language, which provided some mystery as many could no longer speak it fluently. He was a special man to the Aboriginal communities from Ingleba to Nundle—a very significant member of the Aboriginal community in New England, well known in Nundle village, where he lived for some time in the 1940 and 1950s. James Morris' Sarah (Betts) was related to him. He had no children of his own. All the Aboriginal people of New England said he had special powers. He was loved and respected among them.

Doc Woods was centre of so many stories. His two dogs seemed to 'have the healing powers'. They seemed to be benevolent in the community as they 'kept an eye on things', even walking with children in the dark of night until they got home safely—but then the dog would just disappear.

The following was narrated by Maisie Kelly and is used with the kind permission of author Margaret Somerville.

> *Grandfather Joe Woods got two dogs, they were both doctors—One that was like an Alsatian, like a young calf … You'd never see the red one much unless there was danger about. If there was anyone sick this black dog would come along into the house—You got to be very still when he's there, that's fire, that's the cure, you know. They warm their hands at the fire and rub, blow on it … someone got a headache, blow like that, you know, warm it and blow on it. Even my father would do that. Well the dogs come in and blow on you, or lick you. I tell you, as soon as when they come—you could say you're cured; you're right.* (Cohen and Somerville)

Another time:

> *We sat down—my father was real sick there in Walcha once. The rest of 'em had gone to the football. He told all us kiddies to go across the creek and sit on the side of the hill. We made the fire for him, and he lay down at the fire. He said, 'I'll be alright directly, just go over there and wait. You'll see the dog coming.' We sat down on the side of the hill—there's a little crossing with stones and elm trees there—that's where he used to live (the stones and a well are where we used to get our water). But we sat up on the bank and waited. We seen the dog coming—trotting up to 'is hut there, and we knew he'd be alright.*

Yeah, our father had tea cooked for us when we came home. (Cohen and Somerville, p. 82)

Some Aboriginal people in Nundle still talk about Doc Woods and his two dogs. In 2017, Kassie Ninness, who lives in Nundle and is a cousin of Patricia Bartholomew-Lock, declared that the dogs were real. She said Doc Woods did live in Nundle—in a shack in Happy Valley—for a time. She 'never saw the two dogs.' But they were real to her. (Some things are unexplainable!)

Doc Woods was the one people turned to for help! He had no children of his own, so he was everyone's grandfather.

The above quotations are from *Ingelba and The Five Black Matriarchs* (Cohen and Somerville, p. 82), which was published with the permission of the Aboriginal people of Ingleba. They are used with the permission of the authors.

Chapter 40

William Wynter of Taree

Some white people were worried about how the Aborigines were being treated. William Wynter wrote to the paper about what was happening. He wanted to publicise the wrongdoing. But his efforts made no difference.

It is recorded that William Wynter, founder of Taree, wrote the following letter to the editor of the *Sydney Herald*. It was published on 8 July 1842. It spoke of raids on Aboriginal camps by settlers on horseback, and cruelty. This passage captures the terror of these occasions neatly:

Instantly setting spurs to our horses we galloped across the creek and into the camp; we found it untenanted however except for a woman with an infant at the breast, and a child apparently about four or five years old. On our approach they fled up the mountain, the woman carrying the child astride upon her neck. As we neared them they cried out in great fear, and upon our coming close the woman took the infant from her shoulders and clasping it to her bosom threw herself upon her knees bowing her face to the ground thus concealing and protecting her little one with her body and the other child crouching at her side hid its face in the grass. They uttered no sound but their long-drawn respirations showed they were in great terror. I dismounted and taking the child by the shoulders, raised her face from the ground but she set up such a terrible squalling that I let go again, when she dropped quite stiff and stark into her former position and was again silent.

There were those among the European settlers in the 1840s who demonstrated their humanity and concern towards the Aborigines and stood up for their rights. William Wynter was one. He forced a public enquiry about the death of an aged Aborigine, a man, perfectly innocent and helpless, who had been killed by the police under the command of Mr P. G. King.

In court it was reported that a little girl was shot on that occasion; the police had amused themselves by destroying the camp. Nothing came of the inquiry and no police were charged. The Wynter brothers had rescued the old man in vain. Authorities exhumed his body, which showed that he had died from being both shot and bashed.

That day, the law was selectively applied in the white man's favour—once again.

The white police force was usually made up of convicts, and the native police were usually Aboriginal men who had the skill of tracking. They would not have had much background screening or training, so it is unsurprising that police behaviour could be thoroughly undisciplined.[1] Wynter was one member of the public who cared.

Note

- ❖ For a further dramatic account of police brutality, see Massacre on the Ora River, a somewhat local account https://clarenceriver.teachingforchange.edu.au/OraraRiver
- ❖ Reynolds, Henry *This Whispering in our Hearts* 2018 (UNSW)

Chapter 41

A Missionary Who Made a Difference

Reverend Lancelot Threlkeld of Myall Lakes[1] reported events in 1788–1859 in Awabakal country from around Lake Macquarie in New South Wales, south and east of the country occupied by the Nundle and Hanging Rock families, but within their administrative district.

From a white man's point of view, his influence made a bridge of understanding in the districts of northern New South Wales at the time. It did so because he had a Biblical worldview—that is, he believed individual people mattered! However, other white men thought quite differently about missionaries and did what they could to nullify their influence.

Threlkeld's careful records indicate his personal concern for the Aboriginal people's welfare. He had a Christian point of view. He was not interested in statistics. He was interested in the Aboriginal people as individuals. In his work with them, he was modelling the life of Jesus and how He moved among the people.

Reverend Threlkeld was not a conformist. He experienced enormous difficulties on the mission field in the Newcastle district.[2] He worked as a Congregationalist under the London Missionary Society, but he didn't get on with them and the feeling was mutual.

Threlkeld cared about the wanton ways of the white men living around his mission. Like other missionaries, he saw Aboriginal women and girls coming under their influence. Because he had a true Christian worldview, he was trying to make a bridge between the two parts of the local community. He kept careful records of everything he did each day. He was proud of the way he organised his work.

***

To better his efforts, he had learned some of the language. On one particularly bitter day, he tried to interact with one particular child that he saw. It was freezing outside, and she was so thin. He wasn't sure what she said, but she seemed to want blankets.[3]

He gave her two and watched her rush back into the bushes. That afternoon he would go out looking for the child. Perhaps he could find a kindly woman to take her in and shelter her—only if she had no mother, of course. Mrs Brown might be willing—she was always interested in talking with him when he visited her home. He had never seen a Mr Brown, but he thought there were two children. That thin, frightened child might learn some things around the house that might keep her safe—and perhaps get her a job in another home, one day.

When he went out next, the snow flurries had lessened somewhat. He hunted through the bush near his home and eventually found the frightened girl child with her exhausted mother, who was obviously very ill. Mrs Brown was willing to take them both in— 'as a trial, mind. Only a trial.' She put down some old dry bedding on the floor in the corner of the room for them and warmed some broth for the sick woman. Like the missionary, Mrs Brown had learned a few words of language, so she was able to speak a few words of comfort, and there was a spark of connection between the two mothers. The woman drank the soup down—she was obviously very hungry—and fell into a light sleep, but she started up at the slightest sound, and especially when Mr Brown came in from the cold, stamping his feet to get the snow and mud off. He put his boots near the fire to dry out a bit after stuffing them with newspaper. He told his wife he'd been chatting to a young man, along the road where they sold some terrible grog—the chap was alone, without any family at all, and they'd had a drink together. The girl child was curled upon the dry bedding in the corner, her big eyes taking in everything that was happening around her.

Notes

1. See the website *Rev. Lancelot Threlkeld: Reverend Lancelot E Threlkeld, 1788–1859.* https://history.lakemac.com.au/page-localhistory.aspx?pid=1085&vid=20&tmpt=narrative&narid=3586 Research by Dulcie Hartley fills out Threlkeld's very interesting story. He was appalled as he saw how alcohol was destroying the Aboriginal people. He tried desperately to teach the people Christian ways, but it was impossible to have a greater influence than the gangs of rough white men from the local convict camp who roamed the area. See also the site *AustraliansTogether.org.au*

2. And in Tahiti, where he served for some months as missionary.

3. See the Blanket Return Books, *Waters & Moon* p. 133.

Chapter 42

The 1920s on Gog's Top

While Reverend Threlkeld was trying to make a difference around the lake, up in the range, some grandparents were caring for their families, their own people—and Bidja was there.

Elsewhere in the country the other Aboriginal families were still on their guard. They did not have the means to escape from the white men, who had horses.

***

In her later years, Meg Bartholomew told her daughter Patricia the stories from her childhood of when the family lived on several New England stations, where Grandfather Claude had found work. The following are two of these true stories, that Patricia told the author.

Claude and Sarah Duval were living in a large house built entirely of cedar, it was at the highest peak of the Hanging Rock range, where giant old cedar trees grew in abundance. Up there they were still keeping the children safe from the Welfare.

However, the chance of some work came up for Claude and they decided to risk moving the whole family down the mountain to the upper Hunter Valley below, towards Moonan Flat … So next morning they packed up all their things, saddled up, loaded a new pack horse with all Sarah's cooking and her trunk, and set off. It was to be a long day. Young Meg, their daughter, was riding the old pony Dopey. It was slow going—they had to take it steady on the slopes—stones under the horses' feet rolled so easily. There were six horses, two children, including two Aboriginal youths who often worked with Claude. They were picking their way between the tussock grass, up there. Some hours into their journey they were doing well, proceeding slowly, winding between the big tussocks and scrub, when something spooked the young pack horse. Now Sarah had spent the whole day before over a hot wood stove cooking biscuits for snacks to have during the next day's ride. Claude was leading the pack horse on a rope—the rope broke and the young horse took off. It was a sight to behold as all the carefully packed tins of biscuits went everywhere, rolling down into the scrub ahead of them. Sarah's precious trunk[1] went over and over and down into the bush. She cried, 'Oh, not my trunk too!' She was devastated—all that cooking gone to waste, and her precious trunk. Claude swore under his breath. They had been travelling so well!

The boys managed to catch the pack horse; they and Claude were able to get the heavy trunk back from out of the bushes, which made Sarah a little happier—it was dented but not broken open, so her treasures weren't lost. The children gathered round—no one had been hurt in all the excitement, but there was nothing left of the biscuits. If any were left still whole they were trampled by the horses' hooves and their boots during the confusion; they would just have to have only water when they stopped for a spell down the bottom.

It was almost dark when the party came onto Moonan Flat country. They needed to hurry up—it was never wise to be out at night with horses and children around—but at least the family was intact. They were relieved to have arrived at the shack where they would be living. It had been an exciting day for young Meg—she was only seven years old. Dopey had been a safe ride for her. But she was very hungry!

On another occasion, when Meg was eight, the family was living on Giro Station, up in the range.

Bidja, young Meg and a pack of dingoes

A beast had been slaughtered at the station and the meat was to be shared among the families. Claude took the meat along the track to Meg who would carry it to the next family along the valley. Meg was usually a willing child; she was gamer than the boys, and strong too!

She hopped up onto the old pony Dopey's back, grabbed hold of her two-year-old sister, Ethel, as her father lifted the child up; the bag of meat was heavy. The children rode happily up the gully bareback, towards the rough home among the gum trees. But the gate in the fence had to be negotiated, it was made of sliprails, which were difficult for a child to manage.

Meg put the heavy bag of meat up on top of the post. They dismounted, with Meg struggling to get the gate open. She was just about to lead Dopey through when he was spooked—and took off; the children were left there with a big bag of meat and no easy way to get back home, half a mile away. It was way too far for a two-year-old to walk. They were scared—how would they get home?

There was a pack of five dingoes nearby and they soon smelled the meat. Meg realised that they were in great danger, and in a panic the older girl was able to push Ethel up into a tree to safety. She herself only just managed to scramble up too, to save their lives. Dopey arrived home without the children; the adults, Claude and Sarah, raced back along the gully to find them. Fortunately, Grandfather was fencing nearby. He took his shotgun, ran as quickly as he could. He came upon the pack of dingoes scratching high up in the bark to try to get at the sweet-smelling meat. Meg's father shot three of them but two dogs got away. The children were lucky that day. It could so easily have ended in tragedy!

In the camp the mothers uttered their approval of how both youngsters had been kept safe, but they all were alerted to the fact that there were hungry dingoes around, and they reminded the piccaninnies and older children to stay close.

Meg and her brothers were fortunate—they we cared for within the family. Other young people were not so lucky; the white people called them 'half-caste', neither one nor the other—skin colour was seen as very important in early colonial times. The authorities hunted out children who didn't 'look right'. They came around every fortnight, always looking for such children.

∗∗∗

Bidja was there, on walkabout—he had seen the whole thing. When he got back to the camp that evening, his hands and lips moved frantically as he told everyone what he had seen. He'd watched all the activity from behind some rocks, and the children hadn't noticed him. Neither had the dingoes!

∗∗∗

Note

1. Precious trunk: Aboriginal women sometimes keep their precious keepsakes in a trunk. This one may have contained her clay pipe, family photos, maybe hair (which had special cultural significance), and things that had belonged to particular family members.

Chapter 43

Mixed Ancestry Marked Two Women's Lives: They Spoke Up

Patsy Cohen and Ella Simon were two whom the white authorities had taken from their families when they were young. Despite this trauma, they both made a difference: Simon by writing about her father's death and Cohen by sharing her childhood experiences with the historian Margaret Somerville.

Ella Simon

Birpai woman Ella Simon, of the Gloucester district, wrote in *Through My Eyes*:

> *There is no doubt that the Aboriginal people fully occupied and made effective use of our district … There is equally no doubt that the incoming white people had very little understanding of the black men's ways. European thinking was dominated by three hundred years of dealing with the colonised people of India, Africa and the Americas.*
>
> *The European view of these people [Aboriginal people] had many strands. They were thought of as treacherous, primitive, savage, fascinating, feared, hated or loved. They were exploited, destroyed, even worshipped—depending on the outlook of the Europeans judging at the time. Rarely were they accepted for what they were—different but similar, or other members of the human race. Other Europeans*

encountering Aborigines were poor, living on their wits, uneducated, terrified, brutalised themselves, and acting in harsh ways towards Aborigines. The word was 'rape the women and shoot the men'. There were massacres on both sides. For example: In 1826 five shepherds were murdered. The revenge taken was that they [the Aboriginal suspects] were 'put down'—the wording of the day. This massacre occurred at Gangat—an Australian Agricultural Company outpost and Heifer Station (west of Gloucester hinterland)

A great tragedy for young Ella occurred when her father died. No one told her that he had died. Consequently, she never went to the service held in the chapel of the Purfleet (Taree) community. And she was never told where he was buried. The terrible sadness affected the rest of her life. The authorities knew where she was—but no one bothered to tell her. She was not treated like a person at all, just a number. For all intents and purposes, she was invisible.

Patsy Cohen

Patsy Cohen wrote, in collaboration with Margaret Somerville:[1]

Patsy Cohen née Schmutter of Armidale and Ingleba was King Bungaree's great-great-granddaughter, a great-grandchild of Bungaree and grandchild of Clara Pacey.

Patsy's dilemma was in not knowing how or where she fitted into the society of her childhood. Born in Woolbrook in 1937, her father was called up to fight for Australia in 1939, at which stage the Aboriginal Protection Board moved in, removing her from her only parent. She had been living with her mother and brother at Yarra Bay, New South Wales before being made a state ward in 1941.

As a youngster, she says she was difficult to manage and spirited, particularly after being taken from her mother at age four. When she was eight, she moved from one carer family to another—some white, others black. She was also in and out of various homes.

But her father never forgot about her and her sister. He always came searching for the children when home on leave. In a non-mobile phone era it is surprising that the girls and their brother Norman managed to stay in touch, as the court had sent them off in different directions.

Patsy's Aboriginal identity only became real to her when her Granny, Clara Pacey, came into the picture, which she recalls as a terrifying experience.

She first realised that she belonged in a family of blacks when she was confronted at nine years old. She didn't know that she was black because no one had ever told her! Skin colour had never been an issue in her young life. She compared her skin colour with Chinese, Hawaiian and a dark-skinned Aboriginal child in the Bidura Home who was very dark. She knew she didn't look like any of them! 'I knew I was different from other kids, but I didn't know why.'

Eventually, she was to join her mother's family. She met the women who were to become so influential in her young life for the first time on Woolbrook railway station New South Wales. They knew that Patsy was of their family, they saw that she belonged with them, but Patsy didn't understand how they recognised her. She was frightened as the skinny black arms reached out to her in welcome.

She saw an old woman whom she'd never met, Clara Pacey, who was her true Granny. 'I was frightened of them blacks, I had never seen any blackfellas.'

A granny was the most significant family member for a female child learning how to be Aboriginal. When these connections are broken down by distance, confusion over identity or loss of language, things go wrong, as they could have for Patsy.

Familial loss was compounded as some Aboriginal people became assimilated into the white community; which was inevitable. The white members of the various authorities did not realise the profound effect that removing children from their native community would have on the Aboriginal population. It caused a terrible loss of identity.

The authorities may have been well intentioned, but this did not alter the inevitable results of moving family groups from their traditional territories or putting children of several language groups together in a school dormitory. The worst aspect of this practice occurred where children were forbidden to speak in their own languages at all—as occurred at mission stations—because much of their past cultural practice was classed as wicked and to be desisted from. Without their own languages, they were lost—they belonged nowhere.

Patsy Cohen's parents were Ted Schmutter and Sibby, daughter of Walter, the son of Mariah and Bungaree. Thus, her great-grandfather was Bungaree (James Dixon),[2] who led the large gathering at Bowling Alley Point on the Peel River in 1883, and her great-grandmother was Mariah Quinn, sister of Mary Elizabeth who had married James Duval back in 1863.

It is from this stage in her life that Patsy had the fondest memories. She became certain that Ingleba was her country. It wasn't far from Woolbrook, her birthplace. She also felt that way because of her closeness to the many family members from whom she learned about her tribe, traditions and stories, she formed the ideas of where she fitted into the wider world, and with whom she enjoyed love and stability, even though they were often poor in this world's goods.

During the Ingleba event that was organised in 1987, she tried to convey these values and experiences to her then teenage daughter, Angela, so that Angela would always have the foundation that Patsy herself took so long to find. The story of the Ingleba event, along with the Woolbrook Cemetery event and what the process of that evoked, is told at length in *Ingelba and the Five Black Matriarchs* (Cohen and Somerville). It makes for interesting and insightful reading regarding the Aboriginality of that particular group, all of whom had strong connections to the community of Ingleba, and several of whom later lived around Hanging Rock and Nundle.

Patsy expressed her appreciation of various places at Ingleba as having been 'made by the hands that loved me', a powerful sentiment. She spoke of Pop Boney, who was 'everything that a grandfather could be to me'.[3] It is the connection between Maurice Quinn's daughter Mary Elizabeth Duval and the Aboriginal people of the Hanging Rock and Nundle district who are descended from Maryann (who was born at Rimbanda in about 1820) that link Patsy Cohen of Ingleba to Maurice Quinn of Rimbanda Station and to the five Black Matriarchs described in the book she wrote with

Professor Somerville. Other families that have their roots in Ingleba are Widders, Kelly, Green, Pacey, Morris, Davis, Wright and many others.

Patsy Cohen died in 2023 in Armidale. She was a well-known and much-loved woman.

Notes

1. Patsy's story is used with her previously gained kind permission.
2. James Dixon was King Bungaree's baptismal name—though he rarely used it.
3. In Aboriginal culture, adolescent girls usually formed strong links with their grandmothers, but Patsy formed a strong link with her grandfather. With all the moving around that the authorities imposed, it was inevitable that some previously close families became broken.

Chapter 44

Marge Fermor nee Bartholomew Was Not Stolen

Marge Fermor had her own take on the Stolen Generations children. Over our many meetings and many yarns together she showed me a lot that formerly I did not understand at all. I interviewed her when she was ninety-three, at my home in Nundle.

Marge Fermor helped me understand and value her and the other Aboriginal people. She spoke with dignity:

When I stood up to tell my story at the Aboriginal Land Council meeting in July 2013 at Tamworth, I said, My story is a sad one …

I was born at Royal North Shore Hospital on 1 May 1926 and put into the Montrose Babies Home in Sydney.

And if the government had not looked after me, I would not be alive today!

Another baby arrived every two or so years, then mother would go to Sydney—but she came home [to the Hanging Rock district] without the baby. There were six of us: Allan (George), Margaret (Marge), Fred (Peter), Robert Bruce, Kenny and David. I was raised in three institutions: Montrose, Burwood; Bidura Children's Home, Glebe; and Brush Farm, Eastwood.

Granny Duval — Sue Pickrell

I was taught how to clean, sew, cook and keep house. But at eighteen we had to leave Brush Farm and go out to work. I had only five years of schooling, to sixth class. We were not abused at all at Brush Farm. We were treated well: taken on picnics, and excursions to the Botanical Gardens and the Show Boat etc.

Though my family was broken up, three of us managed somehow to stay in touch—Alan, Fred called Peter, and myself—Margaret.

I lived in Sydney till I was eighteen and went out to work, first to Wallacia—Mum put my details in to the government, so she found me, but I was not happy there as I was staying with my mother, and we did not get along—she had not shown me any love while I was growing up at all. We didn't know each other at all. So I went back to Bidura, met Mrs Hargraves of Cronulla. I worked for her for five years.

I never had love for my mother at all—and I do not forgive her for how she neglected me. I had no love from a parent in all my growing up. Everyone needs to know love of a parent while growing up! Later I worked for the Mrs Hargraves's family at Cronulla. I was happy there, for four years.

My mother was Florence, Lilly Bartholomew's sister, who was a daughter of Annie and Adam Bartholomew. I have never found out who my father was, though apparently I look very like one of Ted's daughters, Olive—so maybe I am his daughter? I did challenge him once about it—but never found out the truth. No one could tell me.

When I was twenty-two, mother insisted I go to Hanging Rock to visit my relations. I did not know these people at all. They were very black—up till this time I did not know that I was Aboriginal.

My friend June came with me ... We stayed two weeks. There I met Auntie Lilly Bartholomew—I liked her. She and—my cousins—Myrtle and Tom Smith (Patty, Lyn), Arthur, Norman, Ronnie, Frank were all living pretty rough. I got to know Thelma, my cousin who married Percy Morris (Neil Morris' father). When she had her terrible accident—she was burnt badly when the lamp exploded—she died. So I took the two youngest, Charlie and Peter the baby, and raised them with our children.

Our first two children were christened in Niangala Church: John and Victoria (Vicky) Margaret; our third child was Donald. I had met Ronnie Fermor while I was there for the fortnight. We were married in Sydney at Fairfield Church of England on 28 December 1949. Ronnie and I had three children, John, Vicky, and Donald. Ron died six months before what would have been our sixtieth anniversary.

We raised the children up at Hanging Rock and Niangala. We lived at Niangala South (maybe at Reg Le Brock's). Millie Bartholomew, at Fairfield, was looking after us as Ronnie let us down and we needed money. I went to the Parramatta Court for a judge's ruling so that my family and I could survive. Millie had been reared at Singleton Girls Home—she understood about my life.

I do not consider myself to be of The Stolen Generations because the Welfare did not come and take us from our mother—she gave us away; at least, that is what I think happened.

I have lived in Sydney since Vicky was about twenty (1969) at Bass Hill. One of the hardest things I ever had to do in my life was learn to drive—while we lived where the pine trees are (Ponderosa Park), I was terribly nervous—I had to drive the children down the Port Stephens cutting to get the school bus at Ogunbil. Another time I had my children in a car—I was taking the children to ballet in Nundle—there were other kids in the car with us, too. I didn't know that the driver was 'under the influence'. The car went over the side at the Devil's Elbow corner—right down—it was stopped, caught up on a dead stump. I told the kids to get out of the car—very, very carefully. We all scrambled out and managed to get up the hill to the road. We could all have been killed!

Today, Marge has poor eyesight, but is still good for a yarn! In 2022, she was living with her daughter Vicky Brown on the Central Coast. (Marge passed away in 2023).

Children like Marge weren't stolen children because their parents made sure they would be safe.

Chapter 45

The Bush Kids the Welfare Missed

These children were 'missed' because Auntie Meg and Uncle John Bartholomew kept them safe, out in the bush beyond Cowsby, during the 1950s. How was it that a returned serviceman with a reliable job came to move his family, in the middle of a winter's night, by old car—an Essex—from Armidale into the bush way out from Walcha? The car had no 'mod cons'—no winding windows—and whoever sat in the front had to turn the wipers. In the car 'we had Mum and Dad, with our animals and us three kids' (Patricia Bartholomew-Locke)

John was at work one day—he managed the boilers at New England Girls School in Armidale. The school matron came to him and told him, 'The Welfare are coming to get your children tomorrow.' They had an old Essex; he and his wife bundled the three kids up, as well as the two geese and a pet sheep and the dogs, and drove them along into the bush out from Walcha and Hanging Rock to the simple home—a shed really—made of iron with a dirt floor, which became home for them all for the next several years.

Kassie Ninness (Meg's niece) grew up with Meg and John Bartholomew's children, and much of her childhood was spent living in the bush beyond Bakers Downfall, at Cowsby and at The Gums, Niangala. These were children who would probably have been taken away by the authorities had their parents not hidden them. Kassie was the daughter of Ethel and Alan Brand.

How was it, growing up as a 'half-caste' child in the New South Wales bush in the 1950s? Way out along Cowsby Road, there was plenty of scope for drama and excitement.

The Bartholomew and Brand kids had been drilled by their father (John) that whenever they saw a strange car approaching, they must run and hide. He had dug a big hole where they could be safe. They knew to pull the sheets of iron over themselves and to be very quiet. On one occasion, they hid a long way into the bush for two weeks without any adults to manage them. The Welfare police were cunning: they would ambush any child they might outrun.

The children might have received one year of schooling altogether—or none at all. They had very little correspondence schooling because there was usually no adult there to help them.

John Bartholomew, the son of Adam and Annie Bartholomew and father of Trish Bartholomew-Locke, was an enterprising man. He bought an old truck and built a body onto it, creating a bus. He then drove the bus, taking the kids to sports events. John served in the Australian Imperial Force in World War Two, but his wife 'Auntie Meg' received no pension until her case was pleaded, persuasively, in person, by her persistent daughter. John and Meg received the usual treatment of returned Aboriginal servicemen: John's war service was not acknowledged, which was an injustice, Meg got no pension and he received no promise of an allotment. Also, he was not accepted among his ex-serviceman mates at the pub because of his Aboriginality.

Kassie (also called Kate) recalled her brothers and sisters' christening. All four were to be baptised at Ponderosa Park by Reverend McLean. The youngest, Jack, was about four. He ran away into the pine forest to try to escape, but eventually they found him and brought him back struggling, and he, like the others, had to submit to the splash of cold water on his head.

Kevin Ninness and his wife had the honour of being the first couple married at All Saints Church Nundle. For some reason, the marriage took place at 10 pm. The ceremony was conducted by Reverend Elliot.

Ethel and Alan started the Brand family.

Mixed-race or coloured children could be hidden from the Welfare in the bush for months at a time. The children all worked together at ploughing the 'flats' with a draught horse. A child who was stepped on by the horse could be seriously hurt. The children worked in pairs when ploughing because they weren't strong enough to plough alone. They planted potatoes, turnips, beans and cabbages—vegetables that they harvested by hand and somehow got to market in Tamworth. It was the large potatoes that were in demand—and the family's main income—for those were the spuds that made the best chips. When the spuds were harvested, they were bagged in large hessian bags that had to have the owner's name stencilled on them. When partitions were needed in the hut for privacy, the bags served as room dividers. The sheet-iron walls of the hut had holes because the iron had been used several times before, so they boiled up flour and water to make glue and pasted the large pages of the Women's Weekly or newspapers over the holes to keep out the drafts.

The Bartholomew family might technically have been entitled to some welfare payments, but they did not apply because they were one of the many hidden families in the bush, hiding from the authorities. These families lived rough, but they never went hungry. There were always plenty of home grown vegetables, as well as rabbits, with the occasional kangaroo tail or eel for variety.

Stolen children could be shipped as far away from home as Sydney. Even worse, the girls could be 'spayed' (that word was used!) as if they were animals. It is believed that at least two girls from a Hanging Rock family were operated on. They never had any children, while others often had a family of six or seven. The decision as to which girls to 'spay' was presumably based on skin colour, which can vary considerably in families with both Aboriginal and white heritage.

The accident

What happened? One of the mothers, Ethel, was feeding hay into a chaffcutter. She'd been at it since early morning. She was tired, but she was tough. However, something distracted her for a moment, and the next thing she knew, the machine started to turn her hand into chaff! It crept along her fingers, took her wedding ring, then the next joints and her wrist. Everyone was horrified to see such a thing happening before their eyes!

One child saw what was happening to her mum and had the good sense to run and kick the belt off the pulley on the tractor. Then she put a tourniquet around her mother's upper arm. It was the quick thinking of that eleven-year-old that saved her mother's life that day. Dad was immobilised in shock from seeing all the blood, so he wasn't any help. The children disconnected the chaffcutter from the tractor, put the trailer on instead with some tick (bedding) in it, helped Mum lie down, and set off. The tractor was the only vehicle they had. It was nearly dark, and the track out to the main road to Walcha was long, muddy and twisting.

Now, a 'Fergy' (Ferguson) tractor can't travel fast, and it was getting dark. Twelve-year-old Jack was driving—just a kid from the bush. Luckily, when they got to the junction (Ham's Corner), a local family who had a car, were there. They gathered up the injured woman and drove her the rest of the way to the hospital. Surprisingly, Ethel was still conscious when they got there. The trip from 'home' to the hospital had taken thirteen hours.

The arm was amputated halfway between the elbow and the shoulder. In the hospital, they said that she never complained: 'she was the easiest patient that we had here.' After the operation, she was in the Cottage Hospital in Walcha for some time, and was given the job of stuffing the pillows—using the stumpy arm. She went on to raise six children. Even with her stumpy arm, Ethel still rode everywhere, and she kept on making all the bread for her family. They say she could pack a serious wallop with that stump!

The story of that terrible day lives on in the memories of the family members involved. They were tough and independent-minded—both adults and children. They were survivors.

***

Some people might feel they are superior to the adults of this community, who were the battlers of Hanging Rock—but when a bunch of unschooled bush kids can act as these ones did, with quick thinking, practical skill, courage and love, and rise to the occasion, we of the suburbs might take another look at these pioneers of the back blocks and their kids, who enabled their mother to survive that day, to continue to care for her family. Such kids—and adults—were survivors, and love between the members of Aboriginal families is very strong. It is wonderful that their spirit, the spirit of the bush, can still be found here and there in Australia, in the twenty-first century. When we observe it, we feel grounded as a nation.

Chapter 46

The Two Beardies: Men with Agricultural Influence

Another individual who made a difference in New England was John Duval the Beardie. He was an English convict, assigned to work in New England. He appears to have been unconnected with the James Duval of Rimbanda.

He arrived in New South Wales in 1826, having been transported on *Seostris* and assigned to Captain Dumaresq to work on the Tilbuster Run, near Armidale. He worked alongside a fellow called Richard Chandler. The two acquired several nicknames. As adults, they grew splendid beards, which accounts for them being called Beardies.

When new would-be settlers came to New England, there was a need for men to advise them about suitable land—men with a deep knowledge of the bush and of managing livestock, especially cattle. The newcomers needed advice about selecting choice portions of land, about waterholes and rivers and about the local Aborigines. The skills and experience of the two Beardies were invaluable in assisting new settlers. Was money was exchanged for this service? Probably.

John Duval

The following is John's story:

In the summer Assizes of the County of Stafford in July 1825, there stood arraigned in the dock a farmer of about twenty-eight years, of moderate stature, grey-eyed, with light brown hair and a pale complexion. Trembling, he heard his indictment for breaking and entering the dwelling of one T. Rogers and stealing a waistcoat, a pair of trousers, a pair of stockings and a handkerchief. The jury found him guilty of the burglary, and he was duly sentenced to death—a sentence that was commuted to imprisonment for the term of his natural life. He was later transported to New South Wales, arriving in 1826. Some time after this, he was given a ticket of leave and a conditional pardon. The records can be found in the Mitchell Library.

This man, John Duval, became a servant of Captain William Dumaresq, the acting chief of the colony and a recipient of large land grants, who took up Tilbuster Station in 1835. This means that this John Duval was definitely not the young man who married Mary Elizabeth Quinn in 1863 in Walcha. John Duval was involved in helping to set up pastoral properties in the Armidale area of New South Wales.

Richard Chandler

The second Beardie was Richard Chandler. Part of his story might have happened like this.

It was on a chilly day in the far bush of Tilbuster Station that two Aboriginal youths and Mr Chandler encountered one another. The two young men had just cornered a few stray sheep against a rough stone wall. Chandler saw that the youths had a short spear and would surely kill one, so he acted swiftly, calling them and their yellow dog off with a warning bellow. It scared them, and they took off up among the rocks and then down into the gully. Chandler was pleased that he'd come across them at just the right moment. He would have a good piece of that fat young wether[1] for his own dinner that very day! He had no idea where it had come from; it must have been missed in a muster somewhere further over the range.

Once they'd calmed down a bit, the two youths decided to head for the southern hills, where they called the country 'home'.

***

Bidja and his best mate had walked together for many days, hunting together and curling up near their small fires at night. His mate had helped him feel brave when he went out to find his father. They'd met some family members camped near the falls and had decided to turn for home in the south, to where their extended family would be camped down near the Barnard River. The warmer weather was coming on, and the tribe would be back from their times at the big water—the saltwater where the delicious fish and cockles grew. The two young men knew that their clan would all be together down near the river, deep in the ranges.

Note

1. Wether: neutered male sheep.

Chapter 47

Bush Justice

★★★

Bidja had a weight on his mind. His mother had been abused by a man from another tribe who had been out of control, the rum having taken over his senses. Later she had given birth, and died from her injuries. While he had been growing up, Bidja had been spared the pain and shame of knowing what had happened to his mother, but now it was his time to avenge her suffering. His grandfather had taught Bidja everything he needed to become a strong man in the tribe. For now, he put his pain aside, as it was time for him to make himself a man's spear—he was going to need it. Crafting it took longer than he expected.[1]

At the dawn of the following day, Bidja, with his best mate, put some glowing coals from their small fire into a length of hollow reed to carry with them and set off. The two youths tramped westwards, then clambered down over the rockfall above the small settlement of Nundle to seek out a certain yellow man, as they called him—a Kamilaroi man. They were told, 'he is with a mob away across the plains, near the water they call Currabubula.' They walked until it was nearly dark, then made a small fire and curled up beside the warmth of it. They had blown gently on the coals to keep them alive all the way along on their walkabout that day.

In the morning they would dig for some murnong. They'd certainly need some tucker as they couldn't find a fat possum before it had gone to sleep. Then they followed a track towards the water and spied on the camp in the distance. Was their quarry with those men? Yes—they could see him! They had found the man they were looking for, but was it Bidja's father? The youths slipped down into the bushes and back behind the big rocks. It wasn't the right time to reveal themselves—yet.

Next day, they secretly followed him when he left the camp. Something told Bidja that it was this man who had hurt his mother. Once they got out into the open, Bidja challenged the yella-fella, letting fly with his new long spear. Before the man had time to turn, he was wounded on the leg, and he let out a cry of pain. There was plenty of blood—he couldn't stand on the leg at all. Payback had been made the Anaiwan way—not by inflicting a wound that would kill but with a strong, painful injury that would be sore for many months. The pain would be a reminder of the terrible thing he'd done all those years ago. The shame that Bidja and his grandparents had borne would end.

However, Bidja had wounded his father, which was a serious move to make on a fearsome Kamilaroi man. Bidja would need to leave the area with a yellow dog and make for the mountains or the coast to be safe from his father's tribe's rage.

***

Note

1. The making of a spear: A long straight sapling of stringy bark or black wattle would be used. The sapling would be debarked while it was green. Heat from a fire would be used to make the timber pliable, and the piece could be wedged in a tree fork to straighten it. One end would be sharpened, and sometimes another piece was added—some sharp metal when they could get a piece, which made the spear more dangerous as tetanus could result from an untreated wound. (After the white settlers came, metal objects were sometimes found that could be used on a spear point.)

Chapter 48

Seeking Sanctuary

***

Sensing the urgency, the young man and his friend made for the mountains, the yellow dog still following.

They kept to the Nundle Spur; the ridge country was leading them towards the nature reserve known by the white people as Mt Yarrowyck but by the Aborigines as Bullcorronda. There were caves there and some rock paintings that had been there a very long time. Perhaps his grandfather knew of the pictures; maybe they illustrated some of his story?

After wondering briefly about the meanings of the drawings they saw, the youths tramped southwards towards the rivers and valleys where they would find their own people, towards the camp down near the Barnard River and the Tuggolo Forest. It took them a day of steady walking to reach the camp. Always the yellow dog followed along, its nose to the aromatic earth as it smelled all the intriguing new scents along the way, such as the acrid pong where a wombat had marked its track. They found their people together, and great interest was shown by everyone as the young men used words and gestures to relate their many adventures.

Later that moonrise, a meeting was held of the three related groups who camped in the bushland near the Barnard River. The young man—Bidja—was there. One evening, while watching the dancing, he noticed a fine-looking young woman, Mimi, who glanced his way shyly from time to time. He thought she was beautiful. As the damp of darkness fell, listening for the faint sounds of the night creatures, their faces reflected by the gentle glow of a nearby fire, the two went off up the hill and into the night together, moving carefully around the few rocks, snow gums and stunted bushes in their way, as the moon rose behind them. No one saw them leave the Camp.

Their courtship would be very private. Marriages could only happen according to strict customary marriage rules that were very complex. He didn't know if he could marry her, because he didn't yet know her clan connections or her 'skin name'.

It seemed no one from the camp noticed their relationship growing—which was surprising as the whole large group was camped together on the banks of the Barnard River. The tasty food was plentiful there; the children would enjoy swimming in the water. No doubt grandmother had been keeping an eye on the developing relationship, but she might not have noticed when they used the secret finger language of young people.

***

These were Aboriginal people, whose difference from the white population might not always be explainable in words but could not be denied—there was something about them as a people! Something mystical. They were a challenged people who have had to find their way in two contrasting 'worlds', living within two realities at the same time. Bidja and his Mimi were just two of the present narrative.

Chapter 49

The End of the Story?

✳✳✳

When the time came for the birth, Bidja was to be nowhere to be found. Birthing was women's business; it was not appropriate for a man to be nearby. Bidja knew Minna, his wife's grandmother, would certainly be there to help and support her during the birth; Auntie Lil Fermor might be there too if she was needed—she was a respected midwife.

The young woman bore him a beautiful daughter. The baby came into the cold, raw world of Aboriginal camp life, and the very next evening the young parents strode out, the man ahead of the woman, who was carrying the baby safely cradled in a coolamon, warm in a soft new possum-skin wrap. They were following the Nundle Spur, heading for the country to the north, the country the whites called Rimbanda Station. He knew the way—he was Aboriginal, of course he knew the way! They hurried along, the new mother carrying their precious daughter.

It was a sparkling clear cold night with a full moon. The frost was just starting to crisp up the blades of short grass. In the half-light, kangaroos and wallaroos were nibbling at the sweet green spears between the trees; their shapes could just be seen in the shadowy moonlight. A grass owl, spooked, flapped up into the treetops, its stark white underwing feathers reflecting the moonlight. The baby began to whimper; her possum-skin wrap had slipped down. The young mother stopped to cover and comfort her, then they continued on their way, their baby settled now. They were heading for a camp they knew was close by, where they could take a short rest. They were looking forward to some food—murnong cooked in the ashes. It would still be warm, sweet and juicy. Someone knew they were coming.

When the sun came up next morning, they were well along the track, walking silently, wondering what would happen that day. They expected to meet the young man's great-grandmother, Maryann. They'd heard she was ill, so they hoped they'd get there in time. Being young parents, they wanted to show their daughter to her—and get her blessing.

Meanwhile, up at the Rock that night, the white man's small fire burned weakly in the grate as he sat almost on top of it on the one rickety chair. He was listening to his wife's heavy breathing; she wasn't well. She was an Aboriginal woman. They were raising two grandchildren, who were tucked up in the only bed, warm and snug under soft possum-skin covers. All day the children had been watching the 'yellow men', following the horse up and back on the track where loads of soil and rocks were being moved, making way for the big dam that would hold the water back so the diggers could use it as they looked for the gold. The children were tired and had gone off to sleep quickly. All was quiet—there was just the crackle of the sticks burning in the grate.

His wife sat up with a harsh cough. They both thought they'd heard a dog bark earlier. There must be a quoll or a dingo around—after his chickens! His wife's thoughts echoed his own. But silence fell, and all was quiet again. As he had an Aboriginal wife, he was a 'believer'—he understood about Bidja. Even so, he wondered what had disturbed the dog. Someone or something certainly had been out there.

At the Aboriginal camp, way out beyond The Rock, someone heard the howl of a solitary dingo. And later, in the bush, happy children's voices began calling to each other. They were chasing fireflies, holding them very gently in their hands. When the cold mist of the dawn came down, the children melted away into the shadows, leaving an eerie silence that was softened by just a hint of the friendly spirits.

***

The End of the Story?

Dear reader,

Did you notice Bidja when he saw that a baby had been born safely out in the bush, it may have been around 1820 by white fella time? And did you realise that it was he and his wife - who were moving steadily along the track between the tussocks - the mist still rising? They were hurrying, to get there in time for his grandmother's blessing.

Bibliography

1. Attwood, Bain. *Telling The Truth about Aboriginal History.* Allen & Unwin, 2005.

2. Blomfield, Geoffrey. *Baal Belbora The End of the Dancing: The Agony of the British Invasion of the Ancient People of Three Rivers, The Hastings, The Manning & The Macleay, New South Wales* (revised edition). Alternative Publishing Co-operative Limited, 1986. See pp. 3–19, pp. 106–125, p. 13 (Macleay River outrages).

3. Carruthers, J E *Memories of an Australian Ministry 1868 to 1921*, The Epworth Press, London, 1922; p. 64-65

4. Clayton-Dixon, Callum *Surviving New England: A history of Aboriginal resistance and resilience through the first forty years of the colonial apocalypse*, Anaiwan Language, Revival Program, Armidale NSW, 2019

5. Cohen, Patsy and Somerville, Margaret. *Ingelba and The Five Black Matriarchs.* Allen & Unwin, 1990.

6. Dawson, Robert, active 1830. *The present state of Australia* / Robert Dawson Archival Facsimiles Alburgh 1987

7. Deverell, Garry Worete. *Gondwana Theology.* Morning Star Publishing, 2018.

8. Eldershaw, F. *Australia As It Really Is, In Its Life, Scenery & Adventure, With The Character, Habits, And Customs Of Its Aboriginal Inhabitants, And The Prospects And Extent Of Its Gold Fields.* Darton And Co, 1854.

9. Fox, Matthew, and Hammond, Catherine. *Creation, spirituality & the dreamtime* Millenium Books Newtown 1991

10. Harris, John W. *One blood: 200 years of aboriginal encounter with Christianity: a story of hope* Albatross Books Sutherland, NSW, Australia ; Claremont, CA, USA 1990

11. Harrison, Rodney and New South Wales Department of Environment and Conservation. *Shared landscapes: archeologies of attachment and the pastoral industry in New South Wales* / Rodney Harrison UNSW Press Sydney 2004

12. Jamieson, Donald. *Tales at Old Inglebah.* Donald Jamieson, Tamworth, New South Wales, 1987.

13. Mathews, R. H. *The Burbung of the New England tribes, New South Wales.* Ford & Son, 1896. Describes the ceremony of initiation into adulthood for boys.

14. Milliss, Roger. *Waterloo Creek: The Australia Day Massacre of 1838, George Gipps and the British Conquest of New South Wales.* McPhee Gribble, 1992.

15. Ong, W.J., *Orality and Literacy: The Technologizing of the Word.* New York, NY: Routledge. 1982.

16. Pascoe, Bruce. *Dark Emu, Black Seeds: Agriculture or Accident?* Magabala Books, 2014.

17. Peterson, Nicolas, 1941- and Sanders, Will. (eds) *Citizenship and indigenous Australians: changing conceptions and possibilities* Cambridge University Press Cambridge; Melbourne 1998

18. Pemberton, P. A. *Pure Merinos and Others: The 'Shipping Lists' of the Australian Agricultural Company.* Australian National University Archive of Business and Labour, 1986. Employees and immigrants from the British Isles.

19. Reynolds, Henry. *This Whispering in Our Hearts Revisited* NewSouth Publishing, Sydney, 2018

20. Reynolds, Henry. *Truth-telling: history, sovereignty and the Uluru Statement.* NewSouth Publishing, Sydney, 2021

21. Rolls, Eric C. (Eric Charles), 1923-2007. *A million wild acres* / Eric Rolls Penguin Ringwood, Vic. 1984

22. Russell, Lynette (ed). *A Trip to the Dominions: The Scientific Event that Changed Australia.* Monash University Publishing, Clayton, Victoria, 2021

23. Samways, Louise. *Spirituality without God.* 2002. http://www.louisesamways.com.au/wp-content/uploads/2013/08/Spirituality.pdf. (Throws light on the unseen influences people believe in or find to be true in life—their spirituality.)

24. Sherman, Louise and Mattingley, Christobel, 1931-2019 and Conlon, Max and Naden, Gail and Naden, Glenny and Scales, Inawantji and Baumann, Miriam-Rose and Bible Society Australia. *Our mob, God's story: Aboriginal and Torres Strait Islander artists share their faith / researched and edited by Louise Sherman and Christobel Mattingley; art selection by Max Conlon, Gail Naden, Glenny Naden and Inawantji Scales; with foreword by Miriam-Rose Ungunmerr Baumann,* Bible Society Australia Sydney, NSW 2017

25. State Library of New South Wales. *Manuscripts, Oral History and Pictures Catalogue.* https://archival.sl.nsw.gov.au/home

26. Telfer, William and Milliss, Roger. *The Wallabadah Manuscript: The Early History of the Northern Districts of New South Wales: Recollections of the Early Days.* New South Wales University Press, 1980.

27. Walker, Robin Berwick, *Old New England: a history of the northern tablelands of New South Wales, 1818-1900* Sydney University Press, Sydney, 1966. For Thunderbolt see pp. 4–10, 124–129, 172–175.

28. Waters, Kate and Moon, Korey. *Bullcorronda (Mount Yarrowyck) Aboriginal Cultural Association with Mount Yarrowyck Nature Reserve.* Korey Moon Office of the Registrar Aboriginal Land Rights Act 1983 Glebe, NSW 2016

29. Wright-Burgess, M. J. *The Wright Story: An Historical Account of the Wright Family of Nowendoc NSW.* 2023. eBook is available to download from https://www.facebook.com/profile.php?id=100064196974856

Appendix 1

Tom McClelland OAM's Poetry about Nundle and Hanging Rock

Nundle

Surrounded by mountains and beauty
Where golden wattle blooms
Nundle shares its history
Through a tourism boom.

The Peel Inn is a goldmine
of a very different type.
It was won by John Schofield
in a poker game one night.

The funeral parlour no longer
a relic, has turned the page of time.
Along with all its ghosts—
It's part of Mount Misery Mine.

Granny Duval — Sue Pickrell

'Quiet please!'
Once echoed from the empty chair.
The Court's no longer in session—
There's silence everywhere.

And if Old wares delight you
That'll take you back in time,
just visit Odgers and McClellands
The goods are of one kind.

There upon Jenkins
are antiques of the past,
Their story is part of the legend,
For they were made to last.

And every Saturday morning
The Craft Shop ladies hold their stall;
Selling cakes, biscuits and goodies
to tourists, locals and all.

A visit to the Information Centre
Have gems like no other displayed,
You could browse there for hours
or take a day trip away.

Come each Easter Saturday morning
Go For Gold is on again.
With their acrobats and dragons
the Chinese drive the crowd insane.

On First Sunday in May
Fund Raising is the game
Yet the Great Nundle Dog Race'll
Cause laughter, stitches and pain.

Out along Nundle Creek
is a monument standing tall
Where the Chinese erected on either side
A straight and narrow wall.

But the prospectors keep on coming
They have the Gold Fever touch.
For they who cry 'EUREKA' and
'Bloody Ripper'—thank you much.

Yes Nundle has it all
For those who pass that way—
a Past a Present and Future—
A visit takes more than one day!

Thomas McClelland OAM

Hanging Rock

Hanging Rock is steeped in history,
Many stories remain untold.
The legends have long since gone
But the myths never grow old.

At the top of the mountain
The Pub has no ale;
The Our House Inn is a memory—
Coaches no longer bring mail.

Hidden amongst the scrub
A pair of gallows roughly stand
Where rustlers slaughtered cattle
that belonged to other men.

With beef at bargain prices
Much to the miners' delight.
The evidence was soon devoured,
From the Gold Commissioners' sight.

In the moonlight by 'The Wendron',
tread carefully—make no sound—
just the snap of a twig
Will disturb the Sounding Ground.

As you trudge the Niangala Road
An eerie feeling passes by
Where a clearing holds its secrets—
Enough to make you cry.

Known as the 'Murder Dog'
After events of that night
When the horses grew restless
And broke loose in fright.

In a rage of fury and madness
Followed a scream of high note,
The old man grabbed his dogs
And one by one cut their throats.

On the top of Mt Sheba
A timber Trig Station stands 'lone,
Pointing North, South, East and West
Its directions weathered to bone.

Reigning over Callaghan's Swamps
Standing there in its pride
Is a Cathedral of rock
that only Mother Nature could hide.

With features like no other,
there stood a spectacular sight
That the English called London Bridge
To keep their 'home fires' bright.

Out at Mt Pleasant
the School of Arts has seen its day.
The pupils have all graduated
And been sent on out their way.

The orchard now stands quiet
Having born fruits in the past.
Fossickers seek the pineapple stones[1]
That lie amongst the grass.

Mt Pleasant cemetery is a memory—
no head stones anywhere.
Who will remember these settlers,
Except with thought and prayer?

Up at Foley's Folly
The farmers don't meet of late,
Where once they traded their goods
across the old Butter Gate.

This is just a token
Of Hanging Rock's bygone days;
Its myths, its past, its legends
And its pioneering days.

Thomas McClelland OAM
Tamworth

1. Pineapple stones: fossilised dinosaur droppings

Appendix 2

A Language Lost in Time

By Dr Nicholas Reid, University of New England Linguistics. Appeared in 'Tongue Talks', *Armidale Express Extra* (newspaper), 16 April 2014 – used with the author's kind permission.

Massive disruption to the social lives of local Aboriginal people brought about by disease and lost lands had a devastating impact on Anaiwan culture, and one of the great losses was a unique tongue. The language originally belonging to the area around Armidale is Anaiwan. You've probably seen it on signs, and possibly also noticed variant spellings like Anewan, Aniwan, or Enneewin. We've good reasons to think the name was once Nganyaywana. Although this language has not been actively spoken for a few generations now, Frank Archibald, one of the last people with good memories of Anaiwan, explained to the linguist Terry Crowley that the language name 'began with the ng sound ... the next syllable began with the ny-sound (as in 'onion') ... with the vowel of 'hay' ... the word could either end in n or na ... and the stress was quite strongly placed on this ay sound—so it should sound like nga-NYAY-wa-na or nga-NYAY-wan.' This is probably the word that the variant spellings above were trying to represent.

You'll notice that the most common modern spelling, Anaiwan, is not only shorter, but distinctively misses the initial ng sound. English does not allow words to begin with the ng sound, so English speakers often fail to hear ng at the beginnings of Aboriginal words. This might be a contributing factor to the reduction of Nganyaywana to Anaiwan, but there's also an indigenous influence because Nganyaywana was already naturally losing its word-initial sounds. If you compare its vocabulary with neighbouring coastal languages like Gumbayngirr and Dhunggadi, you'll find many examples of words like coastal mila 'eye' corresponding to ila in Nganyaywana. It might seem an odd thing to do, but linguists who study language change will tell you that this is a very common kind of sound change for a language to undergo. Where a language puts emphatic stress on the second syllable, as we saw in nga-NYAY-wa-na, then it follows that the first syllable becomes weaker, and often disappears entirely. For a more familiar example, note the English reduction of 'amend' to 'mend', and we can even see this force at work across words in the reduction of 'God's truth' to 'strewth'.

The net result of these sound changes was that Nganyaywana words look radically different to their neighbours' words. There was a time back in the 1970s before these changes were well understood, when linguists got all excited because Nganyaywana looked like an 'isolate language'. Like Basque on the Spanish/ French border which is unrelated to all other European languages, it looked briefly as though Australia had its own isolate language mysteriously trapped on the northern tablelands. But now we understand that the words are indeed related, just subject to systematic rules by which the earlier more similar forms can be reconstructed. So the transition of old Nganyaywana to modern Anaiwan is thus not as odd as it might at first seem.

Anaiwan was once a full language that did what all human languages do—convey complex culture, and be a vehicle for rich metaphor, humour, and intellect. Today Anaiwan is one of the least known of Australia's 250 indigenous languages. Less than 300 words are recorded, and we know only the briefest fragments of its grammar. Neighbouring languages like Gamilaraay to the west and Gumbayngirr to the east have extensive dictionaries, well understood grammars, and are taught in several schools. Here though, while we can salvage a few words as street or committee names, put together a simple welcome ritual, perhaps even construct a few rudimentary conversational exchanges, the greater resources that could underpin full language learning do not exist. I sometime sit in the creekland parks and try to imagine the ringing laughter, shouts and talk of Anaiwan people trickling down from north and south hills.

But the resounding hush only highlights the linguistic richness that could have be Armidale's. I cannot begin to imagine what it's like for Anaiwan themselves to live with the loss of such treasure.

Appendix 3

Aboriginal Spirituality

Aboriginal spirituality is the belief that all objects are living and share the same soul or spirit that Aborigines share.

Aboriginal worship occurs along with all the living things surrounding them. Therefore all Aboriginals have a kinship with the environment.

The soul or spirit is common—only the shape is different, but no less important.

Everything is equal and shares the same soul or spirit from the Dreamtime.

The 'authority' for this belief occurred and still occurs 'in the Dreamtime'—in the here and now and in past individual's consciousness.

—Eddie Kneebone (quoted in Fox & Hammond, Creation Spirituality and the Dreamtime p.89)

Compare this with Christian spirituality, which is a belief in the Living God—the Creator.

There is a power of God—the Spirit that (Who) energises all living things. This power raised Jesus from the dead.

The Christian God thinks, feels, speaks and acts into our world.

The Christian God is knowable—personally—and is experienced through a relationship with God's Son, Jesus Christ.

The authority for Christian belief is found repeatedly in the Bible and is not anywhere contradicted.

—Sue Pickrell

***

An alternative understanding of Aboriginal spiritual beliefs is that the Aboriginal people may tap into the magnetic energy fields of the earth using their intrinsic understanding of created beings and spirits, including their songlines and totems, and that perhaps their corroborees and somehow reflect or use the magnetic fields, even in their dancing. For Australia's Indigenous people, in the beginning came the Dreamtime—the beginning of an ongoing process, when there was nothing but a huge energy field. Out of the Dreamtime field came the stars, planets, moon and earth. And from the Dreamtime, other energy fields emerged: the Dreamtime ancestors, like the rainbow serpents that connected the energy fields of earth with those of the cosmos.

Appendix 4

Historical Background: Wool

This appendix provides some historical background about the lives and practices of shepherds.

Shepherding: wool production and shearing in New South Wales in the nineteenth century

James Duval became one of the employees of the Australian pastoral industry. He learned that flocks were kept small so that great care could be taken with the animals' health.

The business of wool production was very important. Sheep were valuable because the fleece (which was termed the staple) was valuable.

James learned on the job. To a shepherd, new green grass on a swamp looked tempting, but it could be low in feed value so that sheep that ran there would have fleeces with a break in the fibre, meaning the wool might be down-valued. Also, sheep that ran on swampy ground in cold conditions often developed catarrh, which weakened them. If a run had a lot of swampy land, a wise owner-manager usually moved his flock well away. He might even change to running cattle instead of sheep.

Lazy ex-convict shepherds got into serious trouble if they grazed the master's sheep in a swamp. A flockmaster (head shepherd) who lost sheep had to pay for them himself. This was a tough penalty, as these men were on low wages.

Dingoes were also a problem on the runs. They ripped the ewes and lambs to pieces but didn't eat the meat. It was terrible waste. The shepherds always had to keep a sharp lookout.

Wool processing: washing the sheep

To get the sheep ready for shearing, the animals had to be washed because clean fleece fetched a much higher price back in England than unwashed fleece. Three hundred sheep were washed at a time and left to 'drip-dry' in a secure holding pen. During the initial washing, the yolk—the lanolin and dirt—was separated from the wool. This waste product was used to soften the water for the final washing, when water pressure was used. Nothing was wasted. Water channels could be made by carving out the centre of a log, and a flow of water could be carried over a gully to give it speed to supply water pressure. This all helped to get the dirty, smelly, wet job done.

***

When Bidja watched as sheep were dunked in the dirty water, he couldn't understand why. For him, sheep were really great tucker!

***

Tension in the shed

In 1869, James Duval found work as a shearer, on one of Goonoo Goonoo Station's properties, but it was not a happy shearing shed.

The job was across the Peel River from Nundle village. James was in his twenties and had a pregnant wife and children to provide for. The day he arrived, there was tension in the air. The men were complaining about poor rations and scabby wet sheep, and the overseer was in a foul mood. The day before, they had worked in the heat and the flies all day, washing the sheep so they could be shorn when they were clean and dry. Wool fetched a good price in London, especially for army uniforms, so the shearing had to be handled with care.

They were down a couple of men, too, as a fire had broken out in a far paddock and some of the shearers had been needed to fight it. If they couldn't put it out, the westerly wind would blow it towards the small homestead in the evening. To make matters worse, some of the sheep had rotten feet from the moist, steamy weather during the summer. The treatment for this was cutting away the rotten hoof and treating it with bluestone. It was a stinking job that had to be done carefully because the rot was contagious. It could go through the whole flock if not thoroughly controlled.

Droughts

During the 1840s, times were tough for graziers, farmers and their men. There were droughts. Properties in lower New England changed hands frequently and for poor prices. Not only the labourers but also the managers moved around a good deal to find work. It was due to drought that a mob of 7,000 Australian Agricultural Company sheep could not be washed at the station and had to be walked across the range to the coast. During the crossing, they were ambushed, the shepherd killed, the mob dispersed (see Chapter 21, Two Strong Men Wrote).

Those trying to eke out a living getting gold struggled too, for when water was scarce, the gold diggings fell silent and life was hard all round.

Around 1880, drought was devastating the whole country; the price of sheep dropped and many thousands were boiled down for tallow, which was essential for lighting in the simple homes, used with a wick in a saucer. With the drought, James Duval lost his job as a shearer.

Appendix 5

Capturing the 'Breelong Blacks' Bushrangers

'Bushranging—the Breelong Blacks', Original copy of a letter from Marcia Ajani, Hanging Rock—appreciated. This is the original wording of an article. It has very irregular punctuation. It is a personal report.

> *I would like to write now about the bushranging—the greatest manhunt in Australian history. The Breelong Blacks—Jimmy and Joe Governor's. Jimmy was a half-caste married to a white girl. They had one child, Jimmy was quite a smart young man doing bush work breaking-in horses etc was once with the Police as a tracker in the winter. 1900 he took a job clearing and fencing for Mr Mawbrey at Breelong. Along with him was his brother and Jacky Underwood. The Mawbreys had two homes having built a new home some distance away and came to the homestead for rations.*
>
> *There was a Governess at the homestead—a Miss Kerz, when Mrs Governor came for rations, she, Miss Kerz would ask her why she married a blackfella and she took offence at being spoken to about it.*
>
> *Jimmy got worked up about things and decided to kill the family. On the 20th July 1900 he started—took Jimmy Underwood with him. They first called at the old home, where Mr Mawbrey and the eldest son and a chap called Fred Clarke camped for the night—seeing the men were all there he asked Mr Mawbrey to send him some food etc in the morning.*

Jimmy then made for the house where the family was—he with a Nulla Nulla and Jacky with a tomahawk—most of the family were in bed—he knocked on the door. Mawbrey opened the door. He hit her on the head, knocked her down, the beds were occupied by Mrs Mawbrey, Percy, Grace, Sid, Hilda, Bert, Cecil Garnet Mawbrey also a school teacher—Miss Kerz Elsie Clark and George Mawbrey a nephew.

I only intended to write about the time they passed Wallabadah where two settlers came on them. The two Governors were sitting down having a meal on the bank of a gully on Wallabadah Station a man named Mr Mc Cullock and another chap came on Jimmy and Joe having a meal—Mr Mc Cullock called out to them to surrender. The Governors grabbed their rifles and slipped into the gully and fired a shot cutting the bark off the side of a tree where Mr Mc Cullock was behind.

Next day they past Rangers Valley keeping to the hills, they would have went to Mr Alf. Swain's only Mr Dick Tanner let a rifle off through the roof. The following day the police and trackers came along to our home at Back Creek and advised my mother and sister to go away. They went to a neighbour's place about 3 miles down the Creek towards Nundle. The Police and trackers got me to shove them across country to Goo-Noo Goo-Noo.

That night a chap from Merriwa and myself came back to Rangers Valley. Next morning the Governors entered our home at Back Creek and what a mess they left ... after doing a lot of damage my Mother left a Sider chest of drawers locked. They burst the drawers open with the butt of their rifles. They took a bullet mould and loading gear, also eggs etc, made a fire and had a meal in sight of the house, then went back to the neighbour's place.

Just across the creek a chap named Harry Shorten ... took his suit of clothes, cut a sack of flour in the middle took some flour.[1] They took some scissors and comb from our house and cut their hair packed the hair off and packed the hair up. The next night ... of mine was working at Wombramurra Station saw a fire up on the side of the mountain ... seen that it should not be there he went to the Police next morning and having ... Trackers six of them and under the care of Sergent Galbraith they were camped on Crawney Road ... at a Mr Ryan's place, next morning Herb Swain and myself and two chaps from Merriwa wanted to go after them but orders were given no one was to get ahead of the Police and Trackers, but a half caste Tracker who was with the Tamworth Police told us 'if you want to see the Governors, at this time' ... we were all up on the side of the mountain where the fire was. They—the Blacks had shot a sheep, cooked the leg had a meal the fire was still alight about 10 o'clock the half-caste said to us 'if you want to see the Bushrangers go back down come up on the other side'. When we heard two shots we rushed up the hill and met some man coming down—he said they had been shot at. They—Mr Jim Heyman, his brother Barry 2 policemen and Dick Young and a blacksmith from Nundle, when we got to the top of the mountain ... There Mr Bill Woodley and Paddy, Dick ... the Govenors were having dinner with them when ... heard the horses they fired two shots and ran down the other side of the mountain and came back over the top again and that night was down at Wombramurra wool shed next morning some school children saw them the Govenors in near Nundle, they then made for the Range again going by the Wet Creek Gap. Two men—George Chapman and Jack Condon was up there waiting for them. Lying behind a log ... the Governors came quite close to them ... from here they turned up at Wingham where two men who had followed them all the way from the start—their names Byers and Woods were waiting in a hut saw them the Bushrangers coming near the hut when Jimmy heard a noise they ran behind a tree poked his head out and Byers shot him in the mouth they got away but did not last long.

Jimmy was caught and hanged in Sydney Joe was shot dead.

Others that they killed—Alex McKay, Kieran Fitzpatrick and a Mrs O'Brien and baby. They also had left Mrs Bennet for dead—but she got better.

Note

1. Bushrangers usually cut the middle of a bag of flour and took it from there because often strychnine was added to bags of flour to discourage theft by Aborigines.

Appendix 6

Myths and Legends of the Goldfields

Myths and legends of the diggings, from the times of the Old People.[1]

The Scratchits

This couple from the Hanging Rock community 'prospected with their chooks'. In the 1940s, they kept a lot of chickens. They usually fed them with a little corn, but when things got tough and they sacrificed one, the remaining chooks had to fend for themselves around the lot.

After killing one particular chook, the wife, who was making ready the pot, told her husband that it felt strangely heavy. It turned out that the old hen had 'seven ounces and nine pennyweight' of shotty gold in her crop.

Mr Scratchit didn't do any work after that except wash the scratchings off the henhouse floor. When the hillside was well scratched over, he ploughed it, and they did pretty well until the surface was eroded away by heavy rain.

After shifting camp, the Scratchits found that their chooks could not live without the gold in their diet; they died. Because gold had been absorbed into their feathers, the feathers were burned and the ashes panned with quicksilver. Fourteen hens yielded nine ounces of retorted gold! (This story is strongly believed to have been true.)

The riddle of Hanging Rock

by Frank Proust

Sydney Morning Herald, July 1946

When blizzards howl on a winter's night old men huddle round a fire in the Pub at Hanging Rock, near Tamworth, and verbally probe the village's million dollar quiz!

High up in the mountain darkness of Hanging Rock a snow-bound rabbit kicks a heavy stone into the night and resumes his battle for life. Another rabbit sleeps in a chamber streaked with gold.

For years nuggets have materialised from 'nowhere' in Hanging Rock. To the old miner they represent gleaming messengers from a vast treasure hidden in the hills. But its location is a mystery, though nuggets continue to flash out in a tantalising challenge to all comers who think they can find the hidden hoard.

HANGING ROCK [is a] picturesque mountain village of the Nundle District named after the rocks of a nearby cliff, which hangs above Oakenville Creek valley. It has a reputation for gold being found along its windswept roads. But, except for a few persistent fossickers the district's hunt for gold has come to a reluctant end. Hanging Rock's once famous Lady Mary Mine is being gradually reclaimed by the relentless undergrowth, while Ruziski's Claim where gold was 'picked up in the grass by the bucketful' is today less important than a memory. Old hands who have not lost faith in their district's gold-bearing capacity have to agree that 'Nature has become very difficult'.

When once was heard the whirl and grind of machinery echoing on the mountainside now only the voice of a biting wind frequents, heralding the approach of Spring, breaking the stony silence. Hanging Rock has good reason to believe however that 'there is gold in them thar hills', for nuggets weighing eight pounds in weight have washed down into the village during storms! One resident, Mrs George Partridge Snr. recently picked up a nugget outside her front door. Another nugget rewarded a Bank Teller waiting at the Bus Stop! Larger pieces of gold have broken off an unknown reef, have come to light in a similarly tantalising manner.

Old timers believe that these 'welcome strangers', roll down the mountain from the direction of the Lady Mary Mine indicating the near presence of large quantities of gold, similar to these once flowed abundantly from the now idle shaft where the rolling gully commences its tobogganing from Hanging Rock—And it remains a mystery.

Mr Victor Dunbar told this story of the local postman

In Nundle, the story is told of a postman who travelled on horseback, who perished during a particularly cold winter somewhere on the track between Hanging Rock and Glenrock. Apparently the most important item in his pack was the grog. He had a well-trained horse which knew how to sidle up to a gate so he could lean out to open it. The story goes that the postie sampled the rum at every tent, camp or hut along the way—so much so that when he finally got as far as Glenrock (fortunately the horse knew the way) the grog was gone—and so was the postie, until he had slept it off.

In one extra-hard winter, in deep snow and somewhere along that fifty-mile track, he and the horse—and the mail—disappeared—never to be seen again.

A true retelling—what was it the boy saw?

One day, when Bobby Partridge was about eight, he was given a basin by his mum and sent out to 'gather cherries from wild trees near The Downfall'; she was going to make a cherry pudding for their large family's dinner. He wandered along the track singing away—his family all were great singers—but as he rounded a bend and got his first sight of the cherry trees, he was shocked to see a huge black hairy animal. He thought it must be a bear! He was terrified, tossed the basin down in fright and ran shrieking all the way home. No doubt there was no cherry pie for dinner that evening!

Sixty years later, in 2017, there was still a debate about what it was he saw: a yowie, a Hairyman or what?

Hairymen/yowies seen on Thunderbolts Way in about 2015?

Two women regularly drove down to Gloucester, where they worked as teachers. They were driving along one morning, keeping a lookout because it was misty that day. Rounding a bend in the road, the driver put her foot on the break—for standing in the middle of the road were two very large hairy creatures like nothing the women had ever seen before. And they drove that route ten times a week! As the women sat, just staring, both creatures slowly ambled into the thick bushes beside the road and disappeared. When they got out of the car to look around, they found two heavily imprinted footprints in the mud.

When the women had recovered somewhat, later that day, they asked themselves: What happened? What kind of creatures did we see?

Everyone in the villages talked about the experience for days, but no one could come up with a answer that seemed verifiable. Everyone was baffled. What had the two women seen? Were they yowies?

A local man photographed them. He made casts of the huge footprints, and he has kept them to this day.

Chinese diggers were afraid of going underground

They claimed that they saw yowies there.

Gerty Fermor

(This description was provided by Gerty's great-nephew George.)

She lived way down in Possum Gully, a gold mine site. She had very long hair—'right down to her waist', said George—she could actually sit on it!

She was only five feet tall and weighed only six stone, but she was very strong. She could carry a 180-pound wheat bag. The wheat was divided into two bags to be carried on each of her shoulders. She carried the load half a mile, resting briefly only once.

She kept pigs, and she knew all their names. The pigs would lie in the creeks. At mealtimes, Gerty bashed a kerosene tin with stick, and ninety pigs came out of the bush. To feed them, she boiled up skinned rabbits with a bucket of wheat in a huge copper boiler.

When a pig was too big to walk, it was loaded onto slide-on runners and winched up the hill to the truck to go to the butcher.

Nearing her death, Gerty had a huge goitre. The family took her to hospital because she was ill, but she never came home.

Shoes

Ethel never wore shoes. Allen Brand said, 'it took me two weeks to get her into a pair of shoes'.

Allen Brand and George Partridge Sr were great drinking mates

One day Allen said to George, 'Let's go fishing down at Swamp Creek!' But when they got there, they kept on going—up and over the mountain and down to the Nundle Pub.

Two days later, they came home, but they had no fish! They'd forgotten what they'd gone for!

Wax matches?

George said, 'I didn't have a pair of shoes till age twelve.'

He also said, 'You could strike one on the soles of our feet, the soles were so hard.'

Walking geese to market (from an account of village life in very early Nundle, 1858)

They kept a few geese. To get them to market, the geese were walked through a pool of warm tar, then through a bed of fine gravel. This put a protective coating on their feet. A cart was loaded with corn, which was slowly dropped onto the ground as the cart was drawn along the road; the geese happily followed. It is said that it took two weeks to get to the market in Tamworth with the geese walking all the way.

The butter gates

Apparently, Mrs Partridge used to saddle up the sulky and take it across the field to a gate in the Wendron fence. There, the women would exchange cream, eggs or vegies with the householder. The cream would be taken to Tamworth to be made into butter.

Now, up on Gog's Top there was another 'butter gate' where the householders from the small farms—small dairies—down in the Ben Halls Creek settlement would do the same sort of thing. The women would ride up the mountain to the summit of Gog's Top and exchange cream and eggs. That was more challenging than going across the paddock in a sulky.

Note

1. Old People: the term used to describe previous generations.